To God Be The Glory

THE DIGITAL MARKETING REVOLUTION FOR BLACK-OWNED BUSINESSES

COPYRIGHT NOTICE

Copyright © 2023 by Go Black Own, LLC. All Rights Reserved. This publication is licensed to the individual reader only. Duplication or distribution by any means, including email, disk, photocopy, and recording, to a person other than the original purchaser is a violation of international copyright law. These are copyrighted materials.

Publisher By

Go Black Own, LLC
525 Route 73
Marlton, NJ 08053

While they have made every effort to verify the information here, neither the author nor the publisher assumes any responsibility for errors in, omissions from or a different interpretation of the subject matter. This information may be subject to varying laws and practices in different areas, states, and countries. The reader assumes all responsibility for use of the information.

The author and publisher make no representations or warranties of any kind, express or implied, about the completeness, accuracy, reliability, suitability, or availability with respect to the book or the information, products, services, or related graphics contained in the book for any purpose. Any reliance you place on such information is therefore strictly at your own risk.

ISBN-13: 979-8373188494

The entire **"GoBlackly: The Digital Marketing Revolution For Black-Owned Businesses"** is proprietary to Go Black Own, LLC. This is published work protected by federal copyright laws and no unauthorized copying, adaptation, distribution, or display is permitted.

GO BLACK OWN PRESENTS

THE DIGITAL MARKETING REVOLUTION
FOR BLACK-OWNED BUSINESSES

WRITTEN BY KYLE D. AMAKER
FOUNDER & CEO AT GO BLACK OWN, LLC

goblackown
A PLATFORM BUILT FOR US. EMPOWERED BY US.

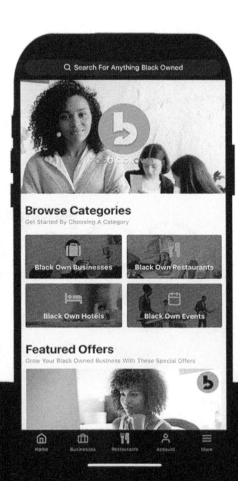

DOWNLOAD YOUR APP TODAY

THE GO BLACK OWN APP

Add Your Black-Owned Business To The Go Black Own Platform For Free, A Platform That Was Built For Us, Empowered By Us. Join The Thousands Of Other Black-Owned Businesses Taking Their Business To New Heights Through The Digital Marketing Revolution.

GoBlackOwn.com

DEDICATION

This book is dedicated to all the black-owned businesses out there. Your hard work, determination, and resilience inspire us all. As a community, we have faced countless challenges and obstacles, but through it all, you have persevered and created thriving enterprises that are making a positive impact on the world.

Your businesses are not just sources of income, but also sources of pride, cultural representation, and community empowerment. They serve as a testament to the entrepreneurial spirit and the indomitable will of the black community.

Thank you for being a shining example of what is possible when we come together and work towards a common goal. Your contributions to society are invaluable, and we are proud to stand with you.

Finally, this book is dedicated to the strength and resilience of our ancestors and future generations. It is our hope that this book will serve as a helpful resource and source of inspiration for those seeking to start or expand their black-owned business through digital marketing.

TABLE OF CONTENTS

DEDICATION 9

PREFACE 15

CHAPTER 01: INTRODUCTION 17
- What Is A Black-Owned Business 17
- History Of Black-Owned Businesses 18
- Existing Injustice Towards Black-Owned Businesses 19
- A Surge In Searches & Sales 19
- Support Has Stalled 20
- The Problem With Performative Activism 20
- The Support Black-Owned Businesses Movement 21
- Black-Owned Businesses Limited Access To Capital 21
- Hope Within Our Community 22
- Go Black Own's "Why" 22
- What We Do 23
- Working With You 25
- What Is The Book About 25
- What Will You Learn From This Book 26

CHAPTER 02: DIGITAL MARKETING FOR BLACK-OWNED BUSINESSES 29
- Why Is Digital Marketing So Important 34
- Primary Benefits Of Digital Marketing 36
- Challenges Faced In Digital Marketing 38

CHAPTER 03: DIGITAL CUSTOMERS 42
- Privacy – A New Currency 44
- Time Is A New Currency 45
- Ideal Customers Are Worth More Than You Think 46
- Engaged Customers = Customer Engagement 47
- Why Do Customers Venture Online 48
- What Are The Online Expectations 49
- Simplify The World For Your Customers 50
- Managing Customer Expectations 51
- Gaining Insights Into The Customer Experience 51
- Creating A Customer Profile 52
- What To Include In Your Customer Profile 53
- Knowing The Stages Of The Customer Experience 54
- Preparing Your Customer Experience 58

CHAPTER 04: BUILDING AN ONLINE PRESENCE 61
- What Is A Domain Name 63

BUILDING A WEBSITE	64
WEBSITE HOSTING	66
WEBSITE SECURITY	66
PROFESSIONAL EMAIL ADDRESS	67
IDENTIFYING YOUR BANDING ASSETS	68
MANAGING SOCIAL MEDIA ACCOUNTS	70
LOCAL & NICHE DIRECTORIES	71
DEVELOPING A BRANDING ECOSYSTEM	72

CHAPTER 05: SEO & SERP 75

WHAT IS SEARCH ENGINE OPTIMIZATION (SEO)	76
WHAT IS SEARCH ENGINE RESULTS PAGE (SERP)	78
SEO & SERP BENEFITS	80
OTHER TYPES OF SEO	81
SEO FOR MOBILE APPS & ASO	82
SEO FOR LOCAL DIRECTORIES	83
CITATION BUILDING	84
WHAT ARE CITATIONS FOR LOCAL SEO	85
WHAT IS CITATION BUILDING	86
WHY DO YOU NEED TO BUILD CITATIONS	86
GOOGLE'S BLACK-OWNED BUSINESS BADGE	88
TYPES OF LOCAL SEO CITATIONS	88
STRUCTURED & UNSTRUCTURED CITATIONS	88
HOW TO BUILD LOCAL SEO CITATIONS	90
YOUR CITATION BUILDING CHECKLIST	91

CHAPTER 06: PUBLIC RELATIONS (PR) MARKETING 94

HOW DOES PR WORKS	95
LISTEN TO YOUR CUSTOMERS	96
RESPOND TO OTHERS	96
WHAT TO CONSIDER	97
BUILD YOUR OWN VOICE	97
NEWS RELEASES OPTIMIZED FOR SEARCH & SOCIAL MEDIA	98
BENEFITS OF ONLINE NEWS RELEASES	99
SOCIAL MEDIA NEWS RELEASE	99
BLOGGING	100
ONLINE PRESS ROOM	100
PITCHING TO BLOGGERS	101
TOOLS OF THE TRADE	102
SHOULD I OR SHOULDN'T I	103
SUMMARY	103
THE BIGGER PICTURE	104

CHAPTER 07: ONLINE REPUTATION MANAGEMENT 106

WHY DOES ONLINE REPUTATION MANAGEMENT MATTER	107
A FEW PRINCIPLES FOR ONLINE REPUTATION MANAGEMENT	108
TRACKING MENTIONS ABOUT YOUR BUSINESS	110

  WHAT MAKES A WEBSITE USUALLY APPEALING? 111

CHAPTER 08: PAID ADVERTISING 114

  UNDERSTAND WHAT LONG TAIL KEYWORDS ARE 115
  KNOW THE TERRITORY 116
  KEEP YOUR TRACKING READY 116
  CREATE A LANDING PAGE 117
  REVIEW RESULTS REGULARLY 118
  GOOGLE ADS 119
  TYPE OF GOOGLE ADS 119
  IMPORTANCE OF PAID ADVERTISING 123
  AMAZON PPC - PAID MARKETING 124
  PAID MARKETING ON LOCAL DIRECTORIES 126
  APPLE ADS - ON APPLE APP STORE 127
  OTHER PAID MARKETING ALTERNATIVES 128

CHAPTER 09: SOCIAL MEDIA MARKETING 132

  WHAT IS SOCIAL MEDIA MARKETING 132
  BENEFITS OF USING SOCIAL MEDIA MARKETING 134
  GETTING STARTED 137
  FACEBOOK & IG ADS 138
  FACEBOOK ADS 138
  INSTAGRAM ADS 138
  PINTEREST ADS 139
  LINKEDIN ADVERTISING 141
  TWITTER ADS 142
  YOUTUBE ADS 142
  SNAPCHAT ADS 143
  TUMBLR ADS 143
  REDDIT ADS 143
  TIKTOK ADS 144
  WHAT ARE HASHTAGS 146
  WHAT DOES TRENDING MEAN 147
  WHY SOCIAL MEDIA HANDLES ARE IMPORTANT 148
  AVOID BEING CANCELED - CANCEL CULTURE 149

CHAPTER 10: VIDEO MARKETING 151

  TYPES OF VIDEO CONTENT TO CONSIDER 153
  CHOOSING THE RIGHT VIDEO PLATFORM 154
  MAXIMIZING THE IMPACT OF YOUR VIDEO PRODUCTION 155
  VIDEO OPTIMIZATION FOR MAXIMUM VISIBILITY 158
  MEASURING VIDEO MARKETING SUCCESS 159

CHAPTER 11: EMAIL MARKETING 162

  THE PROS AND CONS OF EMAIL MARKETING 163
    STEP 1 – GETTING PERMISSION 165
    STEP 2 – DO THE MATH 166

Step 3 – Segmentation & Analysis 167

CHAPTER 12: MOBILE MARKETING 170

SMS Marketing 171
QR Codes 173
Mobile Websites 173
Mobile Apps 175
Mobile Advertising 177
Digital Business Cards 178
Which Mobile Is Right For My Business 178
Who Is It For 179
What Do They Want 179
What Is My Sales Process 180

CHAPTER 13: MERCH (MERCHANDISE) MARKETING 182

Branded Merch Fits In Your Marketing Strategy 183
Gain Brand Awareness Through Branded Merch 183
Branded Swag Is An Extension Of Your Brand 183
Branded Merchandise Creates Client Loyalty 183
Its Already Built Into Your Other Strategies 184
Advertising With Merch Is Cost-Effective 184
Generate Sales And Increase Leads 185
10 Reasons To Include Merch Into Your Marketing 185
At The End Of The Day... 187

CHAPTER 14: OFFLINE MARKETING 189

Network/Contacts 190
Speaking Engagements 190
Cold Calls 191
Print Publications 192
Trade Shows/Associations 192
Print Advertising 193
Uses Of Offline Marketing 193

CHAPTER 15: CUSTOMER RELATIONS MANAGERS (CRM) 196

So What Is A CRM? 196
How To Use A CRM 197
Find A CRM Tailored Towards Your Industry 198
Best Practices 198
Sales 198
Emails 199
As A Sales Funnel 199
Landing Pages 200
Mobile Apps 200
As Part Of Email Marketing Campaigns 201
How To Decide On A CRM 201

CHAPTER 16: CREATING A DIGITAL MARKETING PLAN 203

Benefits Of Planning 203
Many Types Of Plans 204
How Different Plans Fit Together 204
Long-Term Plans Vs Short-Term Plans 205
Digital Marketing Planning 206
The Key Components Of Strategy 208
How Do You Ensure Excellent Execution 211
Internal Marketing 212
Risk Management & Contingency Planning 212
Digital Marketing Plan Summary 213

CHAPTER 17: TRACKING YOUR DIGITAL MARKETING PLAN 215

Traffic 216
Conversion Rate 217
Cost Per Acquisition (Cpa) 218
Return On Investment (Roi) 219
Utilizing The 5 Google Analytics Report Suites 220
Analyzing The Sources Of Your Traffic 221
Identifying The Source Of Site Visitors 222
Creating Goals To See Who's Taking Action 225
Segmenting Your Audience With Google Analytics 227
Horning In On Your Audience 230
Analyzing Demographic Data In Detail 231
Affinity Category Report 234
In-Market Report 234
Putting It All Together 235

CHAPTER 18: CONCLUSION & CONSULTING 237

Reviewing What We've Learned 238
Final Recommendation 253
Do You Need A Consultant 254
How Does Consulting Work 254
To Bring It Home 255
We Are Grateful 256

RESOURCES 258

Digital Marketing Checklist 260
Online Resources 267
Hash Tags To Include In Your Social Media Post 279
Black News Outlets 280
Black-Owned Business Directories 283
Black Business Organizations 286
Grants For Black-Owned Businesses 289
Banks For Black-Owned Businesses 291
Free: How To Grow Your Black Owned Business Using Digital Marketing Webinar 294
Glossary 295

PREFACE

GoBlackly is a movement driven by Go Black Own, that aims to empower black-owned businesses through the digital marketing revolution. This involves using digital channels such as the internet and social media to reach and engage with customers. As digital marketing becomes increasingly important for businesses of all sizes and industries, black-owned businesses are using these tools to grow and succeed.

Throughout the book, we will delve into various digital marketing strategies and tactics that can help black business owners reach their target audience, build brand awareness, and drive sales. We will cover topics such as search engine optimization (SEO), social media marketing, email marketing, paid advertising, and much more.

Our goal is to provide practical and actionable advice that black business owners can use to effectively leverage the power of digital marketing to grow their businesses. Whether you are just starting out or have been in business for a while, we believe that you will find valuable insights and tips in this book that will help you succeed in the digital world. With the right strategies and tactics, you can join the digital marketing revolution and take your black-owned business to new heights.

GOBLACKLY IS A MOVEMENT DRIVEN BY GO BLACK OWN, THAT AIMS TO EMPOWER BLACK-OWNED BUSINESSES THROUGH THE DIGITAL MARKETING REVOLUTION.

CHAPTER 01
INTRODUCTION

This book is designed to help black-owned businesses increase sales, grow their business, and attract new customers by effectively utilizing digital marketing. We are glad that you are reading this book, as it demonstrates your ambition to develop your business and fully utilize the power of the internet.

We are excited to share the information in this book, which we believe can have a significant impact on the growth of your black-owned business if implemented correctly. But before delving into the main content of the book, it is important to have a background on where we come from. This will help us to discuss where we are headed and the importance on why our platform focuses on black-owned businesses.

WHAT IS A BLACK-OWNED BUSINESS

A black-owned business is a business that is owned, operated, and controlled by black individuals. Black-owned businesses can be found in a variety of industries and sectors, including retail, manufacturing, healthcare, finance, and technology.

In the United States, black-owned businesses make up a significant portion of the small business landscape. According to the U.S. Census Bureau's Annual Survey of Entrepreneurs, there were 2.6 million black-owned businesses in the United States in 2019, representing 9.0% of all businesses. Black-owned businesses also employ a significant number of workers, with 3.3 million employees in 2019.

Supporting black-owned businesses can be an important way to promote economic empowerment and equality within the black community. Many people choose to support black-owned businesses as a way to invest in and contribute to the success of the black community, as well as to promote diversity and inclusion in the business world.

HISTORY OF BLACK-OWNED BUSINESSES

The history of black-owned businesses in the United States dates back to the early 1800s, when black entrepreneurs established businesses in a variety of sectors, including retail, manufacturing, and services. However, black-owned businesses have faced significant challenges and barriers to success throughout history, due to discrimination and segregation.

During the Reconstruction era following the Civil War, black-owned businesses flourished, with the number of black-owned businesses increasing dramatically. However, the rise of Jim Crow laws and segregation in the late 1800s and early 1900s led to a decline in the number of black-owned businesses.

In the mid-20th century, the civil rights movement and the passage of anti-discrimination laws helped to create more opportunities for black-owned businesses.

However, black-owned businesses continue to face barriers to success, including limited access to capital and other resources, as well as ongoing discrimination and biases.

Despite these challenges, black-owned businesses have made significant contributions to the economy and continue to play a vital role in the business landscape in the United States.

EXISTING INJUSTICE TOWARDS BLACK-OWNED BUSINESSES

As of February 2020, only 4% of the 22.2 million businesses in America were black-owned. Additionally, only 1% of black business owners were able to obtain loans in their founding year, compared to 7% of white business owners. The COVID-19 pandemic has also had a disproportionate impact on black-owned businesses, with 41% of them closing compared to 20% of white-owned businesses.

These statistics reflect the ongoing injustices faced by the black community in the United States. A Citigroup report notes that "the 400 years of enslavement of black populations in the Americas has residual effects that persist to this day." Inequalities in wages, housing, and education continue to hinder the success of black-owned businesses.

However, the Black Lives Matter movement in June 2020 led to a significant increase in sales for black-owned businesses.

A SURGE IN SEARCHES & SALES

After the death of George Floyd in 2020, there was a significant surge in searches and sales for black-owned businesses. According to data from Google, searches for "black-owned businesses" increased by over 250% in the weeks following Floyd's death. There was also a significant increase in sales for black-owned businesses on platforms such as Etsy, with sales jumping by over 200% in the same time period.

This trend has been attributed to the Black Lives Matter movement and a renewed focus on supporting and uplifting black-owned businesses. Many consumers have expressed a desire to use their purchasing power to support black-owned businesses and promote racial justice.

The surge in searches and sales for black-owned businesses is a promising sign, but it is important to recognize that this support needs to be sustained in order for these businesses to continue to thrive. By continuing to prioritize and support black-owned businesses, consumers can play a role in creating a more equitable and inclusive economy.

SUPPORT HAS STALLED

Unfortunately, there is a concern that the increased interest in and support for black-owned businesses may not be sustainable. Google Trends data shows a decline in interest in supporting black-owned businesses. For example, the search term "Black-Owned Restaurants Near Me" reached its peak during the week of May 25, 2020, but by the week of October 4, 2020, searches had decreased by 95%. Similarly, searches for "small black-owned businesses" have consistently trended downward, with a 99% decrease since May 2020.

The decline in overall interest in supporting black-owned businesses raises questions about the authenticity and motivation behind the initial surge of support during the Black Lives Matter protests. The rapid loss of enthusiasm for supporting black-owned businesses suggests that for many consumers, it may have been nothing more than a superficial form of activism rather than a genuine commitment to supporting these businesses.

THE PROBLEM WITH PERFORMATIVE ACTIVISM

Performative activism refers to when someone speaks out about a particular issue, often on social media, primarily to create and maintain a positive image for themselves rather than genuinely advocating for the cause. It involves a distinction between insincere and genuine allyship. While it is important to recognize that many instances of performative activism may be well-intentioned, there is a significant difference between "meaning well" and "doing well." Performative activism tends to be more focused on maintaining a positive image than on taking meaningful action to support a cause.

Why It Matters: News outlets, social media, and e-commerce platforms rushed to find ways to support the black community, including the promotion of black-owned businesses but it was never clear whether that support was authentic or whether it would last.

An example of "meaning well" without achieving much change might be posting a black square on Instagram, while an example of "doing well" could be donating to bail funds or lobbying legislators for reform. The apparent decline in sustained interest in actively supporting black-owned businesses and taking meaningful action, as opposed to just expressing good intentions, suggests that many Americans may be engaging in performative activism.

THE SUPPORT BLACK-OWNED BUSINESSES MOVEMENT

The support black-owned businesses movement is a grassroots effort to encourage individuals and organizations to support and promote black-owned businesses. This movement can take many forms, including online campaigns and initiatives to highlight and promote black-owned businesses, as well as efforts by individuals to shop at and support these businesses in their local communities.

The support black-owned businesses movement is often driven by a desire to promote economic empowerment and equality for the black community, and to address ongoing challenges and barriers faced by black-owned businesses, such as limited access to capital and other resources, and ongoing discrimination and biases.

There are a number of initiatives and campaigns that have been launched as part of the support black-owned businesses movement, including the #BuyBlack movement and the launch of the Go Black Own platform. These initiatives aim to provide information about black-owned businesses and encourage people to support them.

Overall, the support black-owned businesses movement is a grassroots effort to promote and support the success of black-owned businesses and contribute to the economic empowerment and equality of the black community.

BLACK-OWNED BUSINESSES LIMITED ACCESS TO CAPITAL

Black-owned businesses have historically faced limited access to capital, which has hindered their ability to grow and thrive. A number of factors have contributed to this limited access, including discrimination and biases in the lending process, as well as a lack of diversity in the financial industry.

One study found that black-owned businesses are significantly less likely to receive loans from traditional financial institutions than white-owned businesses. This can make it more difficult for black-owned businesses to access the capital they need to start or grow their businesses.

In addition, black-owned businesses often face higher interest rates on loans and may have less collateral to offer as security. These factors can make it more difficult for black-owned businesses to secure the financing they need to succeed.

Overall, limited access to capital is a significant barrier for black-owned businesses and can hinder their ability to grow and thrive. Efforts to address this issue, such as increasing access to alternative forms of financing and promoting diversity in the financial industry, can help to support the success of black-owned businesses.

HOPE WITHIN OUR COMMUNITY

There is certainly hope for black-owned businesses to succeed online. While it is true that black-owned businesses may face unique challenges and barriers to success, there are many resources and strategies available to help them succeed in the digital space.

One key factor for success is having a strong online presence, which includes having a professional website and active social media accounts. Black-owned businesses can also use digital marketing strategies, such as social media marketing, content marketing, email marketing, and search engine optimization (SEO), to reach a wider audience and promote their products and/or services.

Additionally, black-owned businesses can seek out support and resources from organizations and communities that are dedicated to supporting and promoting black entrepreneurship. These organizations can provide valuable guidance and assistance with things like marketing, financing, and networking.

Overall, there is great potential for black-owned businesses to succeed online, and with the right strategies and resources in place, they can thrive in the digital space.

GO BLACK OWN'S "WHY"

The Black Lives Matter movement gained momentum in late May 2020 following the death of George Floyd, with protests and calls for justice taking place across the country. During the following two months, black squares became a common sight on social media, and Instagram Stories were filled with "action items" encouraging people to donate to bail funds and support local black-owned businesses.

The COVID-19 crisis has disproportionately affected black-owned businesses, which were already facing pre-existing inequities. As a result, black-owned businesses have had to rethink their models or completely change their approach in order to survive. The increased attention on racial justice and equity during this time has also presented challenges and added to the uncertainty faced by black-owned businesses.

Go Black Own, LLC was founded in June 2020 with the goal of empowering black-owned businesses around the world by providing them with the tools and resources they need to grow online. This includes the first all-in-one mobile app for black-owned businesses and comprehensive digital marketing services.

Black-owned businesses have always had the talent and capability to deliver high-quality products and services. However, they have often faced barriers to accessing broader markets and opportunities. Go Black Own believes that a key to overcoming these barriers is understanding digital marketing and how to effectively use various digital channels that are tailored to black-owned businesses. By creating an ecosystem of channels, we believe that black-owned businesses can succeed online.

WHAT WE DO

Go Black Own, LLC is a platform that provides internet-related services to black-owned businesses. We are also the creator of the first all-in-one mobile app for black-owned businesses. The Go Black Own Mobile App allows supporters to search for black-owned businesses, restaurants, hotels, and events in their area, as well as stay informed about news related to black-owned businesses and shop in the first-ever black-owned marketplace.

The black-owned marketplace on the Go Black Own Mobile App is the first of its kind. It provides a platform for black-owned businesses to sell directly to supporters, including products and services, restaurant menu items, and tickets to black-owned events. This allows black-owned businesses to have a dedicated space to sell their offerings and connect with their target audience.

To download the free Go Black Own Mobile App, please go to the link below or visit the Apple Store for iPhone users and the Google Play Store for Android phone users. Search for "Go Black Own".

Link to download the Go Black Own App:

Linktr.ee/goblackown

We also offer digital marketing services to help black-owned businesses increase sales, grow their business, and attract new customers.

OUR SERVICES INCLUDE

Custom Web Design

Every website we create is unique to your business. Templated websites are boring, cheap, and generic. Since we're not that, we create custom websites from scratch that are meant to generate leads and sell services.

Digital Advertising

Using retargeting ads to get in front of people who've already shown interest in the things you're offering is HUGE. We consult and manage Google Ads, Facebook Ads, Instagram Ads, and Linked-In Ads. We cannot say these are right for every business, but we can certainly help you find out.

Graphic Design

We specialize in creating gorgeous, memorable logos, social media designs, email marketing templates, and print materials that leaves an impression and reinforce the positive sentiment of your brand. Stay consistent with a brand that your clients will remember.

SEO

Being found at the top of Google requires a strong strategy based on research. If you're looking to rank competitively for your services, let us help you navigate, and create a strategy that aims to capture your target market's attention.

Local Search

App-based searching for local food, repair, and delivery services are more popular than ever. We help you prioritize, navigate and integrate these app-based platforms into your overall marketing strategy.

Social Media

Do you have a social strategy in place to keep your searchers engaged, informed, and interested? Let us help you determine an appropriate strategy for Facebook, Instagram, and Linked-In.

Mobile App Development

Do you have an iPhone or Android phone, or have you spent any time around someone who does? Then you've undoubtedly got a feel for how addictive apps can be. Now, creating your own app can be a great way for your black-owned business to attract customers.

eCommerce

If you have a product that you're looking to sell online, we're here to lead your black-owned business to digital commerce success. It all begins by setting up a time with us to discuss the goals of your product.

Consulting

We don't expect you to know what you need — that's why we're here to help as your consultant. Together we'll discuss your deeper business purpose and break down the barriers that lie between you and your goals. We look forward to taking this journey with you.

WORKING WITH YOU

While Go Black Own would be happy to work with you and help your black-owned business succeed online, this book is not intended as a sales pitch. Instead, the goal is to provide valuable knowledge and information on how to effectively market your black-owned business on your own.

If you implement the strategies outlined in this book, it is our hope that you will be able to achieve success on your own. While we would love to have you as a client, that is not the primary focus of this book.

WHAT IS THE BOOK ABOUT

The primary objective of this book is to introduce black-owned business owners to the world of digital marketing. While this is not the only goal of the book, it is the reason why it was written.

It is crucial for black-owned business owners to understand the importance of digital marketing and how it can help them achieve their goals. It is necessary to break out of the comfort zone of traditional marketing and embrace new opportunities like having a website and using social media. In the past, it may have been sufficient to rely on word of mouth and reputation within social groups, but the business landscape has changed and it is important to adapt to new forms of marketing.

A key principle of traditional marketing is that marketing efforts should be focused where the most potential customers are. In today's digital age, the internet is where the majority of the population and target audience can be found. Therefore, it is important for black-owned businesses to shift their marketing efforts to the digital realm in order to reach and retain their audience, as well as attract new customers. Digital marketing is rapidly becoming the new standard for traditional marketing in the modern age.

It is important for black-owned businesses to understand the value of high-quality pictures, reviews on websites, fresh content, and search engine optimization in digital marketing. The internet is a powerful tool that can provide more information than any other form of marketing, and it is crucial for black-owned businesses to take advantage of this.

This book is not just for black-owned business owners looking to grow their businesses. It is written in a way that is accessible to anyone interested in learning about and understanding the trends of digital marketing, regardless of their tech or marketing expertise. The goal is to provide useful information and insights that can help anyone gain an advantage through the adoption of new marketing techniques. Digital marketing has become increasingly popular and is still growing at a rapid rate, with many companies investing heavily in it because it has proven to be effective and produce widespread results.

This book covers all aspects of digital marketing, with a focus on providing clear, practical guidance and DIY ideas on how to choose the right strategies and hire the right digital marketing agency. By the end of this book, you should have a thorough understanding of digital marketing and be able to apply this knowledge to your black-owned business to help it grow and succeed. The strategies and tactics outlined in this book have been tested and proven effective in our own businesses, and are now being shared with other black-owned business owners.

WHAT WILL YOU LEARN FROM THIS BOOK

The primary goal of this book is to help you establish and maintain a strong online presence for your black-owned business as a brand, using the latest online marketing techniques. The book aims to provide a comprehensive overview of digital marketing and help you understand how to use various online marketing strategies to drive the growth and success of your business.

The book is organized into smaller learning sections or steps, including:

- How to market your black-owned business on various digital platforms.
- How to deal with digital marketing as you run your black-owned business and adopt new marketing techniques.
- How to track marketing efforts that you conduct in the online world.
- Grow your black-owned business in a way that can be sustained in the oncoming digital era.
- Use of the cloud software CRM (Clients Relationship Management) to grow and be able to value your black-owned business, perhaps even for an exit strategy.

The next chapter will provide an overview of digital marketing and explain what it is and what fields it encompasses. The book will then delve into the importance of identifying who is your ideal customer, building an online presence for your black-owned business and provide guidance on how to do this through strategies such as SEO, organic traffic building, local search citation building, online reputation management, and paid advertising. The book will also cover social media marketing and its benefits for black business owners, as well as email marketing, CRM marketing, lead generation, and conversion optimization.

Then we will take a look at the different types of digital marketing:

- PR Marketing
- Social Media Marketing
- Email Marketing
- Video Marketing
- Mobile Marketing
- Merch (Merchandise) Marketing
- Mobile Marketing
- Offline Marketing
- CRM Marketing

By the end of the book, you will have gained a thorough understanding of the various digital marketing strategies outlined in the book and will be equipped with the knowledge and skills needed to apply these strategies to your black-owned business in order to drive growth and success.

THE DIGITAL MARKETING REVOLUTION EMPOWERS BLACK-OWNED BUSINESSES TO COMPETE AND SUCCEED THROUGH THE USE OF TECHNOLOGY AND STRATEGIES.

CHAPTER 02

DIGITAL MARKETING FOR BLACK-OWNED BUSINESSES

Digital marketing is a broad term that refers to the use of digital channels and technologies to promote products and services. It includes a variety of tactics, such as search engine optimization, social media marketing, email marketing, and more. In today's world, it is crucial for businesses of all sizes and industries to have a strong online presence in order to reach and engage with customers.

Black-owned businesses in particular can benefit greatly from digital marketing. The internet offers a level playing field for small businesses to compete with larger ones, and it allows black-owned businesses to reach a wider audience beyond their local community. In addition, digital marketing can help black-owned businesses to build their brand and establish themselves as experts in their industry.

There are a few key reasons why digital marketing is particularly important for black-owned businesses:

Accessibility

Digital marketing allows black-owned businesses to expand their reach and target audiences beyond just their local area, as it can be accessed by anyone with an internet connection and a device. This allows for the potential to reach customers globally.

Cost-Effectiveness

Digital marketing allows for a more cost-effective approach to reaching customers, as opposed to traditional methods. For instance, using social media for marketing is free, and paid advertisements can be specifically targeted to certain groups to maximize their effectiveness.

Measurable Results

Digital marketing allows for easy tracking and measurement of results. This can help black-owned businesses to see which tactics are working and which ones are not, and make adjustments as needed.

Visibility

A strong online presence can help black-owned businesses to increase their visibility and attract new customers.

Digital marketing allows black-owned businesses to reach and engage with customers through online channels, such as email, social media, and apps. One of the key benefits of this approach is the ability to track and measure the success of campaigns in real-time, allowing businesses to adapt and optimize their marketing efforts as needed. By using digital marketing, black-owned businesses can effectively promote their products or services to a global audience at a lower cost than traditional marketing methods.

Digital marketing also allows black-owned businesses to track and analyze the effectiveness of their marketing campaigns in real time. This includes monitoring metrics such as views, engagement, and conversions, as well as understanding the preferences and behaviors of target audiences. By gathering this data, businesses can optimize their marketing strategies to better reach and convert their target audience.

Digital marketing for black-owned businesses involves the use of online channels and assets to promote products or services. These channels include social media, email, apps, podcasts, electronic billboards, digital television, and radio. By analyzing metrics such as views, content effectiveness, and location preferences, black-owned business owners can effectively target and engage their audience. Digital marketing assets include websites and online branding elements, while tactics refer to the specific strategies and actions taken to reach customers through these channels.

Digital marketing assets and tactics are important tools for black-owned businesses to understand and utilize in order to achieve their goals. By effectively utilizing websites, online branding, and various digital channels like text messaging, instant messaging, and social media, black business owners can effectively reach their target audience and measure the effectiveness of their marketing efforts in real time.

ASSETS

These are the resources available to you to utilize in your marketing efforts.

- **The company website**
- **Blog posts**
- **E-Books and whitepapers**
- **Infographics**
- **Interactive tools**
- **Social media channels** (Facebook, LinkedIn, Reddit, Twitter, Instagram, TikTok etc.)
- **Earned online coverage** (public relations, social media, and reviews)
- **Online brochures**
- **Videos**
- **Branding assets** (logos, taglines, graphics, and fonts)

TACTICS

Search Engine Optimization (SEO)

This is the process of making your website optimized in a manner that it shows up higher in the search engine results and thus increases the amount of traffic that your website gets.

Content Marketing

This involves two things; the creation of content about your products, services or brand and the promotion of that content to generate brand awareness, increase traffic growth and customers.

Inbound Marketing

This type of marketing uses the assets of digital marketing and the theory of push and pull marketing. In inbound marketing, online content is used to attract target customers onto a certain website, or rather; it focuses on pulling customers instead of pushing a message.

Social Media Marketing

This refers to the efforts made to promote your brand or portfolio or even your content on social media platforms. The aim is to increase brand awareness, divert traffic to other places and generate a following that can boost your customer base.

Pay Per Click (PPC)

In this method, traffic is diverted to your website every time an ad is clicked because you have paid a publisher to do so. Google Ads is the most common type of PPC service.

Affiliate Marketing

This type of marketing functions on a commission system so it is performance-based. Participants who generate sales, leads, or traffic to their partner receive a commission for marketing your products or services on your website.

Native Advertising

Native advertising usually refers to advertisements that are focused on the content or open with the content and are present on a platform simultaneously with other content that is non-paid. For example, posts that are sponsored by BuzzFeed are one way to do this but some groups of people also include social media posts as a part of this advertising.

Marketing Automation

Since many actions of marketing have to be repeated continuously such as email, social media, and various website actions-- it is better to have these tasks automated. Thus, marketing automation refers to the software that exists to automate these marketing processes.

Email Marketing

A lot of companies use emails to market their products and services or to communicate with their customers. Through emails, content is usually promoted. Discounts and events are made known to divert people toward the company website.

Online Public Relations (PR)

This is similar to traditional PR building. The only difference is that this occurs in the online space. So digital marketers will aim to secure earned online coverage with publications, blogs, and other content-based activities.

Video Marketing

Video marketing is a powerful tool for black-owned businesses to reach new customers, promote their products and services, and build their brand. To effectively use video marketing, businesses should identify their target audience, determine their goals, determine their budget, choose the right platforms, create engaging content, and optimize their videos for search engines and social media platforms. By following these steps, businesses can effectively use video marketing to achieve their business objectives and reach their target audience.

Mobile Marketing

Mobile Marketing is the use of mobile devices, such as smartphones and tablets, to promote products or services. This can include SMS text message marketing, mobile app marketing, and mobile website optimization. Mobile marketing allows black-owned businesses to reach their target audience on the go and can be particularly effective for local businesses. It is important for black-owned businesses to ensure that their mobile marketing strategies are optimized for the specific devices and platforms they are targeting, and to track and analyze the performance of their mobile marketing efforts in order to continually improve and refine their strategies.

Merchandise Marketing

This is a strategy that involves using physical products, such as clothing or accessories, to promote a brand or business. This can be done through various methods, such as selling the merchandise directly to consumers, using it as a reward for customer loyalty or participation in a promotion, or giving it away to influencers or media outlets for exposure. Merchandise marketing can be an effective way to increase brand awareness, engage with customers, and drive sales, particularly when the merchandise is well-designed and aligns with the values and identity of the brand.

Overall, digital marketing is an important tool for black-owned businesses to grow and succeed in today's world. By leveraging the various digital channels and technologies available, black-owned businesses can reach a wider audience, build their brand, and increase their revenue.

WHY IS DIGITAL MARKETING SO IMPORTANT

Digital marketing allows businesses to reach a larger, more diverse audience than traditional marketing methods. This can be especially useful for black-owned businesses, which may not have as much visibility in traditional media channels. By using digital marketing techniques such as search engine optimization (SEO) and social media marketing, black-owned businesses can increase their online visibility and reach a larger audience of potential customers.

In addition to reaching a larger audience, digital marketing also allows businesses to target specific audiences based on factors such as location, demographics, interests, and behavior. This can be especially useful for black-owned businesses looking to reach specific segments of the population. For example, a black-owned business that sells natural hair care products might use targeted online advertising to reach women who are interested in natural hair care and live in a particular geographic area.

Digital marketing also allows businesses to track and measure the success of their marketing efforts in real-time. This can be useful for black-owned businesses looking to optimize their marketing efforts and allocate resources effectively. By using tools such as Google Analytics, businesses can track the traffic to their website, measure the impact of their social media campaigns, and identify which marketing tactics are most effective at driving sales and engagement.

Digital media has become so prevalent in our community that anybody can have access to loads of information at any time and any place they want. It is becoming an increasing source of many things, including but not limited to: news, entertainment, shopping, social interaction, etc. Before such technology was available, marketing communication consisted of messaging customers the details of your products or services. This message would only contain what you wanted them to know. Things are different now.

Marketing itself is based primarily on the interaction between sellers and buyers-- and even buyers amongst themselves. Through the power of digital marketing, consumers are now aware of not just what buyers tell them or what a company says about its brand but also what other people are saying about the product or brand.

Any interaction that occurs among friends, relatives, peers, or even fellow consumers about a brand is primarily important. This is because people are more likely to believe those interactions than the company itself. By getting a second opinion, consumers place a higher value on brands. The onset of digital content has given the consumer a power they've never had: the ability to conduct research about what they want and then make decisions with more information than ever before.

Another thing that digital media has done is to enable better communication channels with product or service providers. This allows for brands to make themselves more tailored, relevant and personalized to consumer preferences.

Another way to look at or judge the importance of digital marketing is to think of it as something that has just begun. The past trends and statistics I mentioned earlier in the chapter show that digital marketing is still on rising, and from the looks of it, will continue to do so. The future of traditional marketing is digital marketing. Success consists of managing and controlling more types of audience interactions than just email and messages.

To simplify, these can be summarized in the Five D's that black-owned businesses need to assess consumer interactions:

Digital Devices

These are the devices used by customers to interact with black-owned businesses. These include anything from smartphones and tablets to desktop computers, televisions, and gaming devices as well.

Digital Platforms

These are the spaces that can be accessed using digital devices where the interactions can take place like Facebook, Google, and Twitter etc.

Digital Media

Digital media consists of channels that are either paid, owned, or earned for reaching the consumer base and engaging them through advertising, promotions, and social networks.

Digital Data

This is all the insights and statistics that companies collect from the interaction going on in online spaces. These include audience profiles and patterns of interaction, many of which are governed by law in most countries.

Digital Technology

This is the technology that companies use to create the interactive experiences for audiences when they come to interact with websites and apps or even in-store kiosks.

PRIMARY BENEFITS OF DIGITAL MARKETING

One of the main benefits of digital marketing for black-owned businesses is the ability to increase online visibility and reach a larger audience of potential customers. By using tactics such as search engine optimization (SEO), social media marketing, and online advertising, black-owned businesses can effectively promote their products or services and reach new customers who may not have been aware of their business otherwise.

Digital marketing also allows businesses to target specific audiences based on factors such as location, demographics, interests, and behavior. This can be especially useful for black-owned businesses looking to reach specific segments of the population. For example, a black-owned clothing business might use targeted online advertising to reach fashion-conscious consumers in a particular geographic area.

In addition to targeting specific audiences, digital marketing provides businesses with valuable insights into customer behavior and preferences. Tools such as Google Analytics allow businesses to track the traffic to their website, measure the impact of their social media campaigns, and identify which marketing tactics are most effective at driving sales and engagement. This information can be used to optimize marketing efforts and allocate resources more effectively.

Digital marketing is also generally more cost-effective than traditional marketing methods, as it allows businesses to reach a larger audience with a smaller budget. Additionally, digital marketing is highly flexible and can be easily adapted to meet the changing needs and goals of a business. By leveraging the various tools and platforms available, black-owned businesses can effectively promote their products or services and grow their business in the digital age.

In the past, advertising involved placing an ad in a newspaper and trying to gauge its effectiveness by estimating how many people saw it and whether it led to increased sales. However, these methods were not always reliable in determining the return on investment (ROI) of the ad. With digital marketing, it is easier to track the impact of marketing efforts and make more informed decisions about how to allocate resources. Black-owned businesses can benefit from digital marketing by reaching a wider audience, using cost-effective methods, and measuring the success of their campaigns.

In contrast, this is where all the benefits of digital marketing come in. You can now measure your ROI in real time.

Here is a classification of these benefits:

Website Traffic

With traditional or offline marketing, it can be challenging to determine how many people are engaging with your brand unless they directly contact a salesperson or your company. This is similar to trying to determine the best times for television or radio advertisements based on when the audience is most likely to be watching or listening. However, with digital marketing, it is possible to track the exact number of people who view your website and gather data on their device, the other pages they visit, and where they came from. This information, known as digital analytics data, can be used to determine which marketing channels are most effective and where to focus your efforts.

Content Performance

Like print media, digital marketing can generate leads for your products and services through the use of online content such as blogs and articles. In the past, print media relied on ads, brochures, and letters to generate leads, but now these efforts can be tracked online through the number of views or hits each piece receives. Digital marketing also allows for the collection of voluntary contact information from individuals who download something from a website, providing a legitimate way to create leads.

Attribution Modeling

Utilizing effective marketing strategies and the right tools enables a company to trace their sales back to the customer's first digital interaction with the brand. This not only allows for better understanding of the customer journey, but also enables the creation of a database that can help identify trends about the target consumers and streamline the purchasing process, ultimately leading to increased sales.

CHALLENGES FACED IN DIGITAL MARKETING

One challenge that black-owned businesses may face when it comes to digital marketing is limited resources. Many small businesses, including black-owned businesses, may not have the budget or personnel to devote to extensive digital marketing efforts. This can make it difficult for them to compete with larger companies that have more resources at their disposal.

Another challenge is a lack of knowledge or experience with digital marketing. Some black-owned businesses may not have the knowledge or experience to effectively implement digital marketing strategies, which can make it difficult for them to get the most out of their marketing efforts and achieve the desired results.

Competition is also a challenge in the online marketplace, and black-owned businesses may face competition from both larger companies and other small businesses. This can make it difficult for them to stand out and attract the attention of potential customers.

In addition, digital marketing platforms and algorithms are constantly evolving, which can make it challenging for black-owned businesses to keep up and effectively adapt their marketing strategies. This can be especially difficult for businesses with limited resources or knowledge of digital marketing.

Finally, some digital marketing platforms may not be accessible or may have limited reach in certain areas or demographics. This can make it difficult for black-owned businesses to reach their target audience and effectively promote their products or services.

Despite these challenges, there are many ways that black-owned businesses can overcome them and effectively use digital marketing to reach new customers and grow their business. Some strategies may include partnering with other businesses or organizations, seeking out training and resources to improve digital marketing skills, and staying up-to-date with the latest trends and best practices in the industry.

Digital marketing is not a one-size-fits-all solution for marketing and as it continues to evolve, it may present some challenges. However, it is clear that the use of digital marketing will continue to grow and this may bring new challenges.

Some potential issues to consider include:

Increasing Data Volume

With the increasing reliance on online platforms for all types of transactions, it is important for black-owned business owners to collect data from various sources to get a complete picture of the customer journey. However, this can be a challenge because consumers generate a large amount of data on digital channels, making it difficult to sort through and analyze. The volume of data is also constantly growing, adding to the complexity of this task.

The Proliferation Of Digital Channels

Like many people, consumers often use multiple digital channels and devices to meet their online needs. However, different devices have different features, interfaces, and protocols, making it challenging for black-owned business owners to keep track of multiple devices and channels simultaneously. While it may be easy for consumers to use different devices for different purposes, it can be more challenging for black-owned businesses to manage this complexity.

Intensifying Competition

As is common with any new market, digital marketing becomes saturated as more and more businesses enter the space. Many digital channels are free or inexpensive, making them accessible to black-owned businesses of all sizes. However, as more businesses join the market, it becomes increasingly difficult to stand out and capture the attention of consumers. As a result, black-owned businesses may need to spend more in order to be visible and avoid getting lost among the competition.

WRAPPING UP

Digital marketing is a powerful tool for black-owned businesses to reach and engage with potential customers. By leveraging the various tools and platforms available, businesses can effectively promote their products or services and reach new customers online. While there may be challenges to overcome, such as limited resources, competition, and changing algorithms, there are also many strategies that black-owned businesses can use to overcome these challenges and succeed in the digital marketplace.

By developing a comprehensive digital marketing strategy and staying up-to-date with the latest trends and best practices in the industry, black-owned businesses can effectively use digital marketing to reach new customers and grow their business.

DIGITAL MARKETING IS THE GREAT EQUALIZER FOR BLACK-OWNED BUSINESSES. IT GIVES US THE POWER TO REACH A GLOBAL AUDIENCE, SHOWCASE OUR PRODUCTS AND SERVICES, AND BUILD OUR BRAND ON OUR OWN TERMS.

CHAPTER 03
DIGITAL CUSTOMERS

In this chapter, we will examine the thoughts, concerns, and motivations of online customers and how your black-owned business can respond to these behaviors. We will also explore on-site behavior, the online purchasing process, and the various factors that can influence it. Finally, we will discuss the future of digital customer interactions and how black-owned businesses can stay attuned to their needs.

Understanding customers is crucial for effective marketing. Savvy black-owned business owners have a deep understanding of their target customers and can closely analyze their buying behaviors. This is especially important for online customers, as the geographical and cultural diversity is often greater, and their attitudes towards acquiring information and making purchases online may differ from their offline behaviors. Therefore, it is important to closely monitor online customers to ensure success in digital marketing efforts.

Online customers are becoming more vocal and are quick to speak out if a brand fails to live up to its promises. With the rise of social media, customers have gained more control over the conversation around brands and have a platform to share their thoughts and concerns. Despite being pressed for time and overwhelmed with information, they have found a new sense of energy and are more likely to communicate about their experiences with a product or service. It is not uncommon for even high-quality products or services to have a small percentage of negative reviews, with some estimates suggesting that up to 5% of reviews may be negative (scoring less than a 5/10).

Customers have often been treated poorly by black-owned businesses, leading to frustration and anger. Surveys show that marketing efforts have declined in effectiveness over the past decade, and customers are becoming less patient and forgiving. This has created a customer service time bomb that black-owned businesses need to address in order to avoid negative consequences.

Contrary to what one might expect, marketing skills have actually declined in recent years. Automated customer service telephone systems and poorly designed websites have contributed to this trend, leaving customers to navigate complex menus and navigate through error messages and complicated web designs. This can lead to frustration and anger, and customers may vent their grievances on blogs and hate sites, leading to negative word-of-mouth or "word-of-mouse" and further damaging the brand. The customer service time bomb is ticking as black-owned businesses struggle to meet the needs and expectations of their customers.

Customers will not put up with poor service and will readily turn to competitors when given the opportunity. With the rise of social media, customers can also communicate with each other and share their experiences with a brand, both positive and negative. Social network sites enable these discussions and customers may do so for a variety of reasons, such as sharing opinions, seeking fame, or making new connections. Your business should be aware of these customer conversations and be prepared to respond to them, as they can have a significant impact on the brand's reputation.

Customers have gained a greater level of control over communications through user-generated content (UGC), which is not fully controllable by businesses. Social media platforms, which allow for social interaction, will continue to grow in popularity. Customers have been empowered by social media and are increasingly using it to share their experiences and opinions.

As customer needs and media consumption patterns change, black-owned businesses must adapt. In the past, TV was a passive medium that was "pushed" to viewers. On the other hand, the internet is a "pull" medium, where users actively seek out and retrieve content. This shift has led to a desire for more interactive and participatory media experiences, as well as the ability to choose when and how to view content and make purchases. As a result, black-owned business owners are seeing a significant increase in consumer sovereignty, as customers are able to compare prices, share information about quality and brand messages, and challenge black-business owners directly. This shift from a "push" to a "pull" model has significant implications for black-owned businesses and how you approach marketing.

Customers are continuing to change the way they consume media, with a growing preference for using small screens, such as mobile devices. In fact, more entertainment is now consumed on mobile devices than on larger screens.

Some customers use virtual worlds to socialize, escape their existing social groups, and even alter their physical identities. These platforms can be particularly appealing to people with disabilities, as there are no physical barriers or discrimination and users can become anyone or anything they wish, engaging in activities such as dancing, playing games, and doing business just like anyone else.

In the digital landscape, privacy, trust, and time are becoming increasingly valuable to customers. They are cautious about sharing personal information and value black-owned businesses that protect their privacy. Customers also value their time and do not want to waste it, so black-owned businesses that can save them time are likely to be more appreciated. However, customers may resent being asked for too much information or being asked for information before a relationship has been established. It is important for your business to respect your customers' privacy and be mindful of the information you request.

PRIVACY – A NEW CURRENCY

Customers value their privacy and do not appreciate intrusive marketing that invades their time and space. They prefer to choose when and where they receive information or advertisements. However, they are open to receiving relevant assistance from companies that can genuinely save them time or enhance their lives or work. Customers appreciate personalized, tailored communication, such as opt-in emails or personalized websites, as it helps build trust in the relationship.

Do people trust other people more than websites? It is true that people tend to trust well-known and well-respected brands, as evidenced by the willingness to provide personal information such as credit card details and home address when making purchases from sites like Amazon. Trust in a brand can be maintained as long as the brand's promise is not broken. Customers may feel more comfortable with websites that remember their name and preferences, as it helps establish a sense of personal connection. Some websites even display team members in order to emphasize the human element and remind customers that "people still do business with people." It is important for your black-owned business to consider how you can establish trust with your customers and maintain it over time.

As online customers face the threat of privacy invasion and identity theft, trust has become even more important. The profitability of mobile subscription fraud has attracted criminal activity, and criminal gangs are targeting mobile operators as telecom fraud becomes a major problem. There are also concerns that social networking websites can leave individuals and black-owned businesses vulnerable to fraud, as personal data can be compiled from public profiles that customers post about themselves. It is important for your business to prioritize trust and ensure that you are taking steps to protect your customers' personal information and prevent fraudulent activity.

TIME IS A NEW CURRENCY

Customers who have a lot of disposable income but little time want to find information quickly and complete transactions easily. They value their time and avoid wasting it on slow or confusing websites or apps. Well-designed websites that offer relevant and valuable content and services can build relationships and foster loyalty by keeping customers engaged.

Visitors are becoming more selective about the websites they visit, but they tend to spend more time on the ones they choose. These "sticky sites" offer material and services that are genuinely helpful to their customers, who are then willing to spend a larger portion of their budget on a wider range of products from a single site. It is more cost-effective and profitable to sell to an existing customer than to try to acquire a new one, and this is especially true online, where it can be ten times more profitable. You can also consider using brand extensions, alliances, and marketing partnerships to expand your product range and meet the needs of your customers.

Even though customers have a wide range of options to choose from, they are starting to narrow down their preferred websites. This presents an opportunity for black owned businesses to create "sticky" websites that keep visitors engaged with easy-to-find, relevant information and services. It is important to consider what elements of your website might attract a visitor to come back for a second visit and establish a strong relationship with the site or brand. The second visit is the beginning of the relationship, and by cultivating it effectively, you can gain a competitive advantage and build strong relationships with your online customers that can help protect you from competition.

Now, it is important to understand your customers. It is helpful to identify both good and bad customers. Bad customers may haggle over prices, pay late, complain frequently, take advantage of promotions, and leave as soon as they find another company. On the other hand, ideal customers pay on time, give advance notice, share information, and provide useful feedback. They are enjoyable to work with. But who are they? What makes them different? What do they really want? How can you help them even more? Are they online? Targeting, satisfying, and retaining ideal customers is crucial to the success of a business.

IDEAL CUSTOMERS ARE WORTH MORE THAN YOU THINK

According to Pareto's 80:20 principle, 80% of a company's sales come from only 20% of its customers. Some estimates suggest that the top 20% of customers can generate 140% of profits, while the other customers may actually result in losses. The best customers for a black-owned business may be worth 30 times more than the worst customers. This highlights the importance of identifying and targeting the most valuable customers for your black-owned business.

It is essential to understand who your best customers are and whether they are all online. To do this, you need to create a profile of your ideal customer, including their characteristics, location, needs, spending habits, and any other distinguishing features. You should also consider how to recognize these customers in a database and what questions to ask them about themselves in order to get to know them better. The goal is to understand your customers better than they understand themselves.

In order to effectively market to your customers, it is important to understand their mindset, attitudes, aspirations, expectations, and motivations. You should also be aware of any barriers they may have to buying online, such as fears or phobias. You need to understand how your offerings fit within the context of their needs, lives, and jobs, both online and offline. This will help you tailor your marketing efforts to effectively reach and engage your customers.

You also need to know their purchasing process the stages they move through and the information needs they have at each stage. You should also be aware of how they acquire information, what channels they use, the words they use to search for products, and what words and images are most likely to lead them to take action. It is also important to understand how their perception affects which offers they consider and which they filter out.

Online customers differ from offline customers in many ways. While they live in a fast-paced, information-heavy world, they are also more empowered than ever before with access to more information, clear pricing, and greater rights. They value their time and attention, leading to the popularity of permission-based marketing and the decline of intrusion-based marketing. Keep in mind that the assumptions you might have about offline customers may not hold true for online customers, and even the same customer may behave differently online versus offline.

ENGAGED CUSTOMERS = CUSTOMER ENGAGEMENT

By understanding and effectively influencing customer engagement, you can build brand loyalty and create a business that is driven by customer needs. This will give you an advantage over your competitors.

The most valuable customer does not necessarily have to be a high-volume buyer. An irregular buyer who is an influencer and posts ratings and reviews can still be very valuable, as their reviews can sway the purchasing decisions of many others. By keeping "engaged customers" engaged, they are more likely to become brand advocates. It is important to identify these engaged customers and establish a brand ambassador program to strengthen the relationship and encourage word-of-mouth marketing.

By tracking the number and frequency of blog posts, forum discussions, reviews, and profile updates, you can identify opportunities and potential future issues. Instead of solely focusing on buyers, it can be beneficial to target brand evangelists. Some black-owned companies even ask customers to rate a product or write a review as part of their post-sales outreach to identify more engaged customers who are willing to participate. This self-selection process helps to identify these individuals.

Customers who are not interested in a product are likely to have a weaker commitment or emotional attachment to the company that provides it. In contrast, customers who are engaged with a product are more likely to have an emotional connection to the brand. It is important to understand a person's sentiment, opinion, and affinity towards a brand, which can be demonstrated through their repeat business, product ratings and reviews, participation in discussion forums, and willingness to recommend the brand to others.

Consider the following question: "Are we effectively measuring the level of engagement of our various online audiences and using this information to identify our most passionate advocates and provide them with more targeted communications?"

WHY DO CUSTOMERS VENTURE ONLINE

People go online for a variety of reasons, including socializing, staying informed about current events, shopping, being entertained, and gaining knowledge. One of the most popular ways to socialize online is through email, chat rooms, blogs, and social networking sites. The sheer volume of emails sent daily and the increasing use of text messages demonstrates the strong desire for social connection, which is a fundamental human need.

The second most common activity online is researching products, whether for online or offline purchase. To accommodate this behavior, it is important to make it easy for people to browse online and then buy offline, a process known as mixed-mode buying.

Internet users are proactive and enjoy having control over their experiences. Comparison shopping allows them to exercise this control and gain knowledge about products and services through sharing information with others and using comparison sites or shopping bots. It is important for black-owned businesses to be aware of the comparison sites relevant to your products and services and to monitor them regularly.

Contrary to popular belief, not all online shoppers dislike traditional in-person shopping. They simply value being able to find good deals and having control over their purchases. Online shopping may become increasingly popular due to its convenience, especially for busy individuals who appreciate the time-saving aspect of it. The time saved through online shopping can be used to meet a variety of other needs.

The third most common activity online is entertainment, with adult entertainment, games, and music being the most popular forms. People also frequently use the internet to stay updated on the latest news about their favorite bands, sports teams, or celebrities.

It is not surprising that popular websites offer a range of services, including socializing through email and chat, searching for product information through search engines and product guides, shopping, participating in online communities, and playing games. These activities reflect the key desires of internet users: socializing, obtaining product information, making purchases, and being entertained.

WHAT ARE THE ONLINE EXPECTATIONS

Online customers have higher expectations when it comes to service, convenience, delivery speed, prices, and product selection. They also want to feel in control, secure, and safe during their online shopping experiences. However, if these expectations are not met, it can lead to disappointment and damage the reputation of a brand. It is important for your businesses to strive to meet or exceed the expectations of your online customers.

Online customers expect fast service and speedy delivery from black-owned businesses. The nature of the internet and the various technologies associated with it contribute to this expectation of speed. If a black-owned business does not meet these expectations, customers may become disappointed, frustrated, and even vocal in their dissatisfaction. Even if the delivery time is the same as it would be in a physical store, online customers often expect additional perks, such as price discounts or a wider selection of products. Meeting the raised expectations of online customers can be challenging, but it is important for black-owned businesses to strive to do so.

When buying a book online, customers have several expectations that a black-owned business should aim to meet. These include minimizing the time spent on the website and delivering the promised product. In addition to these key expectations, there may be other requirements that you should consider in order to satisfy your online customers.

Online customers reasonably expect the website and purchasing process to function smoothly and efficiently. They expect to be able to find and purchase the products they want with ease. If a black-owned business fails to meet these expectations, it can lead to disappointment and a negative experience for the customer. The internet can be a challenging environment for black-owned businesses to meet customer expectations, both high and moderate.

Unfortunately, it is common for black-owned businesses to fall short in terms of providing excellent customer service. Poor customer service, rather than price or features, is often the main reason why customers do not remain loyal to a company. It is important for your business to prioritize customer service in order to retain your customers.

As more people access the internet through mobile devices, it is reasonable for customers to expect websites to be mobile-friendly. However, not all black-owned businesses have optimized their websites for mobile use. Mobile-friendly sites enhance the customer experience and can be seen as a form of customer service. It is important for you to consider the growing need and expectation for mobile-friendly websites.

Customers do not expect to encounter cluttered and unorganized websites when accessing them on mobile devices. If they do, they are likely to leave the site and go to one that is mobile-optimized and provides a better user experience. Black-owned businesses should ensure that their mobile websites are clear and concise, with the key tasks that customers expect to be able to complete easily accessible. These tasks might include finding key messages, accessing site pages, calling your business by phone, and viewing the full website. While customers do not expect to see all the pages of a full website on a mobile site, they do expect to be able to find the main tasks quickly and easily.

SIMPLIFY THE WORLD FOR YOUR CUSTOMERS

When designing for mobile devices, it is important to create simple and user-friendly customer experiences. Consider ways to surprise and delight your mobile customers through the use of digital enhancements. Make sure that the mobile experience is easy, quick, and, if possible, enjoyable. This will help to create a positive overall customer experience.

It is worth noting that websites built using blog engines like WordPress can easily become mobile-friendly by installing a widget. This widget detects traffic from mobile devices and automatically presents a simplified, mobile-friendly version of the website. This is a quick and effective way for black-owned businesses to ensure that their website is reasonably mobile-friendly.

The most important expectation for online customers is good customer service, which should be provided throughout the entire customer journey, including before, during, and after the purchase process. It is crucial for black-owned businesses to make an effort to deliver excellent customer service in order to meet the needs and expectations of their customers. Now, let's examine customer fears and phobias.

MANAGING CUSTOMER EXPECTATIONS

Customers' expectations can be managed, met, and exceeded. How do we do this?

Here are three stages:

Understanding Expectations

To effectively meet the expectations of demanding customers, it is necessary to first understand what those expectations are. This can be achieved through customer research and site benchmarking. By using standard frameworks to identify the gap between expectation and delivery, black-owned businesses can prioritize the most pressing issues and work to resolve them. Using scenarios can also help to identify the expectations of customers when using your services on your website.

Setting & Communicating The Service Promise

One way to manage customer expectations is to establish an agreement, either formal or informal, about the level of service that can be expected. This can be done through customer service guarantees or promises. It is generally better to under-promise and over-deliver than the opposite, as a black-owned business that delivers faster than promised is more likely to earn the loyalty of its customers. For example, a candle retailer that delivers a candle in two days instead of the promised three days will likely be more highly regarded by the customer than one who promises one day but takes two.

Delivering The Service Promise

To maintain credibility and retain customers, commitments must be fulfilled through on-site service, support from employees, and physical delivery. If these commitments are not met, the online reputation of the black-owned business may suffer and customers may not return.

GAINING INSIGHTS INTO THE CUSTOMER EXPERIENCE

It's common for people to do research online before making important purchases, such as buying a car, hiring a babysitter, or changing the coffee supplier for their office. This could involve reading reviews, seeking recommendations from friends and family on social media, and learning about the features, options, and cost of the product or service. With more and more purchases being made online, it's important for black-owned businesses to have an online presence in order to take advantage of this trend.

The internet is not only helping black-owned businesses generate leads and sales, but it is also being used to increase awareness and interest in their products and services. Smart black-owned companies can use the internet to turn casual buyers into loyal supporters who not only make additional purchases themselves, but also encourage others in their network to do so as well. This new digital environment is having an impact on organizations beyond just their lead and sales generation departments.

Marketing is still about building a positive relationship with potential and current customers. This process is known as the customer profile. In this chapter, you will learn how to create a customer profile for your black-owned business and how digital marketing fits into that profile. The rest of the book will teach you how to design and implement marketing campaigns that guide customers through the various stages of the customer profile. Despite the many changes brought about by technology, the fundamental goals of marketing remain unchanged: to establish mutually beneficial relationships with prospects, leads, and customers.

CREATING A CUSTOMER PROFILE

In order to effectively market to your audience and turn them into loyal fans and advocates, it's important to have a clear understanding of your ideal customers. This includes their goals, the obstacles they face in achieving those goals, and where they go to consume information and entertainment. Creating a customer profile, also known as a buyer persona, marketing persona, or target audience, can help you gain this clarity. Throughout this book, we will use the term "customer profile" to refer to this concept.

A customer profile is a fictional representation of your ideal customer. It's likely that you will have multiple customer profiles for each marketing campaign, as your product or service may appeal to a diverse range of people. Marketing campaigns that rely on broad, generic categorizations, such as age, gender, or profession, often fail to resonate with the audience because people are complex and don't fit neatly into predetermined boxes. It's important to create customer profiles that take into account the unique characteristics and needs of your ideal customers in order to create effective marketing campaigns.

It's vital that you create a detailed and specific customer profile in order to create personalized marketing campaigns that will be of interest to your audience and address their needs. Creating a customer profile has a significant impact on every aspect of your marketing strategy, including:

- **Content Marketing:** What blog posts, videos, podcasts, and so on should you create to attract and convert your customer?
- **Search Marketing:** What solutions is your customer searching for on search engines like Google, YouTube (yes, YouTube is a search engine), and Bing?
- **Social Media Marketing:** What social media sites is your customer spending time on? What topics does your customer like to discuss?
- **Email Marketing:** Which customer should receive a specific email marketing campaign?
- **Paid Traffic:** Which ad platforms should you buy traffic from and how will you target your customer?
- **Product Creation:** What problems is your customer trying to solve?
- **Copywriting:** How should you describe offers in your email marketing, ads, and sales letters in a way that compels your customer to buy?

Having a clear understanding of your customer profile is essential for improving every aspect of the marketing and sales process that involves customer interaction. This is because you are targeting a specific individual, who is likely to purchase your products and services, and it is important to understand their characteristics in order to effectively communicate with them and inspire them to take action. By getting a clear picture of your customer profile, you can tailor your marketing messages to better resonate with your audience and encourage them to make a purchase.

WHAT TO INCLUDE IN YOUR CUSTOMER PROFILE

The customer profile possesses five major components:

- **Goals & Values:** Determine what the customer is trying to achieve. What values does he or she hold dear?
- **Sources Of Information:** Figure out what books, magazines, blogs, news stations, and other resources the avatar references for information.

- **Demographics:** Establish the age, gender, marital status, ethnicity, income, employment status, nationality, and political preference of the avatar.
- **Challenges & Pain Points:** What is holding the customer back from achieving his or her goals?
- **Objections:** Why would the customer choose not to buy your product or service?

To create an accurate customer profile, you may need to survey or talk to current customers. However, even if you don't have this information, you can still move forward by making assumptions and creating a draft customer profile. You can then refine this profile as you gather more data and feedback through surveys and interviews. It's important to begin using the customer profile you have created, even if it is not yet complete, so that you can start benefiting from it. Make sure to add research to your to-do list in order to gather more information and improve your customer profile over time.

Naming your customer profile can help you to better visualize and understand this fictional character. It can also provide a way for your team members to discuss and refer to each customer profile.

IDENTIFY YOUR TARGET AUDIENCE
It's important to have a clear understanding of who your ideal customer is, so you can tailor your marketing efforts to appeal to them. This can include factors such as age, gender, location, interests, and income level.

KNOWING THE STAGES OF THE CUSTOMER EXPERIENCE

If your black-owned business has even one customer, you have a customer journey in place, whether or not it was created intentionally. This journey may be referred to as a marketing or sales pipeline in your organization. Regardless of what it is called, it is the process that customers go through when interacting with your black-owned business.

The goal of your marketing is to guide potential and current customers through the various stages of the customer journey, whether you refer to it as a marketing or sales pipeline or some other term. By carefully mapping out this journey, you can identify any bottlenecks or obstacles that may be hindering the flow of prospects to leads, leads to customers, and customers to loyal fans. Becoming intentional about the movement of people through this journey is essential for the success of your black-owned business.

Sequence is crucial in marketing, especially in digital marketing, and it's important to move prospects smoothly and subtly through the various stages of the customer journey. It's unlikely that you will be able to convert a stranger into a devoted customer immediately, but you can gradually build the relationship over time. To guide people through the stages of the customer journey, follow these eight steps:

Step 1: Generating Awareness

Before becoming a repeat customer or loyal advocate for your black-owned business, every individual was once a complete stranger who was unaware of the problems your company solves, the products you offer, or your brand values. The first step in the journey from being a cold prospect to becoming a devoted fan is awareness. Later in this book, we will discuss specific tactics for increasing awareness. Some digital marketing tactics you may consider using if raising awareness is a challenge for your black-owned business include:

- **Advertising:** Advertising, both online and offline, is a reliable and effective method of raising awareness.
- **Social Media Marketing:** Billions of people access social media sites such as Facebook, Twitter, and LinkedIn every day. Social media marketing is an inexpensive method of raising awareness.
- **Search Marketing:** Billions of web searches on sites such as Google and Bing are processed every day. Basic search marketing techniques direct some of that traffic to your website.

Step 2: Driving Engagement

Simply making a cold prospect aware of your black-owned business is not sufficient. You need to actively capture their attention and engage them through your marketing efforts. For a black-owned business owner, this often involves providing valuable content, such as:

- Blog posts
- Podcasts
- Online videos

A person may spend a varying amount of time at any stage of the customer journey, ranging from a few minutes to several years. For example, a prospect might discover your blog and engage with it for an extended period before moving on to the next phase of the journey. On the other hand, some people may progress quickly through multiple stages of the journey in a short period of time. It's normal for a healthy business to have groups of people at different stages of the journey at any given time.

Step 3: Building Subscribers

The next step in the customer journey is to move a prospect from being simply aware and engaged with your black-owned business to becoming a subscriber or lead. A subscriber is someone who has given you permission to communicate with them.

Black-owned business owners can build lists of subscribers by connecting with people on social media platforms, such as Facebook and Twitter, by attracting podcast subscribers on services like iTunes and Stitcher, or by generating subscribers through webinar registrations. Offline companies may build their subscription list by offering aware and engaged prospects the opportunity to receive physical mail or request a consultative sales call or product demo.

In the digital marketing world, the most effective method of generating leads is often email subscription. Email is a cost-effective and high-converting way to guide a prospect through the remaining stages of the customer journey.

Step 4: Increasing Conversions

The aim at this stage is to increase the level of commitment from the prospect by asking them to invest a small amount of time or money in your black-owned business. This could involve offering low-cost products or services, hosting webinars, or providing product demos. These types of offers can help to build trust and demonstrate the value of your black-owned business to the prospect.

Up until now, the relationship with the prospect has been relatively passive, as they have simply been made aware of your black-owned business and engaged with your content. In stage 4, the goal is to deepen the connection between the prospect and your black-owned business, rather than simply focusing on profitability. This stage is about building trust and establishing a stronger connection with the prospect.

Step 5: Building Excitement

Your marketing efforts should aim to encourage customers to take advantage of the offer they accepted in step 4. This process is known as customer onboarding. Whether the conversion in step 4 involved a commitment of time or money, the relationship with the customer or prospect is more likely to be successful if they received value from the transaction. By creating excitement and helping customers to succeed, you can often reduce cancellation rates.

It's important to ensure that the value of the offers you make to customers far exceeds the price they pay. Offer high-quality products and services and develop marketing campaigns that encourage their use. If customers aren't using your products or services, they are unlikely to continue purchasing from your black-owned business or promoting your brand to others.

Step 6: Making The Core Offer Sale & More

By this stage, prospects have built a relationship with your brand and may have invested some time or money in your company. These individuals are much more likely to consider purchasing a more complex, expensive, or risky product or service from you. This transition from passive prospect to buyer is known as ascension.

Many black-owned businesses stop their marketing efforts after this stage, either by asking cold prospects to make significant investments in a company they don't yet know, or by neglecting to continue marketing to customers after they have made a purchase. The former approach is like proposing marriage on a first date, and is unlikely to be successful. The latter approach fails to turn a one-time buyer into a repeat customer. It's important to continue marketing to your customers and building relationships with them in order to encourage repeat business.

If you have successfully navigated the first five stages of the customer journey, you may find that some of your leads and customers are ready to make larger purchases, sign up for recurring subscriptions, or become loyal repeat buyers in the ascension stage. This is because you have built a relationship with them and effectively conveyed the value that your black-owned business can offer. When you market to your customers in this sequence, you are on the path to turning them into advocates and promoters of your brand (as discussed in the next two steps).

Step 7: Developing Brand Advocates

Brand advocates are enthusiastic supporters of your black-owned business who provide testimonials about their positive experiences with your brand. They are fans of your company and will often defend your brand on social media and leave positive reviews for your products or services on websites like Go Black Own and Official Black Wall Street.

Your ability to create brand advocates depends on the strength of the relationship you have with your leads and buyers. By the time you reach this step, you and your customer should have a close, mutually beneficial relationship that has been built over time and requires ongoing effort to maintain.

You can build a strong relationship with your customers by adding value, delivering on the promises made about your products, and providing responsive customer service. By consistently offering high-quality products and services, you can turn people into brand advocates and ultimately turn them into brand promoters.

Step 8: Growing Brand Promoters

Brand promoters are even more enthusiastic about your black-owned business than brand advocates, and will actively spread the word about your brand online through social media and blogging. They may even go as far as to tattoo your logo on their body. The main difference between a brand advocate and a brand promoter is that the promoter is more active in promoting your black-owned business, while the advocate is more passive.

For brand promoters, your company has become a significant part of their life. They trust and rely on your brand because it has consistently provided exceptional value through its products and services. These individuals have invested not only their money, but also their time, in your black-owned business. They believe in what you offer and are committed to promoting your brand.

CREATE PERSONAS
Personas are fictional characters that represent your ideal customer. Use the data you have gathered to create detailed personas that describe your customers' characteristics, behaviors, and needs.

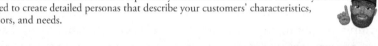

PREPARING YOUR CUSTOMER EXPERIENCE

For successful black-owned businesses, the customer journey is not a coincidence but rather the result of intentionally designed marketing campaigns. Once you understand your ideal customer journey, you can use the tactics discussed in the rest of this book to move prospects, leads, and customers from one stage to the next. Smart black-owned business owners carefully plan their marketing efforts in order to guide customers through this journey.

Developing a customer journey roadmap that outlines the eight stages from cold prospect to brand promoter can be a helpful way to plan and visualize the path that your ideal customers will take. Bring together stakeholders in your company to create a customer journey roadmap for one of your main products or services. Consider the campaigns and offers that will be most effective at each stage of the customer journey to increase awareness of your product and guide customers towards their desired "After" state as brand promoters. This roadmap can be a valuable tool in your marketing planning and execution.

AS A FINAL NOTE

Digital customers are an important consideration for black-owned businesses looking to succeed in the digital economy. By understanding the needs, preferences, and behaviors of their digital customers, black-owned businesses can create a customer-centric marketing strategy that effectively reaches and engages with these customers online.

This includes using digital channels such as social media, email, and mobile marketing to communicate with customers, as well as leveraging data and analytics to gain insights into customer behavior and preferences. By adopting a customer-centric approach, black-owned businesses can build long-term relationships with their digital customers and drive business growth in the digital space.

CREATING A CUSTOMER PROFILE HELPS YOU UNDERSTAND AND TAILOR YOUR MARKETING EFFORTS TO YOUR TARGET AUDIENCE'S NEEDS AND BEHAVIORS.

CHAPTER 04

BUILDING AN ONLINE PRESENCE

Now that we have covered the basics of digital marketing and identified your target customer, let's focus on more specific steps that you can take to grow your black-owned business and build a strong brand. By this point, you should have a general understanding of the actions you need to take to move forward. Now it's time to start implementing these strategies and take more concrete steps towards building and expanding your black-owned business.

In order to achieve both short-term and long-term benefits for your black-owned business, it is essential to have the right clients and to focus on branding your products rather than simply selling them. One of the most important steps you can take to accomplish this is to establish or improve your online presence. This will help you reach a wider audience and establish credibility and professionalism for your black-owned business. Whether you are just starting out or already have an online presence, it is important to make sure it is strong and effective.

It is essential for any black-owned business to have an online presence, whether through a website, an e-commerce platform, a social media page, a local listing directory profile, or a combination of these. Even if your company does not conduct business online, having a presence online can help you attract new clients and customers and increase the credibility of your black-owned business. If you do not have an online presence, you are missing out on opportunities to expand your customer base and promote your black-owned business. It is important to consider the various options for establishing an online presence, such as a website, social media, or local listings, and choose the ones that will be most effective for your business.

Black-owned businesses need to build an online presence for a number of reasons. One important reason is that an increasing number of purchases and purchasing decisions are made online. Having an online presence can help black-owned businesses capitalize on this trend and reach a wider audience.

An online presence can also help black-owned businesses establish credibility and professionalism, as it allows customers to easily find information about the company, its products or services, and its values. It also provides a platform for black-owned businesses to engage with their customers and build a community of loyal followers.

In addition, an online presence can help black-owned businesses to stay competitive in today's market by providing a way to showcase their products or services, offer promotions and discounts, and stay connected with their customers.

Here are some of the reasons you might want to build an online presence:

Make It Easier For Potential Customers To Come To You

Having an online presence, whether it's a website, social media page, or local business listing, is essential for any black-owned business in today's digital age. This is especially true for black-owned businesses, as potential customers expect to find information about your company online. By having an online presence, you can reach a larger audience and increase your customer base, even if you don't conduct business online. In fact, many people specifically search for established online businesses, so transitioning to the digital world can make it easier for both existing and potential customers to find and learn about your company.

Make It Easier To Showcase Your Products And Services

In contrast to traditional methods of promoting a company's products or services through physical showrooms or stores, much of this can now be done online. This can be done through your website or social media page, which can increase interest in your black-owned business and make it more convenient for consumers to connect with you.

Make It Easier To Build Relationships With Customers And Potential Customers

By going online, it will be easier and more cost-effective for you to build and maintain relationships with customers. This is because you can easily stay in touch, share updates about your products, and gather feedback without the need for physical meetings or long delays.

Make It Easier To Market Your Brand

Focusing your marketing efforts in one place rather than multiple locations will make it easier to promote your black-owned business and brand. Additionally, targeting your efforts online where a large portion of the audience is currently located will likely lead to more effective results.

A digital marketing agency helps businesses increase their online presence by utilizing all the available features and opportunities on the internet. This includes aligning the nature of your business and its potential with the possibilities offered online, and bridging the gap between the physical and digital aspects of your business to create a cohesive strategy. There are various methods that can be employed to achieve this goal.

A reputable digital marketing agency will discuss each of these methods with you in detail. With that in mind, let's examine the various steps that need to be taken to establish your black-owned business's online presence.

WHAT IS A DOMAIN NAME

A domain name is the web address that people use to access a specific website. It is the name that is entered into a web browser's address bar to visit a particular website. For example, "GoBlackOwn.com" is the domain name for Go Black Own's website.

A domain name is an important aspect of a black-owned business's online presence. It is the first thing that customers will see when they search for the business online, so it is important to choose a domain name that is easy to remember and relevant to the business.

There are many different top-level domains (TLDs) to choose from, such as .com, .net, and .org. The TLD that you choose can help convey the purpose of your website and give customers an idea of what they can expect to find when they visit.

When choosing a domain name for a black-owned business, it is a good idea to consider the target audience and the purpose of the website. For example, if the business is targeting a specific geographic area, it may be a good idea to include the name of the city or region in the domain name.

Overall, the most important thing is to choose a domain name that is memorable, relevant, and easy to type. It is also a good idea to capitalize each letter in the domain name, as this can make it easier to read and remember.

HAVE A DOMAIN NAME MULTIPLE WORDS?
It is generally a good idea to capitalize the first letter of each word in the domain name when marketing, as it makes the domain name easier to read and remember. For example, GoBlackly.com is much easier to read and remember than goblackly.com

BUILDING A WEBSITE

Every black-owned business, regardless of size, should have a website. The first thing you should focus on is creating a space on your website for your logo, message, vision, and any other information you want to convey to your audience about your black-owned business. This will be your business's online brand hub, because the internet is often where people go to find information. Instead of relying on indirect channels or sources for information about your black-owned business and its products or services, it is better to have an official, trustworthy source that customers can visit to learn what they need from you.

Your website may be simple at first, but it should include essential information that current and potential customers may need or want. Make sure to keep all the information on your website up-to-date and complete. For example, it is common to visit a restaurant's website and find that it lacks the current menu, operating hours, or contact information.

Google may have this information, but the restaurant's own website often lacks it. This can be frustrating and may influence someone's decision about where to get their food. The customer wants to rely on information from the restaurant itself rather than trusting a review from another source or looking at a menu from an unverified source, as it may not be accurate or up-to-date. It is important to the customer to know exactly what the restaurant is offering from a reliable source.

To make your website successful, you should optimize the content for user viewing. This includes making the tabs on your website user-friendly, with colors, text, and images that effectively represent your brand. It's also important to include appealing calls to action on your website. Keep these considerations in mind as you design your website.

Incorporate appealing "calls to action" on your website. "Calls to action" are phrases that encourage customers to interact with your website, such as "view our catalog," "download now," or "place order." You often see these on websites to guide customers in their next steps.

You can easily create a basic website using an application like WordPress, which is a free blogging tool but also serves as an effective content management system. Alternatively, you can build a simple Shopify store for your e-commerce business. You can also opt to pay for a premium subscription or add an online shop to your website. It's worth noting that in 2022, 70% of consumers preferred to shop online. While it depends on the nature of your black-owned business, it is often possible to include some elements for placing orders, if not complete shopping, on your website.

The purpose of your website is to provide all the necessary information that your consumers and clients might need or want in an easy-to-use format. While this may seem straightforward, many black-owned business owners may feel overwhelmed by the various options for website design, themes, and content production when they first start building a website. It's important to remember that your initial goal is simply to have an online presence, so don't get too caught up in the details.

Don't worry too much about small aesthetic details, because you can always improve the appearance and content of your website over time. The first version of your website is not permanent, and you can make changes to it quickly, unlike traditional forms of marketing such as billboards and advertisements. Keep in mind that to improve your ranking in search engines, you should regularly update your website with fresh content like blog posts, upcoming and past events, galleries, case studies, new product lines, and seasonal promotions. From my experience running a digital marketing agency, I've observed that clients often spend too much time and energy on the initial website and then want to change it and evolve it as their online presence grows. It's better to start with a simple site and improve it as your black-owned business develops.

WEBSITE HOSTING

Hosting refers to the process of storing and maintaining a website on a server so that it can be accessed by users on the internet. It is an important aspect of digital marketing for black owned businesses because it allows you to create and maintain a professional and functional website that can be used to reach and engage with your target audience. A website is often the first point of contact between a business and its customers, and having a well-designed and reliable website is essential for building trust and credibility.

There are several different types of hosting options available for black-owned businesses, including shared hosting, dedicated hosting, and cloud hosting. The best hosting option for a particular black-owed business will depend on its needs and budget.

In addition to hosting the website itself, black-owned businesses may also need to consider hosting for other digital marketing assets, such as email accounts and online databases. These types of hosting services can be provided by the same hosting company as the website, or by a separate provider.

Overall, hosting is an important aspect of digital marketing for black-owned businesses, as it allows them to create and maintain a professional and functional online presence that can be used to reach and engage with their target audience.

WEBSITE SECURITY

An SSL (Secure Sockets Layer) certificate is a type of digital certificate that is used to secure and encrypt data transmitted over the internet. For black-owned businesses, an SSL certificate can be used to secure a website and protect sensitive information, such as customer data and financial transactions.

Having an SSL certificate is important for black-owned businesses because it helps to establish trust and credibility with customers. When a website has an

SSL certificate, it is indicated by a green padlock icon in the address bar of the browser, which helps to reassure visitors that their information is secure.

In addition to building trust, an SSL certificate can also be important for search engine optimization (SEO). Google and other search engines often give higher rankings to websites that have SSL certificates, as they are seen as more secure and trustworthy. This can help to improve the visibility of a black-owned business's website in search results, which can in turn drive more traffic and potential customers to the site.

Overall, an SSL certificate is an important aspect of digital marketing for black-owned businesses, as it helps to secure your website and protect sensitive information, build trust and credibility with customers, and potentially improve their search engine rankings.

PROFESSIONAL EMAIL ADDRESS

A professional email address is an email address that is associated with a business or organization, rather than an individual. It is typically formatted as "name@company.com," and is used to communicate with customers, partners, and other stakeholders in a professional manner.

Professional email addresses are typically associated with a company's domain name, which is the online address of the business. For example, a business with the domain name "www.yourcompany.com" might have a professional email address such as info@yourcompany.com.

Marketing And Branding

A professional email address can help to promote and build the brand of a black-owned business. For example, if a business has a domain name such as "www.yourcompany.com" and an email address such as "info@yourcompany.com," it creates a cohesive and professional image for the business. This is especially important when marketing the business to potential customers or partners.

Communication And Collaboration

A professional email address can facilitate better communication and collaboration with customers, partners, and other stakeholders. For example, a business can use its professional email address to send newsletters, updates, or other important information to its subscribers. It can also use it to communicate with partners or vendors in a more professional manner.

Security

A professional email address is generally more secure than a free or personal email account. This is because businesses often have access to additional security features and protocols to protect their email communications. This can be especially important for black-owned businesses, as they may be at greater risk of cyber attacks or other forms of online threats.

Productivity

A professional email address can also help a black owned business to be more productive. For example, a business can use email management tools to organize and prioritize its incoming emails, or use integrations with other tools such as customer relationship management software to streamline its operations.

In short, having a professional email address is an important investment for any business, and can help black-owned businesses to establish themselves as credible and professional entities, communicate and collaborate more effectively, protect themselves from online threats, and be more productive.

USING A PROFESSIONAL EMAIL IS A MUST!
Use your own domain name as the email address, rather than using a generic address provided by a free email service ie: gmail, yahoo, aol, etc. This can help give your business a more professional appearance.

IDENTIFYING YOUR BANDING ASSETS

Branding assets are all of the elements that can be used to describe or portray your black-owned business and brand in a way that makes it stand out from your competitors. These assets should create a unique image of your black-owned business and can include things like logos, fonts, colors, taglines, backgrounds, and anything else that can be customized to fit your black-owned business or idea. There are many options available to you when it comes to branding assets, so it's important to do research and make informed choices to create a lasting impact and strong presence for your brand.

For example, colors can signify different meanings and emotions. Each color is connected to a certain feeling or emotion, like how white represents cleanliness, red signifies danger or desire, blue brings about a calming or peaceful effect, and black may indicate gloominess or mysteriousness. These associations are like neural pathways in the brain that lead to specific emotions.

In the same way that color choice can be a branding asset, other elements like fonts and logos can also convey specific associations. For example, an italic font may appear fancy or formal while a bold font may come across as imposing or attention-seeking. When combining these elements, it's important to consider the individual effects of each element and the combined effect they create. This can be time-consuming, but it's important to get it right because these are often the first things that your target audience will notice about your brand. Be sure to consider the effect you want to create and the associations that each element brings.

Many of these effects on the audience are subconscious, so it's important to also consider the relevance of any element you choose to your brand. Don't get so focused on the elements themselves that you forget that they need to align with your business goals. The elements should work together harmoniously to match your brand and business, not just make it look attractive. It's important to consider more than just the visual appeal of the elements.

It's important to focus on branding assets because they will be a key part of your online presence, both on your website and in other places online. Based on customer psychology, branding assets play a significant role in the online experience. When a client visits your website, they should be able to understand your content and relate to the branding assets you are using. Even if they don't visit your website, they may still hear about your business from other sources, so it's important to have consistent branding assets in all your online platforms.

Your branding assets will be used in various places beyond your website, such as packaging, letterheads, and advertisements. When a client or consumer sees your logo or any other branding element related to your company, they may go through a mental process of recalling businesses that could meet their needs. Similarly, when they come across one of your branding assets in a search or elsewhere online, it will create an image of your black-owned business in their mind. What you do with your branding assets will determine what kind of image is formed in their mind. It's important to consider that not everyone will visit your website, but many consumers may come across your logos, offers, and advertisements online in other spaces or forums. These assets may even be the deciding factor in whether they visit your website or not.

MANAGING SOCIAL MEDIA ACCOUNTS

Once you have created your website, you can focus on expanding your digital presence through social media. Social media is an important part of your online presence that can help you generate more revenue and build lasting customer loyalty. It enables customers, potential customers, and other interested parties to engage with you through a channel that is a central part of their daily lives.

There are various channels you can use to drive traffic to your website or promote your brand. These days, people appreciate it when brands have active and well-maintained social media accounts because it makes it easier for them to see updates on their feeds rather than going to a website to check for updates. Having a business profile on every relevant social media platform will help you connect with a wider variety of demographics. Additionally, maintaining social media accounts will encourage you to be more creative with the messages and content you share, as you'll tailor it specifically for each platform.

Not every social media channel will be relevant for every business, but it's worth considering your options. For example, Facebook and Instagram are useful for almost any black-owned business as they are great platforms for posting news, tips, photos, and videos, and answering questions. After establishing these two important accounts, you may also find Twitter, Snapchat, LinkedIn, YouTube, Pinterest, Tumblr, and Foursquare helpful. It's up to you to determine which channels are the best fit for your black-owned business.

For instance, Instagram is a photo-sharing network, so it's particularly well-suited for businesses that rely on photos. If your business needs to focus on aesthetic beauty to attract interest, Instagram may be a good choice. It's important to consider your target demographic when choosing social media channels – Instagram has around 130 to 150 million users in the US, with over two-thirds of them being women between the ages of 18 and 45. To effectively use Instagram, you'll need to have a smartphone to access your account and engage with your audience.

After deciding which social media channels to use, think about the types of content you can share. The more interesting and engaging your material is, the more likely your followers will like, comment on, and share your posts. Engaging with your audience is essential for promoting your brand – not only will it make you more appealing to existing customers, but the more interaction you have, the higher the likelihood that their friends will be exposed to your brand. Friends often pay attention to what their friends are doing on social media, and they may become interested in what you have to offer.

 ENGAGE WITH YOUR AUDIENCE
Building an online presence involves more than just creating content – it's also about building relationships with your audience. Respond to comments and messages, ask for feedback, and interact with your followers to foster a sense of community.

LOCAL & NICHE DIRECTORIES

In the past, being listed in directories like Thomas Book and Yellow Pages, as well as advertising in local newspapers and classified ads, was crucial for a business to grow. Today, these traditional channels have migrated online, and businesses can be found through platforms like Google My Business, Yelp, Go Black Own, Official Black Wall Street, and local African American Chamber of commerce.

Being listed on online directories is crucial for your black-owned business because that is where potential clients go to find businesses to do business with. Many of these directories offer free listings, but some may require a minimum membership fee. You can also pay for marketing to improve the visibility of your listing on these directories. It is common for black-owned business owners to be listed on directories such as Google, Yelp, or Go Black Own without signing up for it themselves.

According to the US Communication Decency Act (Section 230), online platforms are generally protected from liability for content posted by third parties, such as users of their software or platform. This means that your Go Black Own listing was created by your customers, and while you can claim the listing and have some control over it, you cannot delete it because it was created by a third party. Instead, you can claim on Go Black Own that you are out of business, which the platform will verify with their own users. It is generally a better idea to claim the listing, update the information, add images and content, and continue to receive positive feedback from your clients.

There are specialized online directories for various types of businesses, such as Trip Advisor for travelers, Air B&B for homeowners renting out their properties, and Home Advisor for those in the construction and home improvement industry. It is important for your black-owned business to be listed on these niche directories, as it can help you increase your revenue and improve your organic search engine rankings. Every business model has its own relevant niche directories or online forums, and your business should be listed on them.

DEVELOPING A BRANDING ECOSYSTEM

To establish a strong online presence, it is important to unify all of your brand's online elements and activities in a cohesive manner. This includes your website, social media accounts, and any events or stories that contribute to your brand image. Your website should serve as the central hub of this ecosystem, with your other online presence radiating out from it. In order to maintain a sustainable online presence, it is necessary to continually update and engage with your audience.

Black Enterprise is a brand that effectively maintains a constantly evolving online presence through the incorporation of new stories, challenges, content, events, and records. When an online ecosystem is functional and cohesive, it can naturally attract a large audience and foster brand loyalty by providing additional value to customers through digital devices and interactions across various channels. A digital ecosystem consists of the various devices and media channels through which a brand interacts with its customers. By building an ecosystem through these channels, a brand can create a loyal customer base by delivering added value.

To ensure that your online presence remains cohesive after it has been established, it is important to align all elements of your brand. This includes your website, social media pages, brand elements, and mission or vision statement. When all of these elements work together harmoniously, your online presence will become stronger. In the next chapter, we will examine how this occurs through search engine optimization and how it can help accelerate the growth of your black-owned business. It is crucial to maintain consistency across all of your online media spaces in order to achieve synergy and strengthen your online presence.

TO FINALIZE

Building an online presence is crucial for black-owned businesses looking to succeed in the digital economy. By creating a professional and user-friendly website and using social media and other digital channels to connect with customers, businesses can increase their visibility and reach a wider audience. In addition, businesses can use search engine optimization and digital advertising to improve their search engine rankings and drive traffic to their website.

By building a strong online presence, black-owned businesses can effectively promote their products or services, establish their brand, and engage with customers in the digital space. Overall, building an online presence is an essential part of a successful digital marketing strategy for black-owned businesses.

YOUR ONLINE PRESENCE IS YOUR DIGITAL IDENTITY, AND IT'S UP TO YOU TO CRAFT IT INTO A POWERFUL PERSONAL BRAND THAT ACCURATELY REPRESENTS WHO YOU ARE AND WHAT YOU STAND FOR.

CHAPTER 05
SEO & SERP

In order to effectively establish and grow your black-owned business online, it is essential to understand the importance of search engine optimization (SEO) and search engine results pages (SERP). These are two crucial aspects of digital marketing that significantly impact the digital landscape. Some experts even argue that half of digital marketing involves mastering the intricacies of SEO and SERP. Now that we have thoroughly discussed the necessity of building an online presence for your black-owned business, it is time to focus on these key elements.

In this chapter, we will delve into the realm of SEO and SERP. We will cover the fundamental principles and functions of these techniques and examine the advantages they can offer to black-owned businesses in the digital space. After gaining a thorough understanding of SEO and SERP, we will explore how to effectively incorporate these techniques into your black-owned business to start realizing their benefits.

WHAT IS SEARCH ENGINE OPTIMIZATION (SEO)

Search engine optimization (SEO) is a marketing strategy that has gained widespread popularity in recent years. It aims to improve the visibility of a website or web page through non-paid or "organic" search engine results. SEO involves both technical and creative elements to improve a website's ranking, drive traffic, and increase its visibility and recognition on various search engines. The most popular search engine is Google, which has a 70% share of desktop searches and a 90% share of mobile searches. Other search engines include Yahoo, Bing, Yelp, Amazon, and the Apple App Store and Google Play Store.

Essentially, any platform that allows users to search for information can be considered a search engine. While some people may portray SEO as mysterious or complicated, it is simply a measurable and repeatable process based on how search engines function, allowing relevant signals to be sent to search engines indicating that a website or directory listing is worthy of being included in their index. The process by which Google ranks these signals and websites is a separate topic that we will discuss later.

If you want to send signals to search engines through a process like SEO, there will be various components to consider. This includes the words on your website and how other sites link to your pages. In some cases, SEO may simply involve ensuring that your website is structured in a way that makes it easier for search engines to understand and categorize. Search engines look at two main aspects of your website and its content: on-site and off-site. On-site refers to the information and elements that are present on your own website, while off-site refers to information about your site that can be found on other pages or elsewhere on the internet.

However, SEO is not just about creating search engine-friendly websites; it should also provide a positive user experience. These two aspects are closely interconnected.

Search engines operate by using formulas to analyze a large volume of data to determine which web pages should appear first in search results when a user searches for a particular keyword. This data consists of all web pages that are related to or linked to a specific topic, including both on-site and off-site content.

For instance, when Google processes data, it uses complex algorithms to evaluate and rank websites and searches. This allows it to determine the most relevant and trustworthy results for any given search. The algorithm takes into account various factors such as the quality of the website, the number of sites and pages linking to it, the number of pages mentioning the site, the level of trust from sources and users, and so on. There are many factors to consider and a cumulative score is determined based on all of these categories.

Your task is to analyze your target audience and competition, and then reverse engineer the process that search engines use to determine rankings. This will help you understand what they look for and how you can improve your own rankings. Once you have done this, you can begin to organize and optimize the data and content on your website and links, as well as maintain a balance between on-site and off-site content. While it may seem complex at first, it becomes simpler once you understand the process.

Now that you understand how Google's algorithm works, you can focus on improving your ranking by enhancing the quality of the content on your website. This will help you score higher on the factors that the algorithm considers.

Additionally, you can influence your ranking by gaining authority and trust with your audience, so that even off-site content speaks positively about you. This will increase your score in terms of trustworthiness for relevant searches.

To improve your ranking, you need to score highly in various categories, and the higher your score in each category, the higher your overall score will be. You must find ways to improve your scores in all of these categories until your overall score is high enough for the search engine to rank you above your competitors. While this may seem tedious, it helps you refine every aspect of your website and related inbound links.

SEO also puts pressure on you to continuously improve and optimize your website. It is important to pay attention to every aspect of your site and its content, as there are hundreds of categories that can affect your scores. This means you have numerous opportunities to improve your scores and achieve a higher ranking overall.

To better understand and excel in the ranking system, think of the overall cumulative score as a weighted average, as not all categories are given equal importance. The three most important categories to consider are quality, trust, and authority. In terms of quality, Google wants to determine which sites provide valuable and unique content for searchers. It doesn't matter as much if your product is truly different and better than your competitors unless the content you use to describe it is also unique. Google will have no way of knowing that your offering is distinct unless the content is unique as well. Your task is to show Google that your site has content that stands out from other sites in the same categories and for similar search queries.

Next is trust. Google takes trust very seriously, as it does not want to include deceptive sites in its search results. It wants to show credible and trustworthy sources in order to protect its own credibility. However, Google also penalizes or removes sites, stores, and companies that consistently have negative reviews from searches over time. The best way to demonstrate trustworthiness to Google is to have genuine and useful reviews, ensure that the websites linking to you have good reviews and are credible sources, and get high-authority sites to link to you. You should also monitor your audience's satisfaction and ensure that your partners are praising you.

Finally, the third most important category used to rank your site is authority. Google needs to see that you have a strong level of authority in your industry and the type of information, product, or service you offer. This is because Google wants to show its users the most popular sites for their searches. For example, if someone is looking for natural hair care products, Google wants to show the most popular hair care provider to the user. Therefore, your goal is to demonstrate to Google that you are the most popular in your field. To do this, you should build a large fan base and get as many people as possible to like you. You can do this by getting people to share your content, post it on relevant pages and profiles, discuss it on platforms and blogs, leave comments and testimonials, and show pictures of your products or services being used. It is also important to keep interacting with your fan base and keep the conversation going.

WHAT IS SEARCH ENGINE RESULTS PAGE (SERP)

Search engine results pages (SERP) are an essential component of search engine optimization (SEO). When a user enters a search query on a search engine, they are presented with a list of web pages that are relevant to the query. These queries are often specific words or phrases. The pages that appear in response to a search query are known as SERP. It may seem straightforward, but every SERP is unique because search engines like Google, Yahoo, and Bing customize the results for each search. Even if the same search query is used on the same search engine multiple times, the SERP will be different. While the results may be similar, there will always be minor differences.

These differences occur for two reasons. First, search engines attempt to personalize the search experience for each user by considering factors such as location, browsing history, search history, and social settings. Second, search engine results are constantly changing as search engines themselves are always evolving and testing new technologies to provide more tailored and intuitive responses to users.

To summarize, the content on SERPs can be divided into two categories: organic results and paid results. As SEO practitioners, we are primarily concerned with organic results. As mentioned earlier, SEO is focused on improving the organic, or non-paid, visibility of websites in search engine results. SERPs are important because each one is unique, and SEO professionals strive to optimize websites and content in order to rank higher in organic search results.

On a search engine results page (SERP), not all content is organic. While everything on the SERP can be considered a feature, it's important to understand the different types of content. The proportion of organic content on a SERP depends on the nature of the search query. There are three main types of internet searches: informational searches, navigational searches, and transactional searches.

Informational searches are those that are conducted to find information about a particular topic. In these searches, the search engine does not display many advertisements or other paid results on the SERP because informational searches are solely for finding information. Users are not looking to make a purchase, so there is no point in trying to sell them something. Navigational searches, on the other hand, are performed when users want to access a specific website through their search. This can include finding a website whose URL has been forgotten or when users are not sure of the specifics. Finally, transactional searches are those with the highest commercial intent. These searches will have the most paid content on the SERP because they contain keywords related to buying behavior.

It is critical for a website to be on the first page of the search engine results page (SERP), which is why SEO practitioners focus on SERP ranking even if it can be tedious. The data shows that results ranked from 11th to 20th receive less than half the clicks of those ranked from 1st to 10th. In fact, many people only look at the first result. According to statistics, 90% of the world's population does this.

In simpler terms, this means that if your website is ranked as the second result on a SERP, you are missing out on 90% of your target audience immediately.

This means you are missing out on potential customers, sales, and profits. It's clear why it is so important to be the first result on a SERP.

SEO & SERP BENEFITS

We have previously discussed the concepts and mechanics of SEO and SERP. While this understanding is important, it is also crucial to remember that the ultimate goal of these strategies is to improve and grow your black-owned business. Therefore, let's focus on the key benefits that SEO and SERP can bring to your black-owned business in the long run.

One of the main advantages of SEO and SERP is increased website traffic. As we previously mentioned, the top positions on a search engine results page tend to receive more clicks. Therefore, improving your ranking through SEO can significantly increase the traffic to your website. Additionally, using relevant keywords and tags as a description for your website on the results page can improve the click-through rate and the quality of the traffic to your site.

SEO can also be considered a cost-effective marketing strategy. With the use of technology, SEO allows you to target only those users who are actively seeking out your products or services, rather than wasting resources on outbound strategies. This can help save money compared to other methods such as cold-calling or door-to-door sales, which often have higher costs per lead. Additionally, SEO helps generate leads in real-time, making it a more efficient and effective way to reach potential customers.

SEO also allows for easy tracking and measurement of the return on investment (ROI) for your business. The trackable and quantifiable nature of the SEO process enables you to monitor and assess every aspect of your strategy, including the keywords used by customers and their path to your site. This can provide valuable information such as increased rankings, conversions, customer demographics, and time-based purchases, which can all be analyzed and evaluated to optimize your strategy. Overall, the measurable nature of SEO makes it a powerful tool for tracking and improving the performance of your black-owned business.

SEO not only improves the visibility of your website to search engines and their algorithms, but it also enhances the internal navigation of your site. The structure, links, and content are organized to increase the usability of the website. Improved usability is essential for attracting and retaining users, and

SEO helps to achieve this by making it easier for both users and search engines to find and access information on your website.

 INVEST IN SEO
SEO helps increase your website's visibility by improving its ranking on search engine results pages. This includes optimizing content and technical elements and building high-quality backlinks.

OTHER TYPES OF SEO

SEO for Amazon Store & Product Listings

Like Google, Amazon has evolved into a search engine in its own right. As the leading e-commerce platform, Amazon has helped many brands reach customers and sell their products. It is also a useful platform for new e-commerce websites that lack brand awareness and industry influence to sell their products independently. In fact, many brands that did not adapt to the trend of using Amazon have gone out of business because they relied solely on traditional e-commerce and were unable to generate sufficient revenue. While the Amazon SEO algorithm is different from Google's, the principles are the same: Amazon wants to display the most relevant and suitable products on the first page of search results based on users' inquiries.

To improve your Amazon listing, it is important to focus on creating high quality content. This includes using relevant keywords in the title of your listing and providing a detailed and useful description of the product. It is also helpful to include multiple original photos to make the listing more user-friendly and accurate. By making the listing as thorough and helpful as possible, you increase its chances of ranking well on Amazon.

While Amazon Store and product listing optimization shares some similarities with traditional SEO, it also has its own unique features. Amazon was originally designed as a purchasing platform and eventually added its own search engine, called A9. Unlike traditional search engines, A9 is focused on helping shoppers make purchasing decisions rather than just providing information. The goal of A9 is to optimize the shopping experience in order to increase the frequency of purchases made on Amazon. This means that the algorithm prioritizes factors that lead to successful sales rather than just providing information.

To increase the visibility of a product on Amazon, it is important to optimize it according to the factors mentioned earlier.

The product title is a key element of an Amazon SEO strategy because it is the first thing a user sees when searching for a product on the platform. To optimize the title, it is important to include relevant information such as the brand, product line, material, color, size, type of product, packaging, and any other relevant characteristics.

The order in which this information is presented, along with the use of target keywords, is crucial for a successful strategy. However, it can be challenging to fit all of this information into the title due to the limited space available - organic results typically have titles that are 115-144 characters long, right rail ads have titles that are 30-33 characters long, and mobile titles are approximately 55-63 characters long. Therefore, it is important to prioritize keywords and place them at the beginning of the title.

SEO FOR MOBILE APPS & ASO

Mobile apps can now appear as organic search results on search engine results pages (SERPs) due to the rise of the mobile era and Google's mobile-first update. These app listings are ranked based on their relevance and ability to fulfill user queries, regardless of whether users ultimately choose to install them. One unique aspect of these organic app listings is that they can include an install button, allowing users to easily download the app directly from the search engine. Additionally, app links in these listings will take users directly to the app rather than a website's landing page or homepage, which can be especially useful on social media platforms like Facebook, Twitter, or Go Black Own where users may primarily be looking to download an app. As mobile searches now surpass desktop searches and the mobile app market continues to grow, optimizing for mobile apps through SEO and ASO (App Store Optimization) is becoming increasingly important for success in this market.

When optimizing a search engine for a mobile app, it is often helpful to choose a name for the app that is related to the product or service it provides. This can create a "branded keyword" that the app can rank for in search results. In addition to considering the name of the app, it is also important to do keyword research to ensure that the app's description accurately matches the needs of potential users. Another factor to consider is app indexing, which helps to make sure that the app is visible on search engines. Google has even stated that app indexing can be a ranking signal for Android users. App indexing can also improve the visibility of an app by adding an "install" button to its listing.

To optimize the visibility and ranking of your app, it is important to consider both search engine optimization and app store optimization (ASO). ASO is the process of improving the ranking of your app on app store lists. To do this, you can research and use relevant keywords in the name, title, description, and tags of your app. Tools like Keyword Suggestions, Ubersuggest, and OneLook Reverse Dictionary can be helpful for finding the right keywords. It is also helpful to include images and preview videos of your app to give potential users a better idea of what it is about. These techniques can all help to improve the visibility and success of your app.

Paying attention to and responding to user reviews on app stores can greatly contribute to app store optimization (ASO). This includes both positive and negative reviews, as well as maintaining a consistent flow of new reviews for your app. By actively engaging with and addressing user feedback, you can improve the visibility and ranking of your app on app store lists.

SEO FOR LOCAL DIRECTORIES

The widespread availability of high-speed internet has led to increased user participation in online reviews, which can be particularly influential when it comes to local businesses such as restaurants, event venues, and recreational activities. There are many online directories, such as Google My Business, Yelp, Yellow Pages, Local.com, Manta, BBB, Go Black Own, Official Black Wall Street, and Angie's List, that list these types of businesses. Like other types of online search, SEO can be applied to these local directories to improve the visibility of a business. However, competition for top search results on these directories can be fierce, as they often have millions of listings.

When optimizing local directories for SEO, it is important to first determine which directories are most relevant to your business and target audience. While there are some major directories that should be considered by any business (such as GMB, Yelp, and Facebook), it can also be helpful to focus on more specialized platforms depending on your industry and target audience. This can be a time-consuming task, as there are many options available, but it is worth taking the time to research and select the most suitable directories for your black-owned business, either manually or with the help of automation software.

To optimize local directories for SEO, you should include keywords, photos, and relevant content in the same way that you would for any other SEO strategy. It is often recommended to include keywords at the beginning of the business description and close to your business name. In some cases, the business name itself may contain a relevant keyword related to the products or services it offers.

When creating a listing on a local directory, it is important to include as much relevant information as possible, such as the contact number, address, and business hours, to make the user experience as smooth and efficient as possible. As with a blog or product page on a website, it is also essential to add the listing to the appropriate categories (maximum three). This will help users to find the listing more easily and improve the visibility of your business. User reviews are an important factor in optimizing local directories for SEO.

These can be acquired over time or actively encouraged by black-owned business owners. It is important to remember that, while positive reviews can be helpful, they are not the only factor that determines ranking. Even businesses with some negative reviews can rank well if the reviews are managed effectively. Some local directories, such as Go Black Own, also offer paid options for promoting your black-owned business.

Finally, strong growth for a black-owned business often depends on brand awareness. By optimizing your website for SEO and search engine results pages (SERPs) correctly, you can significantly increase your brand awareness. Using relevant keywords and tags can help users to associate those keywords with your brand. Additionally, a top ranking in search results can make your website more trustworthy in the eyes of users. When combined, these factors can improve the overall perception of your site and increase brand awareness.

CITATION BUILDING

The fundamental aspect of local SEO citation building and achieving success in local search is simply stating the basic information about your black-owned business, such as its location, hours of operation, and contact information.

But how can you ensure that search engines are aware of this basic information about your black-owned business in order to make it appear in local search results?

Why is it important to make this information visible to search engines? Even though your primary focus is on serving your customers, it is also important to consider that many people are now searching for local businesses online. Therefore, it is essential to optimize your online presence for local search in order to reach potential customers.

There is evidence to support the importance of local search for black-owned businesses. Google and Ipsos have conducted extensive research on the topic. Some of the ways in which local search can benefit your business include:

- 88 percent of consumers search for local information on mobile devices
- 51 percent of on-the-go searches have local intent
- Conversions are more than twice as likely after a local search (compared to searches without local intent)

What Does All This Have To Do With Building Citations?

Citations can increase your reputation and significance, which is crucial because Google considers it to be a key element in determining local search rankings, according to its local search guidelines.

Prominence reflects the level of recognition that your black-owned business has on the internet, and Google takes into account the amount of information it can find about your black-owned business on the web when determining your prominence. This includes links, articles, and other information about your black-owned business that search engines can find in directories, also known as citation information. Google, Yahoo, and Bing all utilize this information to list your black-owned business in local search results.

In addition, citations make up about 13% of how search engines like Google determine your local search ranking, making them one of the top four factors that search engines consider when ranking your black-owned business in local searches.

WHAT ARE CITATIONS FOR LOCAL SEO

Citations in local search marketing refer to mentions of your black-owned business on other websites. For example, if your black-owned business is listed on the Go Black Own platform, this counts as a citation. Mentioning your business in a blog post or online newspaper article also counts as a citation.

Citations are vital for black-owned businesses because they serve as indicators that search engines can trust your business.

Creating citations is essential for black-owned businesses that want to appear in local search results, as search engines such as Google and Bing rely on the information found in citations to list your black-owned business. To increase the chances of being found in local searches, it is important to ensure that search engines have access to accurate information about your black-owned business so that they can display it to consumers who are conducting local searches.

How do you do this?

This is where citation building comes into play for local SEO.

WHAT IS CITATION BUILDING

Citation building involves disseminating consistent, accurate, and relevant information about your black-owned business to listing directories so that search engines and consumers can find your local business. This process can be thought of as similar to link building.

Web crawlers trust your black-owned business when they find links to your website, and the same is true for citations. When web crawlers find your business listed in reputable directories, they know they can trust your black-owned business.

WHY DO YOU NEED TO BUILD CITATIONS

Citation building helps to establish credibility for your black-owned business online. As previously mentioned, citations are valuable to search engines because they indicate that your business is trustworthy.

Citations are beneficial for consumers because they can use them to locate local businesses through directory searches. For example, a consumer may use GoBlackOwn.com to find a black-owned business in their area.

To be found by consumers, it is important for your black-owned business to be listed in relevant directories. Search engines also rely on these citations to ensure that they provide accurate information about your business when consumers search for you.

In order for consumers to easily find accurate information about your black-owned business, it is important for the information to be consistent across directories. It's worth noting that local search is very important:

- 50 percent of consumers who performed a local search on a smartphone visited a store within 24 hours
- 54 percent of Americans have substituted local search for phone books

Consumers may be searching for your black-owned business online, and the information they find can influence what search engines display about your black-owned business in search results. It's important to note that search engines will consider the information from citations, whether it is correct or not, when determining what to show about your black-owned business in search results.

Citations can be incorrect for a variety of reasons, such as if your black-owned business has moved or changed phone numbers and the old information is still present in citations. Even small mistakes, like a missing or misplaced apostrophe in your business's name, can cause inaccuracies. Additionally, it is possible that your black-owned business is already listed in various directories, even if you have not added it yourself, but the information may be incorrect. This can lead to confusion for consumers or damage their trust in your black-owned business.

 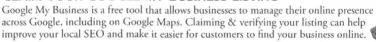

CLAIM YOUR GOOGLE MY BUSINESS LISTING
Google My Business is a free tool that allows businesses to manage their online presence across Google, including on Google Maps. Claiming & verifying your listing can help improve your local SEO and make it easier for customers to find your business online.

A recent study found that unmanaged listings can cause your black-owned business information to change frequently over the course of a year. To illustrate the importance of this, consider the following example: if a consumer searches for a "soul food" in a specific location and the search engine displays two results for your black-owned business, but each result has a different set of business hours, the consumer is likely to choose a competitor from the search results instead.

It's worth mentioning that inconsistency with your citation information can also lower your local search ranking. Now that we have discussed the importance of citations, let's talk about Google's black-owned business badge on maps and search listings.

GOOGLE'S BLACK-OWNED BUSINESS BADGE

Google recently introduced a new feature on Google Maps and Search listings called the "Black-Owned Business" badge. The Black-Owned Business badge is a visual identifier that appears on Google Maps and Search listings for verified Black-owned businesses. The badge is intended to help users easily identify and support Black-owned businesses in their local community. Business owners can apply for the badge through Google's online verification process. To verify a business, Google requires that the business owner provide proof of ownership, such as a government-issued ID, and proof of their business's legal structure, such as a business license or incorporation documents. Once a business is verified, the badge will appear on their business listing in Google Maps and Search results, making it easier for users to find and support Black-owned businesses.

The feature is part of Google's broader efforts to promote diversity and inclusion in its products and services. Google said in a statement that "We believe that increasing visibility for Black-owned businesses can lead to greater economic opportunities for Black communities, and we hope this feature will help people discover new Black-owned businesses in their area." Google's commitment to diversity and inclusion is not limited to this feature, they have a lot of actions and initiatives to support underrepresented groups.

The feature is currently only available in the United States, but Google plans to expand it to other countries in the future.

Additionally, Google has also made it possible for businesses to add themselves as Black-owned on their business profile in Google maps, which will help users to find and support Black-owned businesses.

TYPES OF LOCAL SEO CITATIONS

Before discussing the various ways in which your black-owned business can be mentioned online and the different types of citations, it is important to understand the information that is typically included in a local citation for a black-owned business.

STRUCTURED & UNSTRUCTURED CITATIONS

Citations for your black-owned business typically include your business's name and phone number. In local directories, this is typically the minimum amount of information that is included. However, many citations also include your business's NAP (name, address, and phone number). It is essential to ensure that your NAP is accurate and consistent across the web, as this will be important for maintaining a professional online presence. Otherwise, you could find duplicate listings for your business, or listings with inaccurate, incomplete or inconsistent information.

Inconsistencies in your black-owned business's contact information can lead to a loss of trust from consumers, who may not know which phone number or address to use or when your black-owned business is open. It is important to maintain accurate and consistent information to avoid this issue.

There are two main types of citations: structured and unstructured. Structured citations are those that follow a specific format and include specific information, while unstructured citations may be more informal and may not follow a set structure.

A structured citation is a citation that follows a specific format and includes certain information, such as a listing in a directory or a page on a website where you can edit the information yourself. An example of a structured citation is a Go Black Own listing page, which includes your business name, address, phone number, and hours of operation.

Unstructured citations are mentions of your black-owned business's name that may also include your location and/or phone number. These citations appear on websites that are not directory listings, such as online articles or blog posts. There are various types of citations and websites where you can find or create local SEO citations for your black-owned business. To get started, it can be helpful to focus on the four main data aggregators, which are important sources of information for search engines and directory listings like Google and Bing.

It's worth noting that the aggregators mentioned earlier are not actually citation sources, but they can help you get started with distributing citation information. In addition to the aggregators, it's important to claim or create and optimize your black-owned business's page on various platforms such as Google My Business, Yelp, Facebook, and Bing. Bing has a useful resource for optimizing your Bing Places for Business listing, which can be helpful if you are new to local search marketing.

HOW TO BUILD LOCAL SEO CITATIONS

Before you start creating new citations for your black-owned business, it's important to first ensure that your existing citations are accurate and up-to-date. To locate your black-owned business's current citations, try searching for your business's name and phone number in quotes like this: "business name" "(xxx) xxx-xxxx". Once you find these citations, you should claim any business pages and edit the information if possible to make sure it's accurate. If your business's phone number has changed in the past or if you have multiple phone numbers, you can also search for just your business's name (or your business name and any old phone numbers) and go through the search results to find and update your listings. You can also use Google's tool to see how your business appears in searches and check the information that's being displayed in your citations. Remember to be careful with your address when creating citations for your black-owned business as well.

In local directories, there are various ways to list a business's address. For example, it could be written as 101 Main St. or 101 Main Street. It is important to ensure that the address you use in listings is not only accurate, but also consistent across all listings. While search engines and directories are usually able to distinguish between "street," "st." and "st," it is still advisable to use the same address, also known as the Name, Address, and Phone number (NAP), in all listings to be on the safe side.

Optimize Listings

In addition to claiming pages on websites like Go Black Own or Google My Business, it is important to optimize your listings by adding more than just the bare minimum information. This includes adding a detailed description and photos of your black-owned business to give customers a better understanding of what you offer. Keep in mind that many of these sites also allow users to leave reviews, so it is important to regularly monitor and respond to both positive and negative reviews. If you receive a negative review, make an effort to address the issue and try to resolve it to the satisfaction of the reviewer.

To be successful, it's not enough to simply be discovered by potential customers through local searches. It's important to also be actively engaged with your customers and make sure they are satisfied with your business. Neglecting negative reviews or failing to address them can have a detrimental impact on a small business. Therefore, it's important to respond to negative reviews and try to resolve any issues that the reviewer has raised. In addition, it's essential to regularly solicit and receive new reviews in order to maintain a positive online reputation.

So What About Building New Citations?

Now that you have claimed your business pages and corrected any incorrect listings, it's time to create new citations. You can begin by using the list of data aggregators mentioned earlier. Additionally, you can look for directories specific to your industry or location, or research which citation sources list your competitors' businesses.

However, it's important to note that not all directories are equally valuable for your business. While it's important for customers to be able to find you on any directory they use, it's not practical or necessary to create citations for every single directory. Instead, focus on creating high-quality citations on the most important and commonly used websites for your black-owned business. For example, if your Go Black Own business page is not fully optimized with accurate and up-to-date information and photos, you may be missing out on potential customers. It's better to prioritize creating a few high-quality citations rather than a large number of low-quality ones.

YOUR CITATION BUILDING CHECKLIST

1. Find the correct address for your black-owned business. Check with USPS to see how, exactly, your address is listed.
2. Save this information in a spreadsheet or Word document to minimize errors and make citation building a little easier. Now once you need to update your listings, you can copy/paste the information into the directory.
3. Search for your black-owned business in Google to find your existing citations.
4. Clean up existing citations before you begin creating new citations.
5. Start building new citations, but be picky! Don't just add a citation to every site out there. Go for the important sites and data aggregators we mentioned.
6. Optimize your business's listings. Whenever possible, add photos, business information, and categories. Don't forget to check for and respond to reviews, and keep listings updated.
7. Keep track of your citations. You can't just build citations once, because one new NAP mistake somewhere could mean incorrect information in your listings. And you don't want consumers to find incorrect information about your business.

Keep in mind that citation building is just one aspect of local search marketing, but it is a crucial one. To improve your online visibility, it's important to ensure that your citations are accurate and that your business is listed on important directories. If you don't have the time or resources to handle this yourself, consider contacting a specialist in local search marketing who can take care of it for you. Remember, citation building may be a small piece of the puzzle, but it plays a significant role in helping customers find your black-owned business online.

IN CONCLUSION

SEO, SERP, and citations are important considerations for black-owned businesses looking to improve their online visibility and drive traffic to their website. By optimizing their website for relevant keywords and phrases, businesses can improve their search engine rankings and attract more qualified traffic.

In addition, by building high-quality backlinks and receiving positive citations from other websites, businesses can further boost their search engine rankings and establish their credibility in their industry. By focusing on SEO, SERP, and citations, black-owned businesses can effectively improve their online visibility and attract more customers in the digital space.

EFFECTIVE SEO IS NOT ABOUT ACHIEVING HIGH RANKINGS IN THE SEARCH ENGINE RESULTS PAGES, IT'S ABOUT DRIVING QUALIFIED TRAFFIC TO YOUR WEBSITE AND CONVERTING THAT TRAFFIC INTO CUSTOMERS.

CHAPTER 06
PUBLIC RELATIONS (PR) MARKETING

In this chapter you will learn about the value of press release marketing for black owned businesses. Press releases can be a powerful tool for getting the word out about your business and attracting media attention. By crafting a well-written and informative press release, you can effectively communicate the unique aspects of your business to journalists and other potential customers. Not only can press releases help to generate buzz and build brand awareness, but they can also be used to announce new products, services, or events, as well as share success stories and milestones. By leveraging the power of press releases, black owned businesses can effectively showcase their value and reach a wider audience.

Historically, PR has focused on carefully crafting and disseminating news releases and managing the image of a black-owned businesses through traditional media outlets like newspapers. However, the widespread adoption of the internet has significantly impacted this approach, leading to a shift in the way information is released and communicated. While traditional PR methods are still used, the internet has created new opportunities for black-owned businesses to directly reach their audience and interact with them online.

The internet has revolutionized the PR industry by providing new tools and platforms for communication. However, it has also disrupted traditional PR practices by giving greater access to information and allowing consumers to communicate through channels of their own choosing, rather than those dictated by black-owned businesses. This shift has changed the way black-owned businesses approach communication, as they must now consider the preferences and behaviors of their audience in the digital space.

Black-owned businesses are increasingly using social media to enhance their PR strategies. They focus on building active relationships and engaging in genuine conversations with their customers or stakeholders. The internet provides black-owned business with a wide range of tools for listening to and interacting with a larger community, which can be very beneficial for black-owned business that are open and transparent in their communication. It also enables black-owned businesses to engage in more immediate forms of communication.

WebPR refers to the various online channels and tactics used to promote a message and connect with customers, such as news sites, blogs, social media, and online newsrooms. It is used to improve brand awareness, exposure, and SEO efforts. As a black-owned business owner, it is important to remember that the people you are trying to reach through your marketing communications and social media outreach are deserving of respect and should be treated as such, rather than simply focusing on driving sales and increasing engagement.

The widespread adoption of the Internet has provided black-owned businesses with new communication tools and expanded the reach of a company's stories to a larger audience. However, the rise of social media, particularly the influence of bloggers, has required black-owned businesses to adapt to new methods of engagement and has presented challenges for traditional PR strategies.

HOW DOES PR WORKS

One key aspect of effective public relations is paying attention to what your customers have to say. This not only gives you insight into their preferences, but it also helps you gauge the effectiveness of your communication efforts.

As mentioned in the section on online reputation management, there are various tools available for monitoring customer feedback online.

Public relations is about building a connection with your customers, and part of that involves actively engaging with them through conversation. To truly connect with your customers, it's important to participate in the conversation where it's happening, whether that's online or in person. By actively responding to customer feedback and engaging in dialogue, you can build trust and establish a positive relationship with your audience.

Using web-based public relations tools can help you establish your own voice and be more transparent in your communications. While you may not have control over every aspect of the message, you can still shape the conversation by being open and honest in your interactions with customers and other stakeholders. This can help you build trust and credibility, and ultimately strengthen your reputation.

LISTEN TO YOUR CUSTOMERS

Online reputation management (ORM) involves monitoring what is being said about your black-owned business on the internet. It's important to regularly check all channels that customers might use to communicate with or discuss the company, including forums, consumer advocacy websites, and personal blogs. By keeping track of these mentions, your black-owned business can stay informed about its online reputation and take steps to address any issues that may arise.

By analyzing the general sentiment related to your black-owned business, not only can a trend be identified, but it will also bring attention to any issues that need addressing.

RESPOND TO OTHERS

Online Reputation Management (ORM) involves the use of various tools to track what is being said about your black-owned business on the internet. WebPR involves actively participating in these online conversations, using a consistent voice, to shape the public's perception of your black-owned business. It is important for black-owned businesses to respond to consumer generated media, which is publicly accessible and searchable, because it can significantly impact the public's perception of your black-owned.

Blogs and forums are essential platforms for responding to online conversations about your black-owned business. By responding in these media, your business can ensure that its response is seen in conjunction with the original message.

WHAT TO CONSIDER

It is important to be transparent and honest in all online communications. Using language that is too PR-oriented or misleading can damage your company's reputation. A genuine and authentic voice is more effective, and it's important to be able to handle both positive and negative feedback. Responding to all conversations, both good and bad, shows that your black-owned business is actively listening and engaging with its audience.

BUILD YOUR OWN VOICE

Even if your black-owned business doesn't have its own website, it is likely to have an online presence through listings in online directories and mentions in consumer generated media. It is important for black-owned businesses to carefully consider the image and message they are presenting online and to use the available tools to strengthen that image.

By using online techniques such as article syndication, news releases, and blogging to establish trusting relationships with consumers over the long term, your black-owned business can improve its credibility online and be better prepared to handle criticism in the future. These tools can also help to drive traffic to your black-owned business website and improve its search engine optimization (SEO) ranking by building links to the site.

Traditionally, black-owned businesses would send messages to journalists who would then share them with the public. However, this practice is no longer the primary means of disseminating information. This presents a great opportunity for black-owned businessses to directly engage with their customers.

WebPR does not mean abandoning traditional PR practices, but rather leveraging the full communication capabilities of the internet.

NEWS RELEASES OPTIMIZED FOR SEARCH & SOCIAL MEDIA

Public relations often utilizes news releases as a way to communicate information to the public. These releases follow a standardized format and were originally meant for journalists to use in their reporting. However, nowadays, many people access news releases directly, rather than reading about them through a journalist's reporting. Black-owned businesses have also recognized the influence of bloggers and may distribute news releases to them as well. The roles of journalists and bloggers are also converging, as some journalists are also bloggers and some bloggers are considered citizen journalists, causing the distinctions between the two groups to become less clear.

Newswires are online platforms that allow for the submission and distribution of news releases. These releases are then syndicated through RSS feeds and can be picked up by news engines like Google News, Yahoo! News, and MSN News. Many people rely on these online news engines as a source for their news, as they aggregate information from various publications and newswires. This makes the news release an important tool for reaching a wide audience.

In addition to generating interest in your black-owned business and its products, online news releases should also lead to an increase in traffic to your website. To do this, it's important to include relevant key phrases and links in the release. This will not only help the release be picked up by news engines, but may also be used verbatim by journalists, which can positively impact your search engine optimization (SEO) efforts. To maximize the effectiveness of your news releases, be sure to optimize them for key phrases and links.

Remember to post your news releases on your own website before submitting them to release sites. This will help establish your black-owned business as an authority on the topic in the eyes of search engines and also make it easier for journalists to find information about your black-owned business.

Similar to writing articles, you will need to include a description and assign keywords to your news release. It's also important to include all necessary media contact information. Each site will have specific requirements for the information that needs to be included. Many news release sites, especially those that are free, do not allow you to format your release in HTML. It's crucial to carefully consider the category you choose for your release and select the one that is most relevant.

Many news release sites offer both a free and paid option. The paid version usually includes additional benefits and may be worth considering if you want to take advantage of these perks.

BENEFITS OF ONLINE NEWS RELEASES

- Online news releases allow for almost instant publishing of news online.
- A well-written news release can garner top rankings in the news engines (Google News, Yahoo! News, MSN News etc). Adequate optimization can also result in SERP rankings.
- Content is syndicated quickly via RSS.
- Links are built naturally and effectively from online publishing.
- Distribution is increased beyond your contact list.
- Reach is far greater than that of a traditional news release.
- Reach and distribution can be easily tracked online.

Here are some news release sites to consider

- blackpr.com
- blackprwire.com
- blackgirlpr.com

CREATE A PRESS KIT
A press kit is a collection of materials that journalists and other media professionals can use to learn more about your business. This can include a press release, bios of key team members, high-resolution images, and more.

SOCIAL MEDIA NEWS RELEASE

Blogs and other media created by consumers, known as consumer generated media (CGM), are sometimes called citizen journalism. CGM has a significant reach and influence, so news releases often end up in the hands of content creators. However, some journalists are disillusioned with the traditional news release format and may view it as overly promotional and lacking transparency. Bloggers, who prioritize timeliness and transparency, may also view news releases as being excessively promotional.

The Social Media News Release (SMPR) is a tool designed to clearly and concisely communicate facts using the features of social media. It is the result of a ongoing dialogue between PR firms and journalists and bloggers. While there are differing opinions on this approach, it represents a PR firm's attempt to listen to the conversation, engage with it, and respond to it. The SMPR is still a work in progress and is being continuously developed.

BLOGGING

Blogging is an effective way for black-owned businesses to establish their own unique voice in the digital world of social media and citizen journalism. In addition to helping with search engine optimization through the creation of fresh, keyword-rich content, blogging also helps companies connect with their customers.

Through blogging, black-owned businesses can actively participate in online conversations and show their familiarity with this form of communication. A company blog allows for regular commentary in the business's own voice and helps businesses learn how to engage with their customers on a more personal level.

ONLINE PRESS ROOM

As the internet makes it easier to access information, it is important for black-owned businesses' web public relations (WebPR) strategy to ensure that relevant information is easily accessible. By making sure that journalists, customers, and investors can quickly and easily find key company information, you black-owned business can more easily join online conversations.

According to a Nielsen Norman study, journalists are successful in finding basic information on a corporate website only 73% of the time. Given the tight deadlines that journalists often work with, having readily available information could be the difference between being covered in the media or not. An online press room can help black-owned businesses meet the needs of journalists and ensure that necessary information is easily accessible.

An online press room must have:

- Company history
- Key executive biographies
- Pertinent background information
- Logos and images in a variety of sizes, resolutions (for web and for

- print) and formats
- All news releases
- Multimedia gallery (video, audio and visual)
- Contact information
- Search function
- RSS / email alerts
- Tagging capabilities
- Information in a variety of formats

By making sure that information is easy to find and accurate, both the public relations team and researchers save time and your black-owned business shows its willingness to communicate openly.

PITCHING TO BLOGGERS

While some journalists may also be bloggers, not all bloggers are journalists. Bloggers do not have the same responsibilities as journalists, such as answering to editors or publishers, and they typically write about topics that they are passionate about rather than for financial gain. They tend to measure their success by the number of comments, trackbacks, and traffic their blog receives.

In order to effectively pitch to bloggers, it is important to understand the differences between bloggers and journalists. Many bloggers who frequently receive pitches have written blog posts that provide guidelines for the public relations industry, and it is beneficial for black-owned businesses to read and take note of these guidelines.

To pitch effectively to a blogger, it is important to build a relationship with them, just as it is with journalists. It's important to remember that both journalists and bloggers are individuals, and it's beneficial to approach them with this in mind.

- Read their blog, and engage.
- Make pitches personal and relevant.
- Provide accurate key information. Be descriptive but concise.
- Do not try to spin a story.
- Show that you are aware of who is talking about you, and who is talking about their blog.

- Be transparent.
- Provide links to images, logos and news releases. Never send large attachments.

Journalists are typically limited in the value of gifts they are allowed to receive and are expected to disclose when they receive free samples of products they review. This is to maintain their reputation for impartiality. In contrast, bloggers, who are self-publishers, have the freedom to create their own guidelines. Some bloggers accept expensive gifts in exchange for coverage, which may appear more genuine because it is coming from a blogger rather than a journalist.

TOOLS OF THE TRADE

The tools necessary for effective engagement in a conversation through WebPR include:

- Tools for listening
- Tools for responding
- Tools for tracking success

One of the most effective methods for monitoring mentions of a brand or company online is through the use of RSS feeds that track relevant keywords. This technique is discussed in more detail in the chapter on Online Reputation Management.

Responding can take place through the various social media channels such as:

- Blogs
- Twitter
- Facebook
- Forums

Utilizing online article directories and news release directories is an essential part of publishing and disseminating information. Maintaining a comprehensive and current online newsroom helps to ensure that relevant information is easily accessible.

The key to successful public relations is building relationships. For journalists, bloggers, and consumers alike, transparent communication is the foundation for effective PR.

SHOULD I OR SHOULDN'T I

It is clear that the media landscape has evolved, and those who want to communicate through new media channels must adapt accordingly. While the Internet expands the reach and distribution of all messages, it also means that companies have less control over these messages. However, the use of public relations on the web allows black-owned businesses to have greater access to customer feedback and a direct way to respond to it.

The PR team will have to put in more effort as there are now more recipients of information. In addition to building relationships with journalists, it is important to also target bloggers and other content creators. The way in which black-owned businesses communicate with their audience is changing, and the power is shifting from the black-owned businesses themselves to those that they rely on to disseminate their messages.

SUMMARY

PR has entered a new phase with the rise of online platforms. WebPR, or the use of online channels such as article directories, news release sites, industry websites, online newsrooms, blogs, forums, and social media sites, helps to improve brand recognition, visibility, and search engine optimization.

The internet has provided tools that can help with the fundamental aspects of effective PR, which involve paying attention to and reacting to the needs and concerns of the audience.

Black-owned businesses can use online reputation management (ORM) tools to monitor online conversations about their brand. In order to effectively respond to customer feedback, companies should actively participate in these conversations, whether through commenting on blogs and forums or through other forms of engagement.

Black-owned businesses can use the Internet to build their own voice online.

Tactics include:

- Online article syndication
- News release directories
- Corporate blogging

WebPR leverages the internet to modernize traditional PR strategies. Optimizing news releases for search engines and social media platforms can help to increase the online presence, distribution, and reputation of a company. It is important to have a well-managed online press room that is easily accessible and full of useful resources.

Thanks to the internet, black-owned businesses no longer have complete control over the way in which their brand is discussed online. With WebPR, however, they can actively participate in these conversations and, through transparency, try to shape the conversation in a way that is favorable to their brand.

THE BIGGER PICTURE

WebPR can be a valuable part of a comprehensive search engine optimization (SEO) plan. When content is optimized for search engines and syndicated, it can help to establish the authority of the source website and generate backlinks. Optimized news releases can have a similar effect, and when they are featured on reputable media outlets, the backlinks they provide can be particularly valuable.

PR and ORM are closely interconnected and rely on each other to be effective. ORM involves listening to online conversations about a brand, while PR involves responding to and seeking to initiate those conversations. It is important for black-owned businesses to strike a balance and not appear overly promotional or disconnected from their audience.

On the other hand, if black-owned businesses spend too much time listening and not enough time engaging in the conversation, they may not be able to effectively shape the direction of the conversation. It is important to find a balance and ensure that the conversation is moving in a positive direction. WebPR can complement a brand's social media strategy by leveraging these platforms to expand the reach of marketing messages. Effective WebPR involves using social media effectively to achieve this goal.

PR IS THE ART OF TELLING A COMPELLING STORY AND GETTING IT IN FRONT OF THE RIGHT PEOPLE AT THE RIGHT TIME. IT'S ABOUT BUILDING RELATIONSHIPS AND TRUST, NOT JUST PROMOTING A PRODUCT OR SERVICE.

CHAPTER 07
ONLINE REPUTATION MANAGEMENT

Now that you have learned how to use SEO, SERP, PR, and digital marketing in general, the next step is to focus on managing your business website and building a strong reputation. This will help to continue the growth of your black-owned business and make the most of the tools you have learned to use. If you feel that there is potential to build a reputation, now is the time to take action.

It is always possible to work on building and maintaining a good reputation for your black-owned business. Managing your reputation involves actively maintaining a positive image and the longer you are able to do this, the stronger your reputation becomes. For example, if a company has a history of excellent customer service and has not had any negative incidents in the past decade, or if a company is known for consistently offering good benefits to its employees, they are both effectively managing and building their reputation over time. This chapter will delve into the process of managing and building a strong reputation for your black-owned business.

This chapter will focus on identifying and implementing strategies to make your black-owned business website and social media pages more attractive and reliable. But before we get into the specific tactics for improving your online reputation, it is important to understand the basics of reputation management and how it applies to both your brand and personal identity.

WHY DOES ONLINE REPUTATION MANAGEMENT MATTER

A reputation exists in both the physical and digital worlds, and in the current age, your online reputation is just as important as your reputation in the real world. This book has emphasized the importance of building and managing your online reputation because it directly impacts your black-owned business and career. Negative content or associations online can harm your black-owned business and career, while a positive online reputation can lead to a successful business with a loyal customer base.

There are four key reasons why it is important to focus on building and managing your online reputation:

1. Literally anyone can say anything about you or your black-owned business online without getting into real trouble, whether it is true or not.
2. People are always going to be looking you up online and make decisions based on what they are able to find.
3. Everything that you do online is going to be recorded forever in the online world, which means that at the end of the day you will need more tools to make sure this does not damage your reputation.
4. Having impeccable online content is surely going to help you but most people do not know how to do it.

As competition in the market grows, it is important to publish engaging content on your website and social media pages in order to attract customers. This means that more and more people, including companies and other customers, will be searching for positive information about your business. In order to stand out in a crowded market, you need to put in extra effort to showcase the value and quality of your products or services.

It is common knowledge in the field of digital marketing that the content you publish should be compelling and attractive to your audience. However, many people struggle with creating this type of content. Online reputation management involves enhancing the positive presence of your black-owned business in all areas of your online presence, as we have discussed in this book.

One important point for black-owned business owners to remember is that outsourcing your content creation to a writer or posting uninteresting updates on your social media pages will not be effective in the long term. It is important to put effort into creating high-quality, engaging content in order to succeed in the digital space.

A FEW PRINCIPLES FOR ONLINE REPUTATION MANAGEMENT

Throughout our experience in online reputation management, We have established a few principles to guide our decision-making and keep our strategies focused. These rules have proven helpful in helping us make difficult decisions and maintaining a strong online reputation.

Search Results Are Algorithmically Generated

As we work on building your online reputation, it is important to understand that the internet is driven by complex calculations and algorithms. With such a vast amount of information available online, it is not practical to rely on manual processes. Instead, search engines and social media platforms use algorithms to predict what their users may be interested in or searching for. These algorithms play a significant role in determining what content is displayed to users and can impact your online reputation.

Popularity Over Accuracy

One downside to relying on algorithms to determine what information is displayed online is that humans may be more accurate in assessing what accurately reflects you. While algorithms can be useful in sorting through large amounts of data, they may not always capture the nuances and complexities of a person or business. As a result, it is important to be proactive in managing your online reputation and ensuring that the information that appears online accurately reflects you and your black-owned business.

Popularity Becomes One Of The Main Measuring Standards

This is why searches performed over a long period of time or past incidents, such as embarrassing posts or lawsuits, can resurface and have a significant impact on someone's online reputation. Even if these events occurred years ago, they may still be prominent in the online world and could dominate the information that is displayed about a person or business. This highlights the importance of continuously managing your online reputation and being aware of the information that is being shared about you online.

Do Not Click On The Repetitive Pages

There may be negative search results or irrelevant sites that appear in your search results. One way to reduce their visibility is to avoid clicking on them. As mentioned earlier, algorithms use popularity as a factor in determining what information to display. If you click on a negative or irrelevant result, the search engine may interpret this as relevance and prioritize it in future search results. To avoid reinforcing negative or irrelevant information, it is important to be mindful of what you click on when searching online.

Avoid Any Association With Negative Or Irrelevant Things

Avoid suggesting to your friends that they visit a particular page, especially if your social media account is connected. This is because the search engine will assume that what interests your friends is also likely to be of interest to you.

Do Not Engage With Detractors Online

As mentioned earlier, it is crucial to manage your online reputation because there may be individuals who try to harm your reputation or business online. If someone writes something negative about you or your company or leaves a negative review, it is best to avoid engaging with them on the same platform and posting a response. This will prevent further attention being drawn to the issue and potentially amplifying it.

Responding to the negative comments or reviews could escalate the situation and make it worse. It is not always clear how sincere the person is or how they might manipulate your words and use them against you and your reputation. It is best to avoid responding to avoid any further damage to your reputation.

Use Social Media When You Can

It is beneficial to create accounts on social media platforms like Twitter and LinkedIn because they tend to rank highly in search results due to their algorithmic processing by search engines. When signing up, use your full name rather than a pseudonym to make it easier for people to find and identify you. Additionally, be sure to keep your profile information up to date. One advantage of these sites is that you have the ability to customize your privacy settings and control the content that is visible to others.

Get Your Story Out There

To effectively promote your materials, it is important to have a strong story and reliable content. If the story or content is weak, it will be difficult to promote and others may not be able to support it or speak positively about it if they do not find it trustworthy or relatable. To establish trust and connect with your audience, it can be helpful to share your story and integrate it with your business. This can include explaining why you started your black-owned business, why you enjoy what you do, etc. Find a story that fits your black-owned business and make it a central part of your brand. If it resonates with your audience, you could consider creating a separate blog or YouTube channel to expand on it.

Protect Your Privacy

You have the power to decide what you share on social media and your own website, but it's important to regularly monitor these platforms and stay up-to-date on any changes to their privacy policies. Additionally, it's a good idea to keep track of any personal identifiable information that may be available about you online, as you don't have control over what others may share about you. To protect your privacy, you may want to opt out of services that sell your personal information and remove your data from people-search sites.

Live Under The Assumption That Everything Lasts Forever

Online reputation management is crucial for many reasons, including the fact that anything you publish online has the potential to be permanently accessible, even if it's no longer relevant. Search results are not always organized chronologically, so old posts or published items may appear at the top of search results in certain situations. It's important to be mindful of this and maintain a positive online reputation to avoid any negative consequences that may arise from outdated or irrelevant information being easily accessible.

ADDRESS NEGATIVE REVIEWS & FEEDBACK
If you receive a negative review or feedback, it's important to respond in a professional and constructive manner. Consider apologizing for any issues, offering a solution, and thanking the customer for their feedback.

TRACKING MENTIONS ABOUT YOUR BUSINESS

Google Alerts is a free tool that allows you to track mentions of specific keywords or phrases across the web, including on social media and in news articles. You can use Google Alerts to track mentions of your black-owned business and receive notifications whenever your business is mentioned online.

To set up Google Alerts, you will need to have a Google account. Once you are signed in, you can create an alert by entering the keyword or phrase you want to track and selecting the type of results you want to receive (such as news articles, blogs, or social media posts). You can also specify how often you want to receive alerts and the email address where you want to receive the notifications.

Google Alerts can be a useful tool for online reputation management, as it allows you to stay on top of what is being said about your business online. You can use it to track both positive and negative mentions of your business and respond accordingly. You can also use it to keep an eye on your competitors or stay up to date on industry trends.

WHAT MAKES A WEBSITE USUALLY APPEALING?

I included this topic last, even though I mentioned it at the beginning, because the other information discussed is more important to consider first. Before you start trying to make your website and social media pages more appealing, it's important to understand and address the issues covered earlier.

Understanding all of the elements that contribute to a successful website will help you improve it. While creativity and design skills are important, they can also be refined. If you're not a designer, you may need to hire one to help make your website visually appealing.

Here are some tips for improving the aesthetic elements of your site:

Design & Color

To effectively engage and keep the attention of a website visitor, the site should have a carefully chosen color scheme and strong design. The colors and color combinations used can influence the emotions and thoughts of the viewer, so it is important to consider the impact of the chosen color scheme.

A well-designed website conveys a sense of professionalism and trustworthiness to the visitor. On the other hand, a poorly designed or cluttered website can turn off potential customers and make it difficult for them to navigate, leading to a loss of interest in the site.

Pictures & Graphics

High-quality images can greatly enhance the visual appeal of a website and give it an advantage over competitors. Many websites still lack well-organized and well-composed photos of their products, offices, or staff. It's also important to consider how the website will look on mobile devices and if there are opportunities to incorporate interactive or engaging images.

Usability

Ease of understanding and navigation are crucial components of a successful website. There's no need to use unconventional language or terms; instead, stick to familiar terms like "Home" or "Main Lobby." The buttons and dropdown menus should be clear and straightforward, and the page layout should prioritize the most important information for that page. A well-organized website makes it easy for visitors to find what they're looking for.

Consistency

To ensure a consistent and cohesive experience for visitors, it is important to establish a design language on the homepage and apply it throughout the rest of the website. This will allow visitors to quickly become familiar with the site and easily understand the content, rather than spending time trying to adapt to a different design on each page.

IN SUMMARY

Online reputation management is an important consideration for black-owned businesses looking to protect and enhance their reputation in the digital space. By monitoring and managing their online presence, businesses can address any negative reviews or comments, respond to customer inquiries and complaints, and highlight positive feedback from satisfied customers.

In addition, businesses can use online reputation management tools and services to track and analyze their online reputation, as well as to proactively manage their reputation by creating and promoting positive content about their business. By focusing on online reputation management, black-owned businesses can effectively protect and enhance their reputation, build trust with customers, and drive business growth in the digital space.

ONLINE REPUTATION MANAGEMENT IS ABOUT PROACTIVELY SHAPING THE CONVERSATION ABOUT YOUR BRAND AND TAKING CONTROL OF YOUR DIGITAL FOOTPRINT.

CHAPTER 08
PAID ADVERTISING

We have covered a number of methods for constructing and maintaining a positive online reputation. These techniques should provide you with a foundational understanding of how digital marketing differs from traditional marketing. When utilized effectively, each of these strategies has the potential to contribute to the success and expansion of your black-owned business.

Digital marketing involves utilizing the internet and other digital channels to reach potential customers. It allows black-owned businesses to connect with their audience despite geographical and time differences. In the virtual world, consumers increasingly rely on the internet for information and expect to find products and services online. Building a strong reputation on digital platforms can attract more traffic and potential customers.

In this chapter, we will delve deeper into how to maintain and grow your online business reputation once you start attracting traffic to your website. It's important to keep in mind that you may not initially attract the desired amount of traffic, but as you become more proficient in digital marketing, you can work towards increasing it. However, it's crucial to sustain and cater to the traffic you do have without compromising its growth.

The next step in attracting targeted traffic to your website after optimizing your search engine rankings is to utilize paid advertising. By paying for advertising, you can ensure that traffic is directed to your site. However, it's important to carefully plan your paid advertising strategy to avoid overspending.

Here are some things to consider in order to maximize the effectiveness of paid advertising:

UNDERSTAND WHAT LONG TAIL KEYWORDS ARE

Keywords are a commonly used tool in paid advertising, so it's important to understand how they work before diving into this strategy. However, it's common for people to use broader keywords in an attempt to attract more traffic, which can actually be more expensive and less effective.

To get the most out of paid advertising, it's more effective to use keywords that customers actually search for rather than those with the highest traffic. This involves identifying and targeting "long tail keywords," or specific, targeted phrases that are more likely to be used by customers.

Long tail keywords are longer and more specific phrases that are formed by adding a head keyword, or a broader term, to another keyword. They make up the majority of search-driven traffic and are more targeted and relevant than head keywords. For example, "digital marketing" is a head keyword, while "digital marketing for businesses" is a little more specific but not a long tail keyword. "Digital marketing for black-owned businesses," on the other hand, is a long tail keyword because it is more specific and less frequently searched than "digital marketing for businesses." Long tail keywords help to narrow down results and increase relevance.

Beginners often make the mistake of choosing the wrong keywords for their SEO or PPC campaigns, thinking it will be easy. However, using head keywords, or broader terms, can be costly and may not provide a good return on investment. Instead, it's more effective to target a larger number of lower traffic terms for the same budget and also target a few high traffic terms. This can help you get a better return on your investment.

To further optimize your paid advertising strategy, it can be helpful to identify keywords that customers might use to search for your website on your own site. By understanding what your customers are searching for, you can invest in more specific keywords that are more likely to lead to a higher return on investment.

KNOW THE TERRITORY

There are many different places where you can purchase advertising space online, each with its own set of strengths and weaknesses. To determine the best place to advertise, it's important to understand the various types of paid advertising available.

Banner ads, also known as display ads, are a type of advertising that is highly visible on web pages. These ads are effective because they often catch the attention of customers who are not actively searching for products or services. For example, when someone is reading a newspaper article online, they may not be actively looking to make a purchase. However, the banner ads on the page may still capture their attention and potentially lead to a sale. While banner ads can be a powerful marketing tool, there is still a chance that they may not be effective for every business.

Text ads are a type of advertising that appears on search engine results pages, such as Google. These ads are typically less expensive than banner ads and are targeted towards customers who are actively searching for a specific product or service. To be effective, text ads should be paired with relevant keywords to ensure they are seen by the right audience. One of the most popular places to run paid text ads is through Google Ads (formerly known as Google AdWords). This platform allows you to show display and text ads that are closely related to specific keywords. Bing and Yahoo! also offer similar platforms for running text ads, which may attract less traffic but may have more qualified users, leading to a potentially better return on investment.

In recent years, social media networks such as Facebook, LinkedIn, and Instagram have become popular platforms for advertising. Among these, Facebook has particularly focused on expanding its ad offerings. On Facebook, ads are targeted based on users' preferences, demographics, location, and other factors, in addition to being associated with keywords. This makes the ads more relevant and effective.

KEEP YOUR TRACKING READY

To get the most value out of your advertising investments, it's important to track their performance and identify areas for improvement. Without this information, it can be difficult to justify the cost of paid advertisements. In the physical world, it can be challenging to track the effectiveness of traditional marketing efforts in real-time. However, in the online world, it's possible to track the performance of your ads in real-time, allowing you to easily make adjustments and optimize your strategy as needed. This can save you time and money compared to traditional marketing efforts.

Just as it's important to regularly maintain and monitor a car to ensure it is running smoothly, it's also important to keep track of an advertising campaign that you have paid for. In order to do this effectively, it's important to have a good understanding of all aspects of the campaign. This includes keeping track of its performance, identifying any issues that may arise, and making any necessary adjustments to ensure that the campaign is running smoothly.

Google Analytics is a powerful tool for monitoring the performance of online ads. It provides a single dashboard where you can create custom campaigns and track their performance using a variety of metrics. This makes it easy to see how your ads are performing and identify areas for improvement.

CREATE A LANDING PAGE

Having a well-designed homepage is essential for any website because it serves as the hub for all content and navigation. However, it can also be beneficial to direct incoming traffic to a specific landing page that stands out. This may seem to contradict the purpose of a homepage, but there are good reasons for using this approach.

One benefit of using landing pages is that they can provide a seamless transition between advertisements and your official website. By customizing the message for incoming visitors, you can create a welcoming and enriching experience for them. Landing pages can serve as a link between ads and your website, allowing visitors to easily navigate to your website after they arrive on a landing page.

Another advantage of landing pages is that they allow you to direct customers more precisely to specific areas of your website, such as a page where they can download a free E-book or sign up for a service. This can help you achieve specific goals and guide visitors to take specific actions on your website.

Another reason for using landing pages is that they can make it easier to track visits to your website. This is useful for keeping digital records and for marketing purposes. By directing incoming traffic to a specific landing page, you can more easily monitor and analyze the effectiveness of your marketing efforts.

Also having a keyword-rich domain name for your landing page can help to improve its search engine rankings, as well as make it easier for potential customers to find and remember. For example, if your business sells organic beauty products, a domain name like "OrganicBeautyProducts.com" would be more descriptive and relevant than a generic name like "MyBeautyStore.com". By using a keyword domain name, you can increase the chances that your landing page will be found by people searching for the products or services you offer.

Using landing pages and tracking user behavior data over time can provide valuable insights into the types of visitors coming to your website and what they are looking for. This information can help you tailor your marketing efforts to better reach and sell to your target audience. It's important to remember to block your custom landing page from search engines to avoid skewing the data on its performance. Linking it to search engines can lead to inaccurate results.

REVIEW RESULTS REGULARLY

It is beneficial to regularly review the results of your black-owned business, but the frequency at which you do so may vary depending on the industry. In the field of digital marketing and advertising, it is generally not advisable to review your data on a daily basis as it can create unnecessary pressure and lead to hasty decision-making. Instead, it is more effective to consider the overall average of results over a longer period of time, rather than focusing on daily fluctuations.

It is important to allow your campaign sufficient time to gain attention and drive traffic. In order to accurately gather trends and information through analytics, it is necessary to track the campaign without making any changes. Over time, you will notice that it takes a certain amount of time to achieve a positive return on investment. This can help you determine an appropriate time frame for reviewing your statistics.

Now that you have a general understanding of the concepts and considerations involved in paid advertising, we can delve further into the specifics of what paid advertising entails in the field of digital marketing. Essentially, paid advertising involves purchasing the right to use ad space online from the owner of that space. The cost of this ad space is often determined through a bidding process, where marketers and space owners compete for the space. There are several types of paid advertising, including pay per click (PPC) or cost per click (CPC), pay per impression (PPI), and display advertisements.

We will examine display advertising in greater detail in the following chapter, along with social media marketing. However, before moving on, it is important to understand the basics of PPC advertising, specifically how Google Ads operates.

GOOGLE ADS

Google Ads, formerly known as AdWords, is a pay-per-click (PPC) advertising service offered by Google. It allows businesses to promote their websites by paying for their search results to appear on a Search Engine Results Page (SERP). This service is popular among all types of companies and allows them to bypass the process of gradually improving their ranking through organic means, and instead, immediately display their website near the top of the SERP.

TYPE OF GOOGLE ADS

Google Search Ads
Google.com

Google Search Ads have been a major source of income for Google for a long period of time. However, it is possible that video and display ads may eventually become more important sources of revenue in the future.

Google AdWords, now known simply as Google Ads, is a platform that enables users to bid for prominent placements in search results for specific keywords. It operates like an auction, so the level of competition for particular keywords can vary significantly. For instance, keywords related to finding a lawyer for asbestos-related cancer (such as mesothelioma) can cost upwards of $800 or more per click, while a local store selling specialized items may only pay an average of one dollar per click.

To consistently rank highly for a specific keyword search, it is not enough to simply bid a high amount in the auction. There are other criteria that must be met, such as having a high "quality score" as assessed by Google. If your quality score is deemed to be low, you may have to pay more for a top position or may not be eligible to participate at all. To improve your quality score, it is important to ensure that your targeted keywords, ad copy, and landing page content are relevant and accurate. Google Ads has automated systems that will reject any content that is deemed to be misleading.

In addition to having relevant and accurate content, it is important to ensure that your website provides a good user experience. This includes factors such as the relevance of your text, the speed at which your pages load, and whether your site is mobile-friendly. If any of these elements are not up to par, it may result in a lower quality score, which can lead to higher costs for your average cost-per-click (CPC).

I often recommend using a Google Ads search campaign to those who want to generate leads quickly and don't want to wait for the benefits of organic SEO to materialize. One advantage of this type of marketing over SEO is that, for Google users, paid ads appear above organic ads in search results. Later in this book, we will delve more into how to set up and optimize these campaigns for maximum effectiveness.

Google Display Ads
(Google Ads on other sites via AdSense)

Once you have gathered sufficient data from using Google search, you can launch your own banner campaign, which can be displayed on a wide range of sites that allow Google advertising. Major news sites, online magazines, and even Yelp are among the many sites that participate in this program.

To effectively participate in this program, it is helpful to have a skilled graphic designer on hand. There are specific dimensions to follow, and you will need to ensure that your message is conveyed effectively across different screen sizes.

Youtube Ads - Video Ads

Like Google Display ads, the Google video platform allows you to advertise on a wide range of websites and also targets audiences on YouTube, one of the busiest sites on the internet. To get started, you will need a YouTube video. You may have noticed that videos automatically play on YouTube when streaming content on a smart TV or smartphone. These are ads that are being actively displayed using this platform. The content you see from advertisers will depend on your profile, as determined by Google based on your demographics and interests. For example, if you watch music videos, you may see ads from other artists in a similar genre or sponsored suggestions for their videos on YouTube.

If you are a dentist, the Google video platform allows you to target people who have recently used Google to search for dentists. It will match you with these individuals and also gives you the option to include a custom call to action within the video and direct them to your website.

This platform offers a variety of options for billing and bidding, such as paying a certain amount per click or per video view, or only being charged when a viewer completes the video. These options allow you to customize your budget and make the most of your advertising spend. Additionally, video advertisements tend to have a higher conversion rate compared to text-based advertisements.

Google Play Store - App Ads

This type of advertising is gaining popularity and can now be seen in free apps that people download on their Apple or Google devices.

The most popular form of advertising so far has been promoting apps on the app store or within other apps. This effectively targets people who own the appropriate type of device.

Video advertising is another effective use of this platform, as it often receives a significant number of views within free apps.

If you are a local business without strong branding or other apps to offer, using Google Play Apps can be a frustrating and ineffective experience due to the high frequency of accidental clicks on false advertisements. Strong branding and additional apps can help increase the effectiveness of using Google Play Apps.

Beware that in many display campaigns, Google may automatically include all app users in their targeting list, which can lead to a waste of budget due to the high rate of false clicks. It is important to carefully monitor your campaign to avoid this issue.

As a black-owned business owner, my advice is to avoid using this feature unless you are specifically targeting app marketers or seeking a large number of video impressions. If you are not experienced with this process, it may be helpful to seek the assistance of a professional to ensure proper implementation.

Google Shopping

Advertising through this channel is only available to those selling physical products, as services do not currently qualify. This narrows the group of potential advertisers to those within a specific niche.

Google Shopping is a platform that allows users to search for and purchase products directly from the search results page. When a user searches for a product, Google Shopping displays a list of closely matching items with prices and review ratings, similar to Amazon. Users can also save their payment information with Google for a quick checkout process. Google Shopping is a competitor to platforms like eBay and Amazon.

To use Google Shopping, you need to sync your website data with your merchant and Google Ads accounts through merchants.google.com. If you need assistance with this process, consider seeking the help of a digital marketing firm.

Gmail Ads

Gmail Ads are a form of online advertising that allows you to reach potential customers through their Gmail inbox. These ads are displayed as sponsored messages in the Promotions tab of a user's Gmail account and are targeted to users based on their search history, demographics, and other factors.

Gmail Ads can be a useful tool if you're looking to reach a specific audience with targeted messaging. They offer a number of features, including the ability to include images and calls to action, and can be tracked and measured for effectiveness using Google Analytics.

Remarketing Ads

Remarketing is a useful and cost-effective way to keep your brand top-of-mind with customers. It involves using data collected from website cookies, including IP address, site activity, geographic location, and other information, to create a targeted group for your ad campaign. This type of targeting allows you to reach a highly focused audience.

One of the advantages of a remarketing campaign is its ability to target potential clients as they visit other websites that are part of Google's ad network. With this type of campaign, you can display customized advertisements featuring catchy copy or attractive banners to these individuals as they browse the internet. This gives you the opportunity to keep your black-owned business top-of-mind for these potential clients and increase the chances of converting them into customers.

Paid search refers to the advertisements that appear within a search engine's results, such as those displayed at the top or side of the page. Google is the most widely used provider of this service. The way it works is that black-owned businesses or individuals select specific keywords related to their business and create an advertisement linked to those keywords. Whenever someone searches for those keywords on Google, the advertisement will be displayed alongside the other search results. It's common for multiple companies to bid for the same search term, so it's possible for a search engine results page (SERP) to show multiple ads from different organizations. The higher you are willing to pay per click, the more frequently your advertisement will appear in the search results.

Google Ads uses a system called the quality score to determine the placement of ads. The quality score is based on the relevance and usefulness of the ad to the user and the search terms being used. In addition, the click-through rate and relevance of the landing page are also considered. For example, if an ad for a specific product leads to the homepage of a website instead of the page for that product, it will be considered less relevant and useful to the potential customer, resulting in a lower quality score.

CHOOSE THE RIGHT PLATFORMS
There are many different platforms available for paid advertising, including search engines, social media, and online directories. It's important to choose the platforms that make the most sense for your business and your target audience.

IMPORTANCE OF PAID ADVERTISING

An efficient marketing campaign should utilize all available advertising channels. While paid advertising can be more expensive than creating your own or earning advertising, it can provide a effective way to reach a larger audience and promote your black-owned business. Paid ads are often displayed to online users in various parts of a webpage, and if you are able to pay more, you can place your ads on more popular websites with higher traffic. In addition, you can customize your ad campaign to better meet the needs of your clients by choosing from different categories.

The online advertising industry is a multi-billion dollar industry, with digital ad spending reaching over $129 billion in 2020, which represents nearly 50% of all media spending. While paid advertising can be an effective way to drive traffic to your website, it is important to remember that you are paying for that traffic and it will stop coming in if your budget runs out. Therefore, it is important to make the most of the window of opportunity provided by paid ads and establish your business before stopping the investment. Paid advertising is a rented form of advertising, so it is important to be strategic in order to avoid losing your investment.

One of the benefits of online advertising is its ability to provide precise measurement and targeted marketing. This means that it is possible to track the revenue generated from each visit and to tailor advertising efforts to specific demographics for more successful results. Additionally, both short-term and long-term values can be calculated to gauge the effectiveness of the advertising campaign.

AMAZON PPC - PAID MARKETING

In addition to SEO, Amazon provides a paid advertising service called "Sponsored Products" or Amazon PPC to help listings stand out in search results. These paid ads can be found above or below organic results or in the right column. Similar to other pay-per-click (PPC) campaigns, marketers only pay for ads that are clicked on and generate views of the advertised product. Properly implementing Amazon PPC can also help improve a product's organic ranking.

Amazon's marketplace receives millions of searches each month that range from short to long phrases. Unlike regular search engines, Amazon users are actively seeking to make a purchase. Paid ads, which use an auction-based approach, are displayed among the organic results in order to distinguish them. Sellers set a daily budget for each ad, with higher bids increasing the chances of their ad standing out. However, it is important for listings to be optimized with the correct use of keywords, relevant information, and content to be successful.

There Are Three Main Types Of Sponsored Ads On Amazon:

Sponsored Product Ads

Keywords play a significant role in advertising products on Amazon. It is important to conduct thorough keyword research to maximize the effectiveness of these ads. Amazon ads are known to have high click-through rates (CTRs) and conversion rates and are typically displayed among the organic search results.

Product Display Ads

These ads are displayed in the "similar products" section on a product page. They are self-serving and linked to an Amazon Standard Identification Number (ASIN). This allows marketers to target specific behavioral segments. Product display ads have their own screen placement and budget settings. The effectiveness of these ads can vary depending on the type of product, the goals, and the intended audience. It is important to carefully consider these factors when using product display ads.

Headline Search Ads

Banner ads, also known as top-of-search ads, are only available for certain product categories. These ads are typically displayed at the top of search results and feature a brand logo. The main goal of banner ads is to encourage buyers to click through to a group of products. They offer a high level of customization, allowing you to showcase multiple products at once and customize the landing destination. Options for landing destinations include brand pages, product pages, URLs, and search result pages, and you can also choose which images and text to display in the ads.

To use Amazon's pay-per-click (PPC) advertising, you must have a seller account, be able to ship within the United States, meet the Buy Box eligibility criteria, and be enrolled in the Amazon Brand Registry.

AMAZON'S BLACK-OWNED BUSINESS BADGE

Amazon's new "Black Owned" badge is part of the company's larger efforts to promote diversity and inclusion within its marketplace. The badge is intended to help shoppers easily identify and support products from Black-owned businesses, making it easier for these businesses to gain visibility and reach a wider audience.

To be eligible for the badge, a business must be at least 51% owned, operated, and controlled by an individual or individuals who identify as Black. Amazon will verify businesses' eligibility for the badge through a combination of documentation and on-site visits.

Once a business has been verified, the Black Owned badge will appear on the product pages and search results for the business' products, making them more easily discoverable by shoppers. This could also lead to more sales and revenue for Black-owned businesses on the platform.

It's also worth noting that this move by Amazon is important in the larger context of the ongoing movement for racial equity and the push for companies to take more concrete steps to support Black-owned businesses. By introducing the Black Owned badge, Amazon is making it easier for shoppers to make conscious purchasing decisions and support Black-owned businesses, which could have a positive impact on the Black business community.

PAID MARKETING ON LOCAL DIRECTORIES
(Go Black Own, Google My Business)

Directory websites such as Go Black Own and Google My Business have gained popularity and now offer paid options for listings. Both Go Black Own and Google My Business have a high level of visibility and are often used by users to make purchasing decisions or to find businesses to visit. Go Black Own specifically caters to black-owned businesses and can be just as, if not more, influential in persuading users to make purchases or visit a business. Due to the high level of visibility of these websites, black-owned businesses may find it necessary to invest in paid marketing options.

Advertising on Go Black Own has some specific features. Go Black Own ads can appear in various locations, including relevant search results pages and even competitors' Go Black Own listing. They can also be displayed on different platforms, including the desktop version, the mobile Go Black Own site, and the mobile app. Recently, Go Black Own ads have added the ability to target by location.

There Are Two Types Of Paid Advertisements For Businesses On The Go Black Own Platform:

The Black Excellence Package and Go Black Own Ads are additional features that can be added to your Go Black Own listing for an enhanced experience. These upgrades allow you to block ads from competitors, create a slideshow to showcase your photos, and use a call to action to send coupons, order forms, and be featured on Featured Friday, where your product and services are highlighted and promoted to users on the platform via email. These features are not available with a free listing.

Go Black Own Ads, on the other hand, charges a monthly fee to display a banner ad within the website & app. You can also track the performance of your paid campaign.

Google My Business also has a paid advertising option, which can be linked to Google Ads. This allows ads to be displayed with a business's physical location on Google Maps search results. In addition to this, GMB also offers paid monthly features to help listings stand out, such as:

"Book" Button On Google My Business Profile

It allows users to check a business availability and book an appointment or consultation.

Promoted Map Pin

A special placement in Google maps when users are looking for businesses in your area.

Verified Customer Reviews

A very useful tool to make sure a user actually visited your location or bought your products.

Google Guarantee

A trust badge to be displayed on your GMB profile that allows a customer to receive a refund from Google if he or she is not satisfied with your product or service.

APPLE ADS - ON APPLE APP STORE

Online stores featuring apps for mobile devices receive millions of visits each year. For example, as of September 2021, there were approximately 2.2 million apps available for download in the App Store. With such a high volume and competition among apps, there is a need to distinguish oneself from the rest and rank higher. This is why, in addition to SEO for mobile apps, Apple ads were introduced on the App Store.

These ads, called Search Ads, were introduced in 2016 to help developers reach potential users using information such as gender, location, keywords, or previous app downloads. In 2017, Apple introduced "Search Ads Basic," a pay-per-install advertising product aimed at smaller developers. Traditional Search Ads were also renamed as "Advanced" to differentiate them from the other paid advertising options on the App Store.

After setting up your campaign, Apple Ads will be displayed at the top of the App Store results when a user searches for a keyword related to the promoted app. The app developer pays for different types of conversions depending on the selected ad. With Advanced Search Ads, you pay every time a user clicks on the app. With Search Ads Basic, you only pay when the app is installed on the user's device.

Similar to other pay-per-click campaigns, Apple will suggest a maximum bid for certain keywords based on historical data from the App Store about the app the developer is marketing. However, Apple does not create profiles or collect personal information to gather this data. The ads are only displayed on the Apple App Store and nowhere else on the internet.

Search Ads can also improve an account's organic rankings because Apple's algorithm considers the number of downloads and speed of installation when ranking an app. Apple views installs from Search Ads as high-quality downloads, which helps improve an account's overall position. Although there are no restrictions on the type of ad or the size of the company bidding, Search Ads Basic has a maximum bid limit of $5,000. There is no limit on the amount of money that can be bid for Advanced Search Ads.

Apple's Search Ads are a good option for small developers who want to increase their app's visibility quickly and easily. With a conversion rate of over 50% and a cost per acquisition below $1.50, Search Ads are among the most affordable and effective pay-per-click options on the internet.

TEST & OPTIMIZE YOUR ADS
Paid advertising can be a significant investment, so it's important to make sure your ads are performing as well as possible. Consider testing different ad copy, images, and targeting options to see what works best for your business.

OTHER PAID MARKETING ALTERNATIVES

Google has been a pioneer in the Pay Per Click (PPC) model and continues to be a leader in this area. There are several other forms of paid advertising on the internet that are not as well-known as PPC campaigns. These alternatives are based on the behavior of individual websites and how they can attract bidders to pay for advertisements on them, rather than relying on the performance of a website or listing on platforms like Google or Amazon.

Adroll

Adroll is a digital marketing technology that focuses on retargeting, which means it bases its actions on a user's previous behaviors. It allows you to create ads on different platforms, including desktop and mobile sites as well as social media.

Media.net

Media.net creates products across various segments within the ad tech industry in order to meet all of a user's needs without relying on multiple vendors. They claim to have originated the display-to-search (D2S) ad format, which monetizes display placements by identifying user search intent and displaying relevant search keywords. These keywords then lead to search ads that advertisers pay for on a Cost Per Click basis.

PropellerAds

This advertising platform is designed for marketers and affiliates who are focused on performance. It is a WordPress plugin that enables site owners to generate revenue from their mobile and web inventory, including mobile apps, widgets, online games, and software. The platform includes a variety of tools, such as Push Notification, Native Banners, and Smart Links, to help users achieve specific goals.

Adversal

Adversal is a CPM (cost per thousand) advertising platform that pays for each ad impression rather than for each visitor. It is known for its pop-under ads, which are difficult to block due to the platform's specialized code.

Viglink

Viglink aims to enhance the value of every link on your website, according to the company's website. It specifically targets bloggers, influencers, and editorial sites. To accomplish this, Viglink employs Natural Language Processing (NLP) technology to automatically connect product references in articles and other content to the highest-paying advertisers.

Skimlinks

Skimlinks is a content monetization platform that targets forums, bloggers, editorial websites, and app developers. It specializes in in-text contextual advertising, meaning it focuses on specific keywords within the content and matches them with relevant ads.

WRAPPING UP

Paid advertising can be a powerful tool for black-owned businesses looking to reach and engage with customers online. By using platforms such as Google Ads and social media advertising, businesses can target specific audiences and demographics and effectively promote their products or services to a large and relevant audience. In addition, by using data and analytics, businesses can track the effectiveness of their paid advertising campaigns and optimize them for better results.

By focusing on paid advertising, black-owned businesses can effectively reach and engage with potential customers, drive traffic to their website, and generate leads and sales in the digital space. Overall, paid advertising can be a valuable addition to a black-owned business's digital marketing strategy, helping them to reach and engage with their target audience and drive business growth.

PAID ADVERTISING AMPLIFIES YOUR BRAND'S MESSAGE AND HELPS YOU REACH THE RIGHT AUDIENCE, BUT IT'S JUST ONE PART OF A WELL-ROUNDED MARKETING STRATEGY.

CHAPTER 09

SOCIAL MEDIA MARKETING

To fully comprehend social media marketing, it is important to be familiar with the topics covered in previous chapters, including creating an online presence, managing online reputation, using press releases effectively, and using paid advertising. Social media marketing encompasses all of these elements. Social media refers to websites and platforms that allow users to interact with each other, like Twitter for sharing short messages, Instagram for sharing and editing pictures, and Facebook which is a comprehensive social networking site that includes these features and more.

WHAT IS SOCIAL MEDIA MARKETING

Social media marketing involves using popular social media platforms, which have the highest number of registered users, as a marketing tool by creating content that users can share on their own social media networks. The goal of this type of internet marketing is to increase brand awareness and exposure, attract a larger customer base, and drive traffic to a business's website.

A key aspect of social media marketing is social media optimization, which involves developing strategies that are tailored to the specific features and functions of each social media platform in order to attract new and unique visitors to a website.

There are two main ways to use social media for marketing purposes. The first is by adding links to social media profiles or sharing buttons to website content, allowing users to easily share the content on their own social media accounts. The second is by actively promoting a company's content on social media through updates, such as tweets, blogs, or statuses. Overall, social media marketing is a form of internet marketing that aims to increase a company's online presence and reach.

As social media has become more popular, social media marketing has also become more widespread. To accommodate this trend, the Federal Trade Commission has updated its regulations to allow for social media marketing. If a company provides free products to a blogger or social media user in exchange for promotion on social media, it must be aware that the online comments generated by this activity will be considered legally as endorsements. Therefore, it is important for both the company and the individual sharing the promotional content to ensure that there are no conflicts of interest and to clearly disclose that the posts do not contain any misleading information. Essentially, the same rules for traditional marketing apply to social media marketing in order to prevent deceptive advertising.

It is essential to understand the connection between search marketing and social media marketing, as both are forms of online marketing that are closely related. Black-owned businesses should pay attention to what is happening on social media because search engines often use social media as a source for new or updated content, such as news stories, blogs, and other types of posts. When search engines search the internet for information, social media becomes an important area to examine because it may contain valuable insights about individuals or organizations. In other words, social media can provide search engines with new information to display in their search results.

Social media can also help with search engine optimization (SEO) by serving as a link building tool. SEO involves using links to attract customers, and social media posts often include tags and links that can support these efforts.

Many people use the search function on social media platforms to find content that they know exists on the site. Each social media site has the ability to search for new content within the platform. If people use this search function, they will receive search results in response to their query. If search engines link to these social media sites, they can also be used for searches. The relevance of the search results on these sites can also be influenced by social connections, whether within a social media network or on a mainstream search engine.

> **TIP**
> **ENGAGE WITH YOUR AUDIENCE**
> Building relationships with your followers is an important part of social media marketing. Respond to comments and messages, ask for feedback, and interact with your followers to foster a sense of community.

BENEFITS OF USING SOCIAL MEDIA MARKETING

Social media marketing is increasingly important for black-owned businesses. By leveraging social media, businesses can reach a larger and potentially untapped customer base. The major social media platforms offer endless opportunities for businesses to increase their exposure, often at a low cost. By dedicating as little as one hour per day, you can significantly improve your traffic and sales without a significant financial investment.

Although it is clear that social media is a crucial part of any marketing strategy, many professionals in the industry are unsure about which strategies and tactics to use. A survey conducted by Social Media Examiner found that 96% of business owners were using social media marketing in some way, but 85% of these business owners were unsure which tools were the best fit for their needs. In the next section, we will discuss the clear benefits of using social media in order to clarify any confusion.

In this chapter, we will explore techniques and strategies that can help establish a strong social media presence. Let's begin by considering why social media presence is so important for any brand. When people understand the value of something, they are more likely to be more focused and creative in how they use it and treat it. By keeping the importance of social media in mind, it will be easier to tailor the techniques and strategies discussed in this chapter to your own brand.

Rise In Brand Awareness

There is no doubt that social media is one of the most cost-effective forms of digital marketing for increasing the online visibility of your brand. Content created for social media is connected to a social media strategy that can improve brand recognition by engaging with a larger number of consumers than search marketing alone. Getting started with social media is easy: simply create a social media profile for your business and begin interacting with other users.

It is advisable to start by creating a profile on one social media site and then expanding to others, so you can get a feel for how each site works. Then, ask your employees, sponsors, business partners, and others to like and share your page or profile. This counts as interacting with your content, as it will appear in newsfeeds and may reach a new network of users. By investing just a few hours in this at the beginning, you can build a noticeable profile on social media.

Rise In Inbound Traffic

Have you ever watched a shepherd guide a herd of sheep or cows towards a specific destination? If so, you may have noticed the shepherd using a horse and dogs to keep the animals together and prevent some from straying from the group. This is similar to how your social media accounts can work. Your main website acts as the main enclosure, where you have set up everything for consumers to interact with. Your social media accounts can be thought of as the herd, with some followers straying from the group as they move towards your main website.

- Your social media accounts can be thought of as the dogs that help guide your audience towards your main website. When you create a new website or add a page to your existing site, it is like taking a great picture of yourself that you want the world to see. However, you don't want to beg for attention. This is where your social media accounts can help. You can use them to redirect traffic from social media to your new website or page.
- Each social media account has its own unique characteristics. A well-crafted post on one of these platforms can have a significant impact. You can spark curiosity in your audience or leave them wanting more. You can also make an offer that is hard for them to resist.

Rise In Search Engine Rankings

In the introduction to digital marketing, I mentioned search engine optimization (SEO) and its importance for black-owned businesses. SEO works by ranking websites or brands with higher traffic higher in search results. Search engine crawlers can determine which pages are consistently receiving traffic and which pages are not. By developing a strong content or advertising strategy for your brand's SEO, you can improve your brand's ranking in search engine results. However, SEO is not the only way to improve your ranking.

By using your social media accounts to consistently engage with your audience and redirect them to your website, you can also boost your ranking in search engine results. This is because your social media accounts will be linked to your website, and any posts you make on social media will include keywords and links to your website. To achieve this, it is important to maintain a consistent presence on social media platforms such as Facebook, Twitter, and Instagram, as well as on your own website.

Relationship Building

In the past, it was widely believed that real relationship building could only occur in person. This was partially true due to the limitations of technology at the time. However, today, many people are online and can communicate in real time. Additionally, the tools that allow for deeper communication and understanding in person, such as finding someone's location or learning about their preferences and behaviors, are also available online. With the increasing use of technology, it is possible to use these tools to establish real relationships with consumers, even if they are not physically present. In fact, you may be able to do even more through online communication.

In addition, social media accounts like Twitter and Instagram allow for personalized interaction with your customer base. By reading their posts and tweets, looking at their pictures, and getting an understanding of their daily lives, you can tailor your marketing strategies to better meet their needs. For example, you can find out what they enjoy doing on the weekends, what places they like to visit, and what their interests are. This information can provide numerous opportunities, such as offering promotions based on their interests or discounts at places they frequent. Furthermore, building real relationships with other brands, journalists, public speakers, and experts in your industry can help expand your ecosystem and establish a strong presence in your field.

Users Become More Receptive To Your Message

One advantage of social media accounts is that they are still primarily used for personal networking, rather than being solely viewed as marketing platforms. These accounts also offer privacy settings to keep advertisements out of sight. As a result, people using these accounts are more likely to pay attention to the messages you are trying to convey, rather than seeing your posts purely as marketing efforts.

Advertisements that constantly pop up or are placed in spaces where they are not expected are often ignored by consumers unless they are actively searching for them. However, when trusted forums or friends share links to your brand or talk about it, people are more likely to pay attention to what you have to say.

> **T-IP**
> **DEVELOP A CONTENT STRATEGY**
> A content strategy is a plan for creating and distributing valuable, relevant, and consistent content to your audience. Consider what types of content your audience is interested in, how often you will post, and how you will promote your content.

GETTING STARTED

Now that you have a good understanding of social media management and how it works, including the importance, terms, differences, and advantages, as well as how to start building a social media presence for your brand, the next question is how to dominate social media and what strategies you can use to make your efforts more effective. The following tips and tricks will help you get started and provide some ideas for improving your strategies.

1. To dominate social media, it is advisable to first focus on one channel, become proficient in it, and then expand your presence to other channels. Managing multiple channels at once can be overwhelming, and you may miss out on a strong consumer base if you are unable to give each channel the necessary attention. Alternatively, you may need to hire a social media manager, which can be costly in the early stages of building your presence.
2. The next step is to automate your tasks. You can use social media account management tools like Buffer, Hootsuite, and SocialOomph to grow your presence. You can also use a content calendar to plan which posts to upload on which days and at what times.
3. Repurpose a single piece of content into multiple formats, such as turning it into a blog, an ebook, a video, an audio podcast, or tweeting key points. This can help you reach a wider audience and get more value out of your content.
4. Set aside a few days each month to produce several videos or blogs, then use these materials to create new content through repurposing.
5. Hold contests, give away products or services, and offer special discounts as part of product promotions to engage with your audience.
6. Opt for Facebook advertising, Instagram ads, etc.

FACEBOOK & IG ADS

(Lead Ad, FB messenger)

In 2019, one effective advertising method was using Facebook messenger. This allowed people to view an ad and immediately connect with a representative through the platform. We have successfully used this strategy for several clients, particularly in the legal industry.

Paid ads on Facebook and Instagram have gained popularity in recent years and can be effective for businesses in a variety of industries. However, eCommerce stores have particularly benefited from using these platforms for advertising.

FACEBOOK ADS

Facebook offers a range of options for paid advertising. You can promote your Facebook Page, specific posts on that Page, or a website through the platform. While Facebook Ads primarily target users within the platform, they can also be an effective way to drive traffic to external websites. Facebook's targeting features allow you to reach specific users based on demographic, location, and profile information. When creating an ad, you set a budget for how much you are willing to pay for each click or impression. These ads are typically displayed on the sidebar of Facebook.

Facebook ads are generally more effective at creating demand rather than meeting existing demand. Unlike search engines or purchasing platforms where users have a specific goal in mind, Facebook's primary purpose is to bring people together, rather than directly answering a query or selling products. Marketing on Facebook, and therefore paid ads, are closely related to the content shared on specific pages that align with the user's interests. Successful marketing on Facebook is subtle, and paid ads are more effective when they lead to conversions that ultimately result in sales rather than trying to directly make a sale.

INSTAGRAM ADS

Instagram is known for being one of the most visual social media platforms, with a focus on photos, short videos, and "stories," rather than written content. It is particularly popular with millennials and younger demographics. As Facebook owns Instagram, black-owned businesses can use Facebook data to target specific audiences on the platform. Black-owned businesses can interact with users through ads, mostly displayed on the home page and in the comments section of photos.

Instagram offers a total of six different ad formats for black-owned businesses to choose from. Four of these formats, known as Instagram feed ads, are displayed in the main feed of the platform, while the other two, called Instagram stories ads, are displayed in the stories feature of the platform.

Feed Ads:

- **Photo Ads:** they feature one image and can be featured in a group of six ads with one different image each.
- **Video Ads:** they can be added in video format or GIF
- **Slideshow Ads:** video ads in a loop featuring up to 10 images. It can include music.
- **Carousel Ads:** two or more images or videos.

Stories Ads

- **Single image:** allowing up to six ads with one different image each.
- **Single video:** 15 seconds long video or GIF

PINTEREST ADS

Pinterest is a unique social media platform that is heavily focused on discovery and navigation. Its images are often not branded, which makes users more open to exploring new products and ideas. Paid ads on Pinterest have specific features that are tailored to this emphasis on exploration and discovery. It's worth noting that these ads are currently only available in the USA, Canada, the United Kingdom, Australia, Ireland, France, and New Zealand.

There are up to seven different types of Pinterest Ads available:

Promoted Pins

Pinterest's paid ads, known as "promoted pins," are typically displayed in the home feed and search results alongside regular pins. However, they are given greater visibility and targeted more specifically to reach a wider audience. Promoted pins are labeled as such and otherwise behave like regular pins, meaning they can be pinned to users' boards, shared, and receive comments.

One-Tap Pins

As of 2022, all Pinterest ads have implemented a one-tap system, which means that when a user clicks or taps on an ad, they are immediately directed to a landing page.

Promoted Carousels

Promoted carousels are groups of two to five images that users can swipe through on Pinterest. Each image can have a different description, title, and landing page, making them ideal for promoting multiple related products. These carousel ads behave like regular pins, except they have dots indicating that they can be swiped through.

Promoted Video Pins

Video pins are similar to promoted pins, but feature video content instead of static photos. They can be displayed in the home feed, search results, and the "more like this" section. Video pins will autoplay when they are 50% in view. Pinterest allows for two sizes: max width and standard videos.

Promoted App Pins

Promoted app pins allow users to directly download a mobile app from Pinterest. They behave and appear like promoted pins, but instead of linking to a webpage, they link to an App Store or Google Play URL and have an install button. Promoted app pins are only available to mobile users.

Buyable Pins

Product pins allow users to find and purchase products directly from a related pin. These pins are available for both desktop and mobile users and are displayed in the same sections as promoted pins.

Story Pins

Story pins can include up to 20 pages of images, links, and text. They appear in users' home feeds with a cover image, title, and "Story" label underneath. These pins can be saved to users' boards like any other pin.

LINKEDIN ADVERTISING

LinkedIn operates differently than other social media platforms like Facebook because it is geared towards professional users. This means that it can be an effective way to target people on a business-to-business basis or to promote professional services. One way to increase brand awareness on LinkedIn is to sponsor notifications to get more people to follow your black-owned business. However, it's important to keep your followers engaged by providing valuable insights about your company, such as articles that add value. If you don't do this, you risk people unfollowing you. Sponsoring notifications to get more followers does not cost any money, but it's important to make sure those efforts don't go to waste by engaging with your followers.

LinkedIn is a social media platform that caters to the business professional community. Originally created as a tool to find new jobs or employees, it has also become a useful platform for inbound marketing. This has been facilitated by the creation of LinkedIn Ads, which allow businesses to reach potential clients and decision-makers with targeted content through paid ads. LinkedIn's user base is made up of professionals and businesses, which allows the platform to monetize ads by helping businesses connect with their target audience. Services are often promoted on LinkedIn, as professionals typically offer their expertise and skills, but it is also common to promote software and other products.

To use LinkedIn Ads, you need to set up a campaign using LinkedIn Marketing Solutions, which is a separate platform from a regular LinkedIn profile. To create ads, you can simply click the corresponding button in LinkedIn Marketing Solutions. After you create your Campaign Manager account, you can create campaigns and organize them into campaign groups. You can set your objectives for the ads, such as getting users to visit a website, engage in polls or follow a LinkedIn page, increase exposure for a video, or generate leads using an online form.

After determining the goals of the campaign, the next step is to identify the characteristics of the intended audience. LinkedIn provides numerous options for tailoring advertisements to specific audiences, including the ability to select from up to 20 different languages. It is also possible to target specific geographic locations, ranging from broad regions to specific cities, counties, or even locations in the immediate vicinity. Other criteria that can be used to target a campaign on LinkedIn include demographics, level of education, industry, and areas of interest.

Linkedin Ads support several different formats:

- **Text ads:** text only ads that feature in the right column or the top of the LinkedIn site.
- **Single image ads:** one image that appears on the newsfeed along with organic content.
- **Carousel ads:** two or more images also on the newsfeed.
- **Video ads:** one video on the LinkedIn newsfeed.
- **Follower ads:** available just for desktop, these ads are useful to promote a LinkedIn Page using a profile data to customize the ad.
- **Spotlight ads:** used for special offers, they also use LinkedIn profile data and are desktop only.
- **Job ads:** they promote open positions using LinkedIn profile data. They're only available on LinkedIn desktop too.
- **Message ads:** delivered to profiles that match a target audience to their LinkedIn inbox.

TWITTER ADS

Twitter Ads can be used for three main purposes: attracting new followers, driving traffic and conversions to a specific website, and generating and capturing leads. This is due to the platform's nature as a place for quickly sending short messages. There are also specific types of ads on Twitter, such as promoted tweets (paid tweets that are displayed to engage new followers), promoted accounts (ads that promote a Twitter account to users who do not yet follow it), and promoted trends (useful for enhancing hashtags and generating trending topics). Twitter Ads can be automated using Twitter Promote Mode, which for a flat fee of $99 will automatically promote the first ten daily tweets from your account to selected audiences.

YOUTUBE ADS

Since its acquisition by Google, YouTube has relied on Google Ads to create its paid advertisements. YouTube ads are effective for generating leads, attracting traffic to a website, increasing product and brand awareness, and expanding reach. YouTube's video ad formats are specific and include TrueView Ads, which automatically play before, during, or after a video and offer the option to skip after five seconds. These ads generally last up to 30 seconds and can also be displayed on other parts of Google's display network, such as apps or games. Non-skippable YouTube ads, which cannot be skipped and last up to 20 seconds, appear at the beginning or in the middle of videos that are more than ten minutes long. Bumper Ads, which also cannot be skipped and last up to six seconds, appear at the end of YouTube videos.

SNAPCHAT ADS

Snapchat is a popular social media platform among the millennial generation, similar to Instagram. Both platforms are primarily used on mobile devices, so Snapchat ads are designed to encourage users to download apps or engage with brands and individuals within the platform. Snap Ads are interactive mobile videos that are often used to promote apps or mobile games.

Snapchat offers three advertising options for brands: Sponsored Lenses, Snapchat Discover, and Snap Ads. Sponsored Lenses allow brands to create their own filters for users to use while promoting the company, while Snapchat Discover places a company's story at the top of users' app feeds. These options can be costly, with Snap Ads costing between $1,000 to $3,000 per month, Sponsored Lenses costing between $450,000 to $700,000 per day, and Snapchat Discover costing $50,000 per day. These high prices may make these options more feasible for larger, well-known brands.

TUMBLR ADS

Tumblr is a platform that is heavily focused on written content and blogs, and it allows for a strong connection between users and brands. One way that brands can advertise on Tumblr is through Sponsored Posts, which are ads that appear in users' dashboards and blend in with organic content. Another option is Sponsored Video Posts, which are similar to Sponsored Posts but feature audiovisual content. Brands can also opt for Sponsored Day ads, which allow them to pin their logo and tagline to the top of all Tumblr users' dashboards for a full day.

REDDIT ADS

Reddit is a platform that is known for its AMAs (ask me anything) and viral content, and it serves as an open forum for discussion on a wide range of topics. Despite not being as well-known as some other social media platforms, it is actually used by 6% of all adults on the internet. One unique aspect of Reddit is that it targets audiences through subreddits, which are niche communities centered around specific groups of people and topics. Reddit offers two types of ads: Promoted posts, which can be further divided into link ads and text ads, and Display ads, which are traditional online display ads in the form of banners or rich media.

TIKTOK ADS

TikTok is a relatively new social media platform that has gained widespread popularity in recent years, with over 800 million monthly users in more than 150 global markets. It has become one of the most downloaded apps in the world, and it offers small businesses a chance to connect with a large and engaged audience. By using TikTok in their marketing efforts, black-owned businesses can strengthen their brand recognition and messaging, showcase their products and services, and engage with a growing, influential audience that could potentially become loyal customers.

The COVID-19 pandemic has led to a surge in internet usage, as people look for new ways to stay entertained and connected while being stuck at home. TikTok offers you a way to directly reach your target audiences and engage in real-time conversations that shape relevant thoughts and interests within a community. By using TikTok, black-owned businesses can significantly increase their reach, attract more potential customers, and ultimately generate increased sales and support their bottom line.

Here are a few ways black-owned business owners can leverage TikTok marketing to boost sales:

Create Authentic & Interesting Content

Creative, short-form video is becoming more popular in social media marketing, as consumers are looking for engaging, authentic content that is relatable and valuable. In today's digital age, people want trustworthy interactions with real people and their real experiences, so it's important for black-owned businesses to be transparent and responsive to changing trends and consumer interests. After becoming familiar with the app and understanding what resonates with your audience, you can create videos that showcase your branding in a modern and creative way.

You should not abandon your company's branding and messaging in an attempt to appeal to potential consumers on TikTok. It's not necessary for your marketing team to participate in the latest dance challenges in order to be successful on the platform. Instead, they can stay on brand and establish yourself as thought leaders on the app, sharing useful expertise that is relevant to your niche market and connecting with users in a genuine way.

As an example, a cake decorator could create short videos showcasing various aspects of their business, such as behind-the-scenes clips of their upgraded kitchen, tips for making the perfect icing, the process of baking their signature strawberry shortcake recipe, or footage of their cakes from a recent catering event. Audio selection and effects can help make mundane tips and tricks more fun and engaging in video form.

Connect With Your Target Audience

TikTok offers black-owned business owners the chance to create content that their target audience is interested in, without having to spend a lot of money on advertising. By consistently creating exciting content, the TikTok algorithm will expose it to more and more people, similar to how Instagram works. Black-owned business owners can consider the most popular topics within their niche on other channels and come up with content ideas based on those conversations. By actively engaging with users on the app, black-owned business owners can build stronger relationships with their following and increase brand awareness.

One of the easiest ways to attract potential customers on TikTok is to use popular hashtags that are relevant to your niche. You can also use TikTok SEO to optimize your channel and increase the chances that your content will be discovered on the Discover or For You pages. Influencer marketing is another effective way to boost user engagement, as influencers and micro-influencers often have a high level of credibility with their followers and can be helpful for startups looking to target specific customer groups. Ultimately, the key to creating effective TikTok content is authenticity, creativity, and a focus on relevant topics for your business, audience, and niche market.

Scale With TikTok Ads

One of the main benefits of using TikTok for marketing is that you don't need to spend a lot of money on professional videographers or editors to create high-quality content, as you might on YouTube. Instead, you can redirect those funds towards TikTok advertising, which allows you to filter your ads by age, gender, and location to directly reach your target audience. Setting up an ad campaign on TikTok is relatively straightforward, thanks to the platform's step-by-step guide in the TikTok Ads Manager. Once you have your campaign set up, reaching your target audience should be quick and easy.

TikTok offers five different types of ads:

- In-feed ads
- Branded hashtags
- Top view ads
- Branded effects
- Brand Takeovers

There are several ways that black-owned business owners can reach their target audience on TikTok, including interest targeting, behavioral targeting, custom targeting, and lookalike audiences. Interest targeting allows you to select topics that are relevant to your audience, and TikTok will target those groups based on their common interests. Behavioral targeting allows you to target audiences based on their behavior on the app within the past seven or fifteen days.

Custom targeting allows you to provide a list of customer emails to reach people who have already interacted with your brand, while lookalike audiences help you reach people similar to an existing audience. By using these methods, you can directly reach audiences who are interested in your niche content and are more likely to engage with and potentially become paying customers.

Using TikTok for advertising can be a fun way for small businesses to engage with potential customers and increase overall brand awareness.

USE PAID ADVERTISING
While organic reach on social media can be limited, paid advertising can help you reach a wider audience. Consider using paid advertising options, such as promoted posts or sponsored ads, to reach a specific target audience.

WHAT ARE HASHTAGS

Hashtags are used on social media platforms to tag or label content and make it more discoverable. In social media marketing for black-owned businesses, hashtags can be used to highlight the business, its products or services, and any relevant events or promotions. For example, a black-owned clothing business might use hashtags like #blackownedbusiness #blackownedclothing #fashionforward to promote their business and attract potential customers. By using relevant hashtags, businesses can reach a larger audience and increase their visibility on social media platforms.

There are several ways to use hashtags in social media marketing:

- **Identify relevant hashtags:** Research and identify hashtags that are relevant to your business and audience. These might include industry-specific hashtags, hashtags related to your products or services, and local hashtags.
- **Use relevant hashtags in your posts:** Include relevant hashtags in the text of your social media posts to make them more discoverable.
- **Use hashtags in your bio:** You can also include relevant hashtags in your social media bio to give people an idea of what your business is about and make it easier for them to find you.
- **Participate in hashtag campaigns:** Keep an eye out for hashtag campaigns related to your industry or target audience and participate in them by using the designated hashtag in your posts.
- **Monitor and adjust your hashtag strategy:** Use social media analytics tools to track the performance of your hashtags and adjust your strategy as needed.

It's important to remember that hashtags should be used sparingly and only when they are relevant to the content being shared. Using too many hashtags or using unrelated hashtags can come across as spammy and may turn off potential followers.

By using hashtags effectively, you can increase the reach and visibility of your social media content and attract more potential customers to your business.

WHAT DOES TRENDING MEAN

In social media marketing, "trending" refers to topics or hashtags that are currently popular and are being widely discussed on social media platforms. Trending topics are often determined by algorithms that track the frequency and popularity of certain hashtags and keywords.

Using trending topics in social media marketing can be a good way to increase the reach and visibility of a brand's content. By joining in on trending conversations, black-owned businesses can potentially attract new followers and engage with users who are interested in the topic being discussed.

However, it's important to use caution when using trending topics in social media marketing. It's important to ensure that the trending topic is relevant to the brand and its audience, and to be mindful of any potential sensitivities or controversies surrounding the topic. Using a trending topic in a way that is inappropriate or insensitive can damage a brand's reputation and alienate potential customers.

WHY SOCIAL MEDIA HANDLES ARE IMPORTANT

Social media handles are the unique names or username that businesses use to identify themselves on social media platforms. They are typically used in conjunction with the platform's URL to create a custom link to the business's social media page.

For black-owned businesses, social media handles can be a powerful tool for building a presence online and connecting with customers. By choosing a handle that accurately represents the business and its brand, black-owned businesses can create a professional and cohesive identity across social media platforms.

Some tips for selecting a social media handle for a black-owned business might include:

- **Choose a handle that is unique and memorable:** A handle that is easy to remember and stands out can help to increase brand recognition and make it easier for customers to find the business's social media pages.
- **Use keywords related to the business's products or services:** Including relevant keywords in the handle can help to attract the attention of users who are searching for those products or services.
- **Keep it short and simple:** Long or complex handles can be difficult to remember and may be truncated on some platforms. Aim for a handle that is short and easy to type.
- **Be consistent:** Use the same handle across all social media platforms to create a cohesive brand identity.
- **Check for availability:** Take some time to research and brainstorm potential handles to find one that fits the business's brand and goals. Consider using a tool like Namecheckr to check the availability of a handle across multiple social media platforms.

Once you have selected a social media handle, it's important to use it consistently across all platforms to create a cohesive brand identity and make it easy for customers to find and follow the business. Be sure to update the handle if the business's name or focus changes to ensure that it continues to accurately reflect the business.

AVOID BEING CANCELED - CANCEL CULTURE

Cancel culture refers to the practice of withdrawing support for, or boycotting, a person, group, or organization that has been accused of wrongdoing or expressing views that are deemed offensive or unacceptable. Cancel culture can have a significant impact on businesses, as consumers may choose to boycott a company that is perceived as being associated with controversial or offensive views or actions.

Black-owned businesses may be particularly vulnerable to cancel culture, as they may be more likely to be targeted by social media campaigns and boycotts due to their race or ethnicity. In some cases, these campaigns may be justified, as they may be in response to legitimate concerns about the behavior or views of the business or its owners. However, in other cases, cancel culture may be used to unfairly target businesses, leading to financial and reputational harm.

It's important for businesses, including black-owned businesses, to be aware of cancel culture and the potential risks it poses. This may involve taking steps to carefully manage their online reputation, engaging with customers and stakeholders to address concerns and address any issues that may arise, and being mindful of the views and actions that may be perceived as controversial or offensive.

BE MINDFUL OF YOUR VIEWS AND ACTIONS
One way to avoid cancel culture is to be mindful of the views and actions that may be perceived as controversial or offensive. This may involve being aware of the potential impact of your actions on different groups of people.

IN CONCLUSION

Social media marketing is a powerful tool for black-owned businesses to reach and engage with potential customers. By identifying and targeting the right audience, creating compelling content, and using hashtags effectively, black-owned businesses can effectively promote their products or services and increase their visibility on social media platforms. Additionally, participating in hashtag campaigns and staying up-to-date with the latest trends and best practices in social media marketing can help black-owned businesses stand out in a crowded online marketplace and drive more business to their doors.

SOCIAL MEDIA MARKETING IS ABOUT BUILDING RELATIONSHIPS AND CREATING A CONVERSATION WITH YOUR AUDIENCE. BY CONSISTENTLY PROVIDING VALUE AND ENGAGING WITH YOUR FOLLOWERS, YOU CAN CREATE A LOYAL COMMUNITY OF BRAND ADVOCATES.

CHAPTER 10
VIDEO MARKETING

Video marketing is the use of video content to promote a brand, product, or service. It can involve creating and sharing promotional videos on social media, hosting videos on a website or video hosting platform, or incorporating video into email marketing campaigns. The goal of video marketing is to engage with potential customers and convince them to take action, such as making a purchase or visiting a website.

Video marketing can be an effective way for black-owned businesses to reach and engage with their target audience.

Here are some key points to consider when developing a video marketing strategy for a black-owned business:

Identify Your Target Audience

The first step in any marketing campaign is to identify your target audience. This will help you tailor your messaging and content to appeal to the right people.

Determine Your Goals

Before you start creating videos, it's important to have a clear understanding of what you hope to achieve with your video marketing efforts. Do you want to increase brand awareness, drive sales, or generate leads? Having specific goals will help you measure the success of your campaigns and make adjustments as needed.

Choose The Right Platforms

There are many different platforms you can use to share your videos, including social media platforms like YouTube, Facebook, and Instagram, as well as video hosting platforms like Vimeo and Wistia. Consider where your target audience is most likely to be found and choose the platforms that will reach them most effectively.

Create Engaging & Informative Content

The key to successful video marketing is creating content that resonates with your audience. This might include informational videos that teach viewers about your products or services, or more personal, behind-the-scenes videos that give them a glimpse into your company culture and values.

Use Video In Email Marketing

In addition to sharing your videos on social media and other platforms, you can also use video in your email marketing campaigns. This can help you grab your audience's attention and increase the chances that they will engage with your content.

Analyze & Optimize Your Efforts

As with any marketing campaign, it's important to track the success of your video marketing efforts and make adjustments as needed. Use tools like Google Analytics and social media analytics to track the performance of your videos and see what's working and what's not. This will help you optimize your strategy and get the most out of your video marketing efforts.

DEVELOP A CLEAR MESSAGE
Before you start creating your video, it's important to have a clear understanding of what you want to say and how you want to say it. Consider what makes your business unique and what value you can offer to your customers.

TYPES OF VIDEO CONTENT TO CONSIDER

There are many types of videos that black-owned businesses can use for digital marketing purposes. Some common types include promotional videos, educational videos, customer testimonials, behind-the-scenes videos, and live videos. Each type of video serves a different purpose and can be used in different ways to reach different goals.

There are many types of videos that businesses can use for marketing purposes. Some common types of videos include:

Promotional Videos

These are videos that are specifically designed to promote a product or service. They may include product demonstrations, customer reviews, or other information that helps potential customers understand the value of what you're offering.

Educational Videos

These videos are designed to teach viewers about a particular topic or issue. They may be instructional videos that show people how to use a product or service, or informational videos that provide background information or explain complex concepts in an easily digestible way.

Customer Testimonials

These videos feature real customers sharing their experiences with your product or service. They can be a powerful way to build trust and credibility, as potential customers are more likely to trust the opinions of other customers than they are to trust marketing messages.

Behind-The-Scenes Videos

These videos give viewers a glimpse into the inner workings of your company or the process of creating your products or services. They can help to build a personal connection with your audience and make your brand more relatable.

Live Videos

Live videos are videos that are streamed in real-time, allowing viewers to interact with the content in real-time. Live videos can be a great way to build engagement and create a sense of community around your brand.

Advertisements

Video ads are short, promotional videos that are designed to grab the attention of an audience and encourage them to take a specific action, such as visiting a website or making a purchase. Video ads can be shown on a variety of platforms, including social media, websites, and TV.

Animated Videos

Animated videos use graphics and animation to tell a story or convey information in a visually appealing way. These types of videos can be effective at explaining complex concepts or ideas in a simple and engaging way.

Video Shorts

Video shorts are short videos that are typically under 15 minutes in length and are uploaded to YouTube. They can be used by businesses to promote their products or services, or to provide information or entertainment to their audience. Video shorts can be an effective way for black-owned businesses to reach and engage with their target audience on YouTube. They can be used to showcase the business, introduce the team, or provide information about the products or services offered.

Each of these types of videos can be used in different ways to reach different marketing goals. For example, promotional videos may be used to drive sales, while educational videos may be used to build brand awareness or establish thought leadership. By understanding the purpose of each type of video and how it can be used, you can create a video marketing strategy that effectively reaches your target audience and achieves your marketing goals.

CHOOSING THE RIGHT VIDEO PLATFORM

There are many platforms that black-owned businesses can use to share and promote their video content as part of their digital marketing efforts.

Some common platforms include:

YouTube

YouTube is a video-sharing platform that allows businesses to upload and share their videos with a wide audience. YouTube is owned by Google, which means that videos on the platform are often well-ranked in search results.

Social Media

Social media platforms such as Facebook, Instagram, and Twitter allow businesses to share their videos with their followers and reach a wider audience through shares and tags.

Websites

Many businesses include videos on their own website as a way to engage visitors and showcase their products or services.

Email Marketing Campaigns

Video can be included in email marketing campaigns as a way to grab the attention of the recipient and encourage them to take a specific action, such as visiting a website or making a purchase.

By sharing their video content on a variety of platforms, businesses can increase the reach of their message and engage with a wider audience. It's important to consider the specific goals and target audience of a business when selecting the platforms to use for video marketing.

In addition to these platforms, black-owned businesses may also want to consider using platforms that are specifically geared towards the black community, such as Go Black Own or the Black Business Directory. These platforms can provide valuable exposure and help black-owned businesses to connect with their target audience.

MAXIMIZING THE IMPACT OF YOUR VIDEO PRODUCTION

Video production is an important aspect of digital marketing for black-owned businesses, as it allows them to create compelling video content that can be shared online to promote their products or services. Video marketing can be an effective way for black-owned businesses to reach and engage with their target audience, and it has been shown to be more persuasive than other forms of content.

In the digital marketing context, video production for black-owned businesses involves creating video content that is optimized for the specific goals and target audience of the business. This may involve creating video ads to promote a specific product or service, or creating educational or informative videos to establish the business as a thought leader in its industry.

To produce effective video content for digital marketing, black-owned businesses should follow a similar process to traditional video production, including planning, scripting, filming, editing, and finishing the video. However, it is important to consider the specific needs and goals of the digital marketing campaign when planning and creating the video content.

Black-owned businesses may want to focus on creating video content that resonates with their target audience and showcases the unique value that their products or services offer. They may also want to consider partnering with other black-owned businesses or influencers to reach a wider audience and showcase the diversity and strength of the black community.

By leveraging the power of video production in their digital marketing efforts, black-owned businesses can effectively reach and engage with their target audience and showcase the value of their products or services.

Video production refers to the process of creating a video, from planning and scripting to filming and editing.

It involves several steps, including:

Planning

The planning stage is the foundation of the video production process. It involves determining the purpose of the video, the goals that it aims to achieve, and the target audience. It also involves deciding on the type of video that will be most effective in achieving these goals, such as an advertisement, an educational video, or a live stream. Additionally, the planning stage involves deciding on the platforms on which the video will be shared, as well as the budget and timeline for the project.

Scripting

After the purpose and goals of the video have been determined, the next step is to write a script that outlines the content of the video. This can include dialogue, voiceover, and any other elements such as graphics or animation. The script should be tailored to the target audience and should clearly convey the message that the video aims to communicate.

Filming

Once the script is complete, the next step is to film the video. This involves setting up the camera, lighting, and any other necessary equipment, as well as rehearsing and filming the video. Filming can take place in a variety of locations, such as a studio, on location, or remotely using video conferencing software.

Editing

After the video has been filmed, it needs to be edited to remove any errors or mistakes and to ensure that it is coherent and flows smoothly. This may involve cutting out unnecessary footage, adding transitions, and adding any necessary graphics or effects. Editing can be done using specialized software such as Adobe Premiere or Final Cut Pro.

Finishing

The final step in the video production process is to finish the video, which includes adding any final touches such as color correction and sound effects. This step is important in ensuring that the video is polished and professional-looking.

By following these steps, businesses can create high-quality video content that effectively communicates their message to their target audience.

 USE CAPTIVATING VISUALS & AUDIO
The visuals and audio in your video can have a big impact on its effectiveness. Consider using high-quality images and video footage, as well as engaging music and sound effects.

VIDEO OPTIMIZATION FOR MAXIMUM VISIBILITY

Video optimization is the process of improving the visibility and reach of a video online, and it is an important aspect of digital marketing for black-owned businesses.

There are several tactics that black-owned businesses can use to optimize their videos for digital marketing:

Use Relevant Keywords In The Video's Title & Description

By including relevant keywords in the title and description of a video, it can be more easily found by people searching for those terms on search engines and social media platforms. For example, if a black-owned business sells natural hair care products, it may want to include keywords such as "natural hair," "hair care," and "black-owned" in the title and description of its videos. This can help the videos to rank higher in search results and be more easily found by potential customers.

Add Closed Captions

Closed captions are a text version of the audio content of a video. They make the video more accessible to viewers who are deaf or hard of hearing, and they can also help to improve the video's search ranking, as search engines can better understand the content of the video. Black-owned businesses can use closed captions to make their videos more accessible and to reach a wider audience.

Use A Compelling Thumbnail Image

A thumbnail image is a still image that represents a video and is displayed on platforms such as YouTube and social media. A compelling thumbnail can help to attract the attention of viewers and increase the chances that they will watch the video. Black-owned businesses should choose thumbnail images that are visually appealing and accurately represent the content of the video.

Include A Call To Action

A call to action is a message that encourages viewers to take a specific action, such as visiting a website or subscribing to a channel. Including a call to action in a video can help to increase its effectiveness at driving conversions. Black-owned businesses should include a clear and compelling call to action in their videos, such as "Learn more" or "Buy now," to encourage their audience to take the desired action.

MEASURING VIDEO MARKETING SUCCESS

Video analytics refers to the measurement and analysis of data related to a video's performance, and it is an important aspect of digital marketing for black-owned businesses. By tracking and analyzing video analytics, businesses can gain valuable insights into the effectiveness of their video marketing efforts and make data-driven decisions to improve their strategy.

There are a variety of tools that black-owned businesses can use to track and analyze video analytics. Many social media platforms, such as YouTube and Facebook, provide built-in analytics tools that allow businesses to track the performance of their videos. In addition, there are third-party tools that businesses can use to track and analyze video analytics from multiple platforms.

Some common metrics that black-owned businesses may want to track and analyze include:

Number Of Views

The number of views a video has received can be an indicator of its popularity and reach. Black-owned businesses can track the number of views their videos receive and compare this metric over time to understand how their videos are performing. If a business's videos are not receiving as many views as expected, it may need to adjust its marketing strategy to reach a wider audience.

Length Of Time Viewed

The length of time viewers watched the video can be an indicator of its engagement and how well it held their attention. If a business's videos have a high average view duration, it may be a sign that the content is engaging and resonating with the audience. On the other hand, if the average view duration is low, it may indicate that the content is not holding the viewer's attention and may need to be adjusted.

Demographics Of The Audience

Understanding the demographics of a video's audience can help businesses to tailor their content to better reach and engage with their target audience. For example, a black-owned business that sells natural hair care products may want to focus on creating content that resonates with women, and it can use video analytics to understand the demographics of its audience and tailor its content accordingly.

Engagement With The Video

Measures of engagement with the video, such as likes, comments, and shares, can be an indicator of its effectiveness at resonating with the audience. Black-owned businesses can track these metrics to understand how their videos are performing and adjust their strategy accordingly.

By analyzing video analytics, black-owned businesses can gain a better understanding of the effectiveness of their video marketing efforts and make data-driven decisions to improve their strategy. This can help them to reach and engage with their target audience more effectively and drive conversions.

IN CLOSING

Video marketing is a powerful tool that can help black-owned businesses reach and engage with customers online. By creating and sharing high-quality video content, businesses can showcase their products or services, tell their brand story, and build a strong online presence. There are many types of video content that black-owned businesses can create, including explainer videos, product demonstrations, customer testimonials, and behind-the-scenes looks.

When creating and promoting video content, it's important to consider factors such as target audience, goals, and budget, as well as best practices for video optimization and promotion. By leveraging the power of video marketing, black-owned businesses can drive traffic, generate leads, and build brand awareness in the digital space.

VIDEO MARKETING ALLOWS YOU TO SHOWCASE YOUR PRODUCTS AND SERVICES IN A MORE ENGAGING AND INTERACTIVE WAY, AND HELPS YOU BUILD TRUST AND CREDIBILITY WITH YOUR AUDIENCE.

CHAPTER 11
EMAIL MARKETING

Email marketing is a type of direct marketing that uses electronic mail to send commercial or fundraising messages to a selected audience in order to promote a brand and increase sales. It has become a necessary tool for black-owned businesses since the emergence of the internet. While any email a business sends to a customer or individual could technically be considered email marketing, the term is generally used to refer to one of the following three activities:

1. Sending emails with the aim to better the relationship of a merchant with its current or previous customers so that you potentially have future business with them.
2. Sending emails with the target of getting new customers for your business or for convincing existing customers to purchase something immediately.
3. Sending emails that have been sent by other companies and adding advertisements to them.

Email marketing can be a powerful tool when done correctly, allowing black-owned businesses to sell products, share news, tell stories, acquire new customers, and more. However, the primary goal of email marketing is similar to other marketing techniques, which is to increase brand loyalty, encourage customers to make purchases, and strengthen relationships with current customers.

 BUILD AN EMAIL LIST
To start an email marketing campaign, you will need a list of email addresses to send your messages to. There are several ways to build an email list, including offering a sign-up form on your website or running a contest or promotion.

THE PROS AND CONS OF EMAIL MARKETING

Email marketing can be an effective and cost-effective way for black-owned businesses to reach and engage with their target audience. One of the main pros of email marketing is that it is relatively inexpensive compared to other forms of marketing, such as direct mail or paid advertising. It can also be easily scaled to reach a larger audience, which can be beneficial for businesses looking to grow their customer base.

Like other forms of digital marketing, email marketing has its own unique set of benefits and drawbacks. It is important to understand these before launching an email marketing campaign. While the return on investment for email marketing can be high, it is not always sufficient to outweigh the drawbacks. It is essential to consider if email marketing will be particularly beneficial for your campaign or business before proceeding. In the next section, we will discuss the process of starting an email marketing campaign. In addition to the high return on investment, email marketing also has other benefits and some drawbacks:

One major advantage of email marketing is that it is relatively easy to measure. When evaluating any marketing efforts, it is important to be able to measure their reach and success. Without this capability, you would not know how many people clicked on your ad, website, or newsletter. The likelihood of people opening your email depends on various factors, such as the subject line length, the sender's authority, the use of persuasive words, and the number of campaigns sent. For instance, sending too many email campaigns in a month may decrease the email open rates.

According to research, the average number of emails varies between B2B and B2C businesses, but in general, the email channel tends to have the highest ability to measure return on investment. Search and online advertisements come in second in terms of their ability to track and measure.

Another benefit of email marketing is the ability to personalize the marketing emails. The prospect of sending as many personalized emails as desired is appealing to many black-owned business owners. Adding personalized touches can also be a way to increase revenue, as personalized emails often lead to higher click rates for consumer products and services. To send authentic personalized emails, it is important to collect as much data as possible about your customers. Personalized emails also have a higher chance of being opened. For example, using a person's name in the greeting, such as "Hello [Name]," can be more effective at catching their attention than simply using "Hello."

Segmentation is also possible through email marketing, and addressing this issue is crucial for a successful campaign. Every black-owned business has customers who have spent more than average but have not made a purchase in a long time. To reach these customers, you need to segment them so that you can tailor your approach to specific groups. However, you will also need more information about them to do this effectively. Segmenting emails makes them more relevant, and also reduces unsubscribe rates. You can segment emails based on demographics, interests, and other factors, allowing you to separately target customers who have not made a purchase in a while.

While these benefits come with some costs, one of the major drawbacks of email marketing is the potential for deliverability issues. This means that if your traffic has increased significantly, you need to ensure that your emails are reaching the inbox directly. The deliverability rate is important if you are sending a large number of emails per month, and it may be wise to purchase a dedicated IP address to protect your authority. Sending too many emails can result in being placed on a spam blacklist, indicating a problem.

Time constraints can be a challenge in email marketing, as it takes time to build an email list. This can be a major issue for black-owned owners who are unable to invest enough time in building the list. One way to address this problem is to generate leads through different methods that direct people to your site, where they must provide an email address to access the results. Blogging is a good way to generate leads, and combining it with other methods such as conferences, webinars, or Facebook ads can also be effective. There are many other ways to generate leads, but the key is to not allow customers to see the results until they provide an email address.

Another drawback of email marketing is the increasing use of mobile phones. Most emails are now opened on a mobile device, which means that black-owned business owners need to be concerned with the design of emails and attachments for mobile viewing. If the media or newsletter is not responsive on mobile devices, people are likely to lose interest. It is important to be careful about every aspect of the email, including the subject line. You should also test how the email will appear on a phone, as the visibility of the subject line may vary depending on the phone being used.

Step 1 – Getting Permission

To begin this process, it is necessary to obtain permission for an email campaign as you will be contacting a large number of people. To do this effectively, it is important to create a comprehensive email list to which you can send your messages.

Some black-owned businesses choose to offer a free item or service in exchange for an email address, while others may provide updates or newsletters with valuable information. Ultimately, the decision is up to you. However, it is important to consider that asking for an email address is a call to action, and simply stating "enter your email address for updates and latest news" may not be sufficient. You will need to provide a compelling reason for users to share their email address with you.

You should anticipate questions such as "What benefits will I receive if I provide my email address?", and "Will I receive spam emails or discounts for giving you my email address?"

To be successful in this phase, it is important to be specific in your messaging. For example, you should clearly state when users will receive the item or service they are signing up for, and provide details about exactly what they can expect to receive. This will help to build trust and encourage more users to opt in to your email list.

The second step in this process is to get "whitelisted," which means that your emails are more likely to be delivered to the recipient's inbox rather than their spam or junk folder. This typically occurs when the recipient saves your email address as a contact in their address book. It is important to include instructions for adding you to their contacts in your first email, so that your subsequent emails are not missed or overlooked. Being whitelisted is essentially the same as being marked as a friend or trusted sender.

It is rare for users to actively remove people from their email lists, so following the steps to get whitelisted can help ensure that your emails are not marked as spam or placed on a blacklist. You may want to refer to instructions from popular email service providers like Mailchimp and AWeber to learn more about this process.

Step 2 – Do The Math

The second phase involves a "numbers game," which means that you must manage the expectations you set with your emails through consistent follow-up efforts. Without follow-up activity, your efforts will be unsuccessful, particularly in email marketing where managing expectations is crucial. This does not mean that you should send more emails than you promised, as this can also lead to a negative response. Instead, you should maintain a consistent pace, striking a balance between meeting the expectations you set and not overwhelming your audience. For example, if you promise to send daily emails with important updates, it is important to follow through on that promise, as failing to do so can damage the perception of your service.

The first follow-up email is especially important because it often determines the response of the recipient. Many email service providers offer the option of creating an autoresponder sequence, which can be a useful tool in this phase. It is a good idea to take advantage of these features to ensure that you are able to follow up with your clients effectively.

The first follow-up email is an opportunity to introduce yourself and your business more fully, and to explain in detail what you plan to do with the client's email address. It is important to be specific and thorough rather than quick and unobtrusive, as this is your best chance to engage the client and set the stage for meeting their expectations going forward. This is a crucial step in the email marketing process, as the success of your campaign will depend on your ability to fulfill the expectations you set with your clients.

Using an autoresponder can be helpful if you tend to forget to email your list. An autoresponder can help you stay on track, especially if you have something to sell and don't want to risk missing an opportunity to reach out to your audience. It's important to have a consistent plan in place to communicate with your email list, as failing to do so can negatively impact your business.

An autoresponder can be useful for programming and scheduling content to be sent over a period of time, such as a few months. This can help you maintain a consistent presence with your client base, and build a relationship with them through regular communication. When you do need to reach out to your clients about something new, you will already have established a connection with them, rather than appearing out of the blue. It's important to avoid overwhelming your clients with too many emails, as this can lead to annoyance and decreased engagement. By using an autoresponder and scheduling your emails appropriately, you can ensure that you are consistently in touch with your clients without overwhelming them.

Step 3 – Segmentation & Analysis

Analytics is a crucial step in email marketing, and it's often overlooked by many marketers. It's important to track various metrics, such as open rates, click through rates, and unsubscribes, to gauge the effectiveness of your campaign. The open rate, in particular, gives insight into the strength of your relationship with your audience. If the open rate is low, it may indicate that your emails are being deleted upon receipt, signaling a need to improve the value and manage the expectations of your emails to encourage them to be opened.

The click through rate measures how successful you are at getting your message across. A low click through rate may indicate that your message is not targeted enough or is being obstructed by some barrier. On the other hand, a high unsubscribe rate indicates that people are actively choosing to opt out of receiving your emails, which suggests a need for improvement in retaining clients and addressing the reasons for the unsubscribes. By gathering more information about why people are unsubscribing, you can work to fix any issues and prevent further losses.

By analyzing email analytics, you can pinpoint where issues may be occurring in your email funnel and make necessary changes, such as revising your message presentation and call to action, and adjusting your auto responder emails. Paying attention to these details can help you identify and address any problems in your email strategy.

Segmentation involves dividing your customer list into smaller groups based on relevant characteristics, in order to target them more effectively and provide them with personalized attention. By breaking down the list in this way, you can engage in more targeted communication with your clients and build stronger, more meaningful relationships.

As you interact with customers over time, you can get a better understanding of their preferences and interests. Some customers may be primarily interested in hearing about updates to your products and services, while others may be more interested in receiving promotions and offers from your company. It's important to be mindful of these differences, as giving customers the option to choose what they receive from you could result in losing them as a customer. One way to address this is through segmentation, which allows you to target specific groups of customers with specific messages. For example, you could use segmentation to send a follow-up email to customers who didn't open your previous message and give them a second chance to engage with your content.

| T-IP | **TEST & OPTIMIZE YOUR EMAILS**
To ensure your emails are performing as well as possible, it's important to test different subject lines, call-to-action buttons, and other elements to see what works best for your business. |

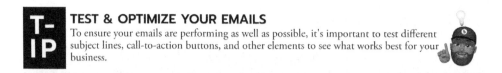

In Closing

Email marketing can be a powerful and cost-effective way for black-owned businesses to reach and engage with their target audience. By building a targeted and engaged email list, crafting compelling email content, and utilizing email marketing tools and software, businesses can effectively promote their products or services, build relationships, and drive sales.

However, it's important for businesses to carefully consider the pros and cons of email marketing, and to make sure that they are getting permission before sending marketing emails to prospects and customers. By following best practices and staying up-to-date with industry trends, black-owned businesses can effectively leverage the power of email marketing to grow their business and succeed in today's competitive market.

EMAIL MARKETING ALLOWS YOU TO DELIVER TARGETED AND PERSONALIZED MESSAGING TO A LARGE GROUP OF PEOPLE AND CAN BE A POWERFUL TOOL FOR BUILDING RELATIONSHIPS AND DRIVING SALES.

CHAPTER 12

MOBILE MARKETING

In today's digital age, promoting your business can be a challenging task. The internet has greatly influenced the way people perceive and respond to traditional marketing methods. The old approaches of intrusive marketing and universal branding messages are no longer effective.

In order to successfully reach potential customers, it is important to meet them where they are and communicate with them on their terms. This shift towards a customer-centric approach should be embraced rather than feared. With the proliferation of social media and other online platforms, it is easier than ever for people to express their preferences and interests, which can be used to tailor marketing efforts.

There are many benefits to using statistical data about consumer behavior in marketing, and one significant advantage is that it is now easily accessible. By conducting a simple search online, you can find a wealth of information about what your potential customers are looking for and need in order to become actual customers. This data can be extremely useful in helping you tailor your marketing efforts and effectively reach your target audience.

Some of the most impressive data coming out of research today is that of mobile marketing.

- In 2021, there were an estimated 7.9 billion mobile phone users worldwide, and this number is expected to continue growing in the coming years.
- Mobile devices account for over half of all web traffic worldwide.
- In 2021, the global mobile app market was valued at over $580 billion and is expected to continue growing in the coming years.
- The average person spends around 3 hours per day on their mobile device, making it an important channel for reaching and engaging with consumers.
- SMS marketing has an average open rate of 98%, making it a highly effective way to reach consumers through their mobile devices.
- In 2021, the global mobile ad market was valued at over $200 billion and is expected to continue growing in the coming years.

Mobile devices play a crucial role in the shopping process due to their increased reliance outside of the home. Consumers often turn to their mobile devices to fulfill immediate and specific purchase needs. This can be especially beneficial for black-owned business owners who want to generate local sales from connected consumers who may pass by their storefronts regularly. The opportunity to reach these consumers at the time of purchase can be very attractive to business owners.

SMS MARKETING

SMS marketing, or text message marketing, is a form of digital marketing that involves sending promotional or informational messages to customers or potential customers via text message. This can be an effective way for black-owned businesses to reach their target audience and promote their products or services.

Benefits of SMS marketing for black-owned businesses include:

High Open And Read Rates

SMS has a high open rate, with about 98% of all texts being opened and read within the first three minutes of being received.

Targeted Messaging

SMS marketing allows black-owned businesses to send personalized and targeted messages to their audience based on their interests and preferences.

Cost-Effective

SMS marketing is generally cheaper than other forms of marketing, such as email or direct mail.

Easy To Track And Measure

SMS marketing platforms provide detailed analytics and reporting, making it easy for businesses to track the success of their campaigns and make data-driven decisions.

Pros And Cons Of SMS Marketing For Black-Owned Businesses:

Pros:

- SMS marketing is a quick and easy way to reach a large audience.
- SMS marketing allows black-owned businesses to send personalized and targeted messages.
- SMS marketing is cost-effective compared to other forms of marketing.
- SMS marketing is easy to track and measure.

Cons:

- SMS marketing requires consent from the recipient before messages can be sent.
- SMS marketing can be perceived as intrusive if not used appropriately.
- SMS marketing is limited to 160 characters, which may not be sufficient for some businesses to convey their message effectively.

Stats:

- The average open rate for SMS marketing campaigns is around 98%.
- The average click-through rate for SMS marketing campaigns is around 36%.
- SMS marketing has a conversion rate of around 45%.

Overall, SMS marketing can be an effective way for black-owned businesses to reach their target audience and promote their products or services. However, it is important to consider the pros and cons and to ensure that SMS marketing is used in a responsible and ethical manner.

QR CODES

QR codes (short for Quick Response codes) are two-dimensional barcodes that can be read by a smartphone or other device equipped with a camera. They can be used to store a variety of types of information, such as a website URL, text, or other data.

In mobile marketing, QR codes are often used as a way to quickly and easily send customers to a specific website or landing page. For example, a business might include a QR code on a print advertisement, product packaging, or storefront window. When a customer scans the QR code with their smartphone, they are taken directly to a mobile website or landing page with information about the product or service being advertised.

QR codes can also be used in other ways in mobile marketing, such as to provide access to special deals or coupons, to allow customers to sign up for a newsletter or loyalty program, or to enable customers to access other types of information or services.

Overall, QR codes provide a convenient and efficient way for black-owned businesses to engage with customers through mobile marketing and to drive traffic to their websites or landing pages.

MOBILE WEBSITES

A mobile website is a version of a website that is optimized for viewing on a mobile device, such as a smartphone or tablet. Mobile websites are designed to be easy to navigate and use on a small screen, and they typically load faster than regular websites because they have fewer features and are designed to be lightweight.

There are several benefits to having a mobile website for a black-owned business. One benefit is that it can make it easier for customers to access information about your business and products when they are on the go. This can be especially important for black-owned businesses that rely on foot traffic or have a physical location, as a mobile website can help customers find directions, contact information, and other details about your business more quickly and easily.

Another benefit of a mobile website is that it can improve the user experience for customers. Mobile websites are designed to be easy to use on a small screen, so customers can easily find what they are looking for and complete tasks such as making a purchase or booking an appointment.

There are also several potential drawbacks to having a mobile website for a black-owned business. One potential drawback is the cost of developing and maintaining a mobile website. Building a mobile website can be time-consuming and expensive, and it may require ongoing updates and maintenance to keep it running smoothly.

Another potential drawback is that not all customers may have access to a smartphone or other mobile device, which could limit the reach of your mobile website. It's important to consider whether a mobile website is the best option for your business based on your target audience and the resources you have available to invest in it.

There are several benefits to optimizing a mobile website for search engines, especially for black-owned businesses.

Here are a few key points to consider:

Improved Search Engine Rankings

One of the main benefits of SEO is that it can help improve the ranking of a website in search engine results pages (SERPs). When a mobile website is optimized for search engines, it is more likely to rank well for relevant keywords and phrases, which can lead to more visibility and traffic from potential customers.

Increased Traffic & Revenue

By ranking well in search results, a mobile website can attract more organic traffic, which can lead to increased revenue for a business. This is especially important for black-owned businesses, which may have less access to traditional forms of advertising and marketing.

Enhanced User Experience

A mobile website that is optimized for search engines is also likely to be optimized for user experience. This includes features such as fast loading times, easy navigation, and responsive design, which can help improve the overall experience of users visiting the site.

Greater Reach & Accessibility

With the increasing use of mobile devices to access the internet, optimizing a mobile website for search engines can help black-owned businesses reach a wider audience and make it more accessible to users on the go.

Overall, SEO can be a powerful tool for black-owned businesses looking to improve the online visibility and performance of their mobile websites. By following best practices and focusing on providing a high-quality user experience, businesses can reap the many benefits of SEO and reach their target audience more effectively.

 OPTIMIZE YOUR WEBSITE FOR MOBILE
With the increasing number of users accessing the web on their smartphones, it's important to ensure your website is mobile-friendly by using a responsive design and optimizing loading speed and usability.

MOBILE APPS

A mobile app is a software application that is designed to be used on a mobile device, such as a smartphone or tablet. Mobile apps for black-owned businesses are designed to help you interact with your customers, promote your products or services, and streamline your operations.

There are a number of benefits that mobile apps can provide for black-owned businesses, including:

Increased Visibility

A mobile app can help increase the visibility of a black-owned business, as it can be easily downloaded and accessed by customers from their smartphones.

Improved Customer Engagement

A mobile app can provide a platform for black-owned businesses to interact with their customers, including through push notifications, in-app messaging, and other features. This can help improve customer engagement and loyalty.

Enhanced Customer Experience

A mobile app can provide a convenient and user-friendly platform for customers to browse and purchase products or services, which can improve the overall customer experience.

Increased Sales

By providing a convenient platform for customers to purchase products or services, a mobile app can help increase sales for a black-owned business.

Pros Of Developing A Mobile App For A Black-Owned Business:

- A mobile app can help increase the visibility and reach of a black-owned business, as it can be easily accessed by users from their smartphones.
- A mobile app can provide a convenient and user-friendly platform for customers to browse and purchase products or services, which can improve the overall customer experience.
- A mobile app can help increase sales for a black-owned business by providing an easy way for customers to make purchases.
- A mobile app can be a useful tool for building customer loyalty and engagement, as it provides a platform for businesses to interact with customers through features such as push notifications and in-app messaging.

Cons Of Developing A Mobile App For A Black-Owned Business:

- Developing a mobile app can be expensive, particularly if a business wants to create a high-quality app with a lot of features.
- A mobile app requires ongoing maintenance and updates to ensure that it remains functional and relevant to users. This can require ongoing resources and time investments.
- There is no guarantee that a mobile app will be widely adopted by users, and if a business's target audience is not likely to use a mobile app, it may not provide much value.

According to recent statistics, the use of mobile apps by small businesses is on the rise. A survey conducted in 2020 found that 63% of small businesses in the United States had a mobile app, and an additional 22% were planning to develop one in the near future. In addition, the survey found that small businesses with mobile apps reported increased customer engagement, improved customer loyalty, and increased sales as a result of having a mobile app.

Overall, developing a mobile app can be a valuable investment for a black-owned business, but it's important to carefully consider the costs and benefits before making a decision.

MOBILE ADVERTISING

Mobile advertising refers to the use of mobile devices, such as smartphones and tablets, to deliver targeted and personalized advertisements to consumers. Mobile advertising can be an effective way for black-owned businesses to reach potential customers and promote their products or services.

There are several benefits to using mobile advertising for black-owned businesses. One of the main benefits is the ability to reach a large and targeted audience. With the widespread use of mobile devices, you can reach consumers wherever they are, at any time of day. This can be especially useful for black-owned businesses that want to reach consumers in specific locations or demographics.

Mobile advertising can also be cost-effective. Many mobile advertising platforms allow you to set budgets and bid for ad space, so you can control how much you spend on advertising. In addition, mobile advertising can be highly targeted, so black-owned businesses can reach the specific audience they are trying to reach, which can help to increase the return on investment (ROI) of their advertising efforts.

There are also some potential drawbacks to using mobile advertising for black-owned businesses. One potential issue is the risk of low conversion rates, as not all mobile ads will be effective at converting users into customers. In addition, mobile advertising can be competitive, with many businesses vying for the same ad space, which can drive up the cost of advertising. Finally, there is the risk of ad fraud, where fraudulent actors create fake ad clicks or impressions, which can negatively impact a business's advertising budget.

Overall, mobile advertising can be a useful tool for black-owned businesses looking to reach a targeted and mobile-savvy audience. However, it is important for black-owned businesses to carefully consider their goals, budget, and target audience before embarking on a mobile advertising campaign.

DIGITAL BUSINESS CARDS

A digital business card is an electronic version of a traditional paper business card that can be shared with others online. Digital business cards can be shared via email, messaging apps, or through special business card scanning apps. They typically contain the same information as a traditional business card, such as the person's name, job title, company, phone number, and email address.

Digital business cards can be a useful tool for black-owned businesses in several ways. First, they can be more convenient than traditional business cards, as they can be easily shared with others electronically and do not need to be physically printed. This can save time and resources. Second, digital business cards can be more environmentally friendly than traditional business cards, as they do not require the use of paper. Finally, digital business cards can be customized and updated more easily than traditional business cards, allowing businesses to keep their contact information current and up-to-date.

To create a digital business card, black-owned businesses can use one of the many online tools and services that are available. These can include business card maker apps, website builders, or graphic design software. By creating a professional-looking digital business card, black-owned businesses can make a good impression and effectively promote themselves to potential customers and partners.

WHICH MOBILE IS RIGHT FOR MY BUSINESS

Mobile marketing offers a wide range of options for black-owned businesses looking to build their customer base, but it can be difficult to determine which option is the most suitable due to the abundance of customized options available.

It is advisable to seek the advice of a professional digital marketing agency before making any decisions, but this guide will provide you with an understanding of the factors to consider when selecting your mobile marketing strategy.

WHO IS IT FOR

To create an effective marketing campaign, it's important to consider the target audience. This involves understanding their demographics, the devices they use, and where they can be found online. By answering these questions, you can narrow down your options and choose the most appropriate methods for reaching your audience. For instance, if you are trying to sell Kindle ebooks, it's likely that your target audience has a tablet, so promoting the books through an SMS campaign may not be as effective as launching an iPad app that enhances the reading experience.

On the other hand, if you are a bar owner, it's unlikely that your target audience will be using an iPad to find your establishment while they are out late at night. Instead, a more effective marketing campaign might be one that utilizes SMS messages. This allows people to easily check their phones while they are out and make a buying decision based on a coupon offer or notification they receive.

Gaining an understanding of your target audience is essential for the success of any mobile marketing campaign.

WHAT DO THEY WANT

To maximize the impact of a mobile marketing campaign, it's important to understand what types of media, information, and incentives your customers want. For example, if your black-owned business involves visual confirmation, such as car sales, restaurant management, or furniture sales, building a mobile-friendly website can help increase sales.

Customers are more concerned with the ease of making a purchase than the design of a website. By providing a mobile-friendly site with mobile-responsive media, you can capture their attention and guide them towards a buying decision. Many people today will even mute their TVs during commercials to spend more time surfing the web on their mobile devices. To appeal to these customers, it's essential to offer mobile-responsive media that meets their needs and preferences.

USE LOCATION-BASED MARKETING
Mobile devices can provide businesses with the opportunity to reach customers when they are near their physical location. Use location-based marketing techniques like geofencing or beacon technology to reach customers near your business.

WHAT IS MY SALES PROCESS

It's important to strike the right balance in marketing efforts, as rushing too quickly could result in a loss if you are unable to convert excitement generated by a high-quality SMS campaign into sales. It's important to ensure that you have the necessary infrastructure in place to support a successful campaign.

Establishing an effective sales process requires careful planning and a clear understanding of your offerings and available resources. Many digital marketing agencies are skilled at creating sales funnel strategies to guide potential customers towards a purchase. It's important to carefully consider all aspects of the sales process in order to maximize the success of your campaign.

An effective sales funnel can generate sales even when you are not actively working on it. The internet offers a variety of sales funnel options that allow you to grow your business around the clock. By combining these funnels with high-quality mobile marketing, you can create a perpetual sales machine that frees up your time to focus on other critical aspects of your business. This can help you increase productivity and drive success.

IN SUMMARY

Mobile marketing is a crucial aspect of digital marketing for black-owned businesses. With the widespread adoption of smartphones, it is more important than ever for businesses to have a strong mobile presence in order to reach and engage with customers. By considering their target audience, goals, and budget, and by implementing a mobile-first approach, black-owned businesses can effectively use mobile marketing to drive traffic, generate leads, and build brand awareness. By adopting a mobile marketing strategy, black-owned businesses can stay competitive in the digital economy and reach a wider audience.

MOBILE MARKETING IS ABOUT REACHING AND ENGAGING WITH CONSUMERS ON THEIR MOBILE DEVICES THROUGH THE MOST APPROPRIATE CHANNELS AND DELIVERING RELEVANT AND TIMELY MESSAGES.

CHAPTER 13
MERCH (MERCHANDISE) MARKETING

Merchandise, or merch for short, is a common element in the business strategies of companies looking to expand. Merch can include a range of items, such as mugs, apparel, stationery, and so on. Merchandise items are often designed to display a company's brand identity. For instance, a mug might feature the company's logo or name as a way to advertise the business for free.

This can help businesses to make an impact on potential customers. Giving away merchandise, particularly for startups, is a cost-effective way to promote a business and increase brand awareness. As a business becomes more established, it may decide to sell merchandise as an additional source of income.

BRANDED MERCH FITS IN YOUR MARKETING STRATEGY

In order to effectively communicate your brand's message to your target audience, you need to consider what marketing strategies will be most effective. It is important to remember that there is no single approach that works for every brand, and you may need to experiment with different methods in order to successfully engage your audience.

Branded merchandise, also known as promotional products or "swag," is a type of marketing that is often overlooked but can be extremely effective. In fact, it is the top-ranked method of advertising for all generations, surpassing even online and print ads. If you are looking to incorporate branded merchandise into your marketing strategy, here are some tips on how to do so effectively.

GAIN BRAND AWARENESS THROUGH BRANDED MERCH

Branded merchandise allows your brand to physically enter the world through tangible items. You can often see branded products being used by people in their daily lives, such as on the subway, on the street, or at home. These items, such as t-shirts, backpacks, and totes, serve as a way to promote and spread your brand message. In addition, a significant 81% of people tend to keep these products for more than a year, further extending the reach of your brand.

BRANDED SWAG IS AN EXTENSION OF YOUR BRAND

Before creating branded merchandise, it is important to consider what your brand stands for, what it looks like, and what services you offer. This information can be useful in designing products that are meaningful and representative of your brand. Branded merchandise can serve as an extension of your brand, so it is important to understand the essence of your brand in order to create effective and cohesive products.

BRANDED MERCHANDISE CREATES CLIENT LOYALTY

Promotional merchandise has the ability to leave a lasting impression on customers, with 82% of people reporting a more favorable view of a brand after receiving a promotional gift. These gifts, such as useful items like desktop accessories or stationery, can not only create a positive association with your brand but also serve as a constant reminder of your company when used regularly. For example, our friends at Hover created a custom-branded handmade lotion with custom packaging as a gift for their partners, which was well-received and serves as a useful and thoughtful item that can be kept on their desks.

 DESIGN APPEALING MERCH
The design of your merch is an important factor in its success. Consider creating visually appealing designs that align with your brand identity and appeal to your target audience.

ITS ALREADY BUILT INTO YOUR OTHER STRATEGIES

Branded merchandise can be a valuable addition to your other marketing efforts, such as events, activations, and trade shows. By giving out promotional items, you create an opportunity for conversation about your brand and give recipients something to remember you by. The versatility of merchandise makes it a useful tool in a variety of marketing strategies, including experiential campaigns, social media posts, giveaways, and blog posts.

ADVERTISING WITH MERCH IS COST-EFFECTIVE

Branded merchandise is often more budget-friendly than traditional advertising methods, which can be costly due to the need to pay for hosting or placement. In contrast, advertising with merchandise is relatively straightforward and requires fewer resources. This can make it a more attractive option for businesses looking to promote their brand on a budget.

If you design branded merchandise that people can use on a regular basis, such as clothing, it can serve as a form of advertising for your brand. For example, if someone wears a shirt with your brand on it, they essentially become a walking billboard for your company. This can be an effective and inexpensive way to promote your brand, as the person wearing the shirt does the advertising for you. Consider designing merchandise that is likely to be shared with others, such as office supplies.

This can increase the reach of your brand, as these items are more likely to be passed along to others than, for example, clothing. It is less common for clothing to be shared between people, so choosing items that are more easily shared can help extend the reach of your brand.

GENERATE SALES AND INCREASE LEADS

Giving away branded merchandise, or "swag," can leave a lasting impression on both current and potential customers. This can help your business generate leads, sales, and loyalty by increasing brand awareness and building positive associations with your company. Whether you are targeting existing customers or a new audience, free promotional merchandise can be a powerful marketing tool. If you are considering creating branded merchandise, there are many templates available online for items such as buttons and other products. These can be useful for companies that are new to merchandise marketing or are looking for temporary solutions until they develop more creative ideas.

COLLABORATE WITH INFLUENCERS
Consider collaborating with influencers who align with your brand and target audience, and consider offering them free or discounted merch in exchange for promotion on their social media channels.

10 REASONS TO INCLUDE MERCH INTO YOUR MARKETING

1. It's A Low-Cost Form Of Marketing

One of the advantages of marketing through merchandise is that it is often more cost-effective compared to other promotional methods. For instance, TV ads have a limited lifespan and can be expensive, while branded merchandise provides longer-lasting exposure at a more reasonable price. This can make it a cost-effective option for increasing brand awareness and coverage.

2. Shows Goodwill Towards Your Audience

Marketing merchandise can also be an effective tool for corporate promotional giveaways, which can help your brand stay current and relevant while reminding customers of your presence and appreciation for their business. These types of promotional items can also encourage repeat orders by inviting customers to come back to your company if they need your services again.

As an example, consider a business that sells iced beverages in the summer. By giving away branded reusable straws, the company can enjoy relatively inexpensive brand exposure while also keeping its brand top-of-mind for the season. This type of marketing merchandise can be a useful and cost-effective way to promote a business and its products.

3. Has A Longer Lifespan

One of the benefits of promotional products is that they can generate long-lasting brand exposure. This is because branded items such as clothing, water bottles, and key rings are often used on a daily basis and are easily visible to others. As a result, they serve as constant reminders of your brand, providing frequent and consistent brand exposure.

4. Shows That You Care About Your Audience

Promotional items are often given away for free to recipients, which can create a positive relationship between your brand and your target audience. By providing useful products at no cost, you demonstrate your appreciation and can foster goodwill. As a result, the relationship between your brand and your audience can strengthen over time.

5. Helps You Become An Industry Leader

Branded promotional products offer the opportunity to be creative and showcase a fun and innovative side of your company. By providing practical or entertaining products to customers, you can differentiate your brand and make it more appealing to a wider audience.

6. Impresses Event, Conference, & Trade Show Visitors

Attending trade shows or sponsoring events can be an effective way to promote your business, and adding promotional products to the mix can help you stand out and attract potential customers. Providing valuable branded gifts can be a memorable and impactful way to make an impression and differentiate your business.

7. Helps you Develop Company and Customer Loyalty

Promotional products, particularly those that feature imprinted logos on apparel, can help increase brand awareness and employee loyalty. These items can also inspire customers and employees to continue supporting your brand. In fact, promotional products can be a powerful tool in building brand recognition and creating a loyal customer and employee base.

8. Appeals To Everyone

Promotional items come in a range of shapes and sizes, which allows you to choose items with a variety of functions that will appeal to different audiences. Whether your target audience is young or old, there is likely a promotional product, such as a gadget, wearable, or gift, that will catch their attention. By using promotional products, you can effectively reach a wider demographic and increase brand awareness.

9. Demonstrates Your Business Is Fun

There are many types of promotional products available in different shapes and sizes, each with its own unique function. These products can be tailored to appeal to any audience, regardless of age. By using custom promotional items, you can capture the attention of a diverse group of people and effectively reach a wider demographic.

10. Reinforces What You Stand For

The tone of your brand should be considered when choosing custom promotional products, as these items can effectively reinforce your brand message. When someone receives a promotional product from your company, they will quickly understand the message you are trying to convey and the nature of your business. It's important to consider your audience when selecting promotional products, as you want them to remember your brand, whether it has a fun or serious tone.

AT THE END OF THE DAY...

Consider incorporating branded merchandise into your marketing plan. These types of products can help to promote your brand and reach your target audience when executed well. When planning your marketing strategy, think about how branded merchandise can help your brand stand out and make an impact.

MERCH MARKETING IS ABOUT USING BRANDED PRODUCTS AND APPAREL TO PROMOTE AND BUILD AWARENESS FOR A BRAND, AND CREATE A COHESIVE AND CONSISTENT VISUAL IDENTITY THAT RESONATES WITH YOUR AUDIENCE.

CHAPTER 14

OFFLINE MARKETING

While offline marketing has been a popular and effective tactic for many years, it has not received as much attention in recent times due to the prevalence of online marketing. Some people may not be familiar with offline marketing or have not yet implemented it in their business. However, in today's competitive business landscape, it is important to consider using a mix of both offline and online marketing strategies in order to stay competitive.

Offline marketing includes various traditional marketing techniques, such as distributing leaflets, advertising on television, and displaying billboards. These methods and others will be explored in more detail later on.

Over the past few years, the world has seen rapid advancements and transformation in various aspects, including marketing strategies and product quality. In the past, people did not have access to phones, but now almost everyone has a smartphone that can perform multiple functions such as making calls, taking pictures, and serving as a calculator and flashlight. This has led to a decline in the use of other forms of communication. The way products are marketed has also undergone significant changes.

Offline marketing refers to the use of traditional media channels, such as television, radio, and print materials, to promote a company's product or service. This type of marketing often includes techniques like telemarketing and advertising through billboards and pamphlets. In this context, we will delve into the most commonly employed offline marketing techniques in detail.

DEVELOP A CLEAR MARKETING MESSAGE
Before you start your offline marketing campaign, it's important to have a clear understanding of what you want to say and how you want to say it. Consider what makes your business unique and what value you can offer to your customers.

NETWORK/CONTACTS

One effective way to generate initial traffic for a new website is to personally communicate with your business contacts or acquaintances about your black-owned business and website. Sharing this information with them can pique their interest and potentially lead them to visit your site and recommend it to others.

While speaking to a small group of people may not yield many results, seeking out opportunities to speak at gatherings related to your field can help attract potential customers and create a strong sense of brand loyalty among your existing customers. This traditional method of marketing is both effective and cost-efficient, as it usually does not cost much to speak about your brand to a group of people in your industry. Despite the availability of newer marketing techniques, this approach can still be a valuable way to generate interest in your product.

SPEAKING ENGAGEMENTS

This method involves promoting your product by speaking about it and trying to generate interest in what you are selling. One way to do this is by choosing larger platforms, such as seminars or exhibitions, where the majority of attendees are in your industry. This approach is similar to the one mentioned previously, where you seek out opportunities to speak about your brand to potential customers.

There are several advantages to participating in speaking engagements, beyond just being able to present your product to a targeted and interested audience. One such advantage is that it allows you to directly engage with your potential customers and present your product to them in a way that captures their attention and interest. When you speak to an audience that is already predisposed to listen carefully to what you have to say, it can be easier to effectively convey the details and benefits of your product.

Speaking engagements can also be a powerful tool for building credibility and leadership within your black-owned business. However, it is important to keep in mind that speaking in front of a large, interested audience can be a daunting task, so it may be wise to start by addressing local associations or smaller crowds to build confidence. This will help you gain experience and prepare you for more challenging speaking opportunities in the future.

In addition to the challenge of building confidence as a speaker, it is also unlikely that you will have many contacts who can refer you to speak at large seminars with large crowds when you are just starting out. It is important to take your time and focus on building both your confidence and your network of contacts before seeking out these types of opportunities. This will enable you to make the most of this traditional marketing method.

COLD CALLS

Cold calling may be a somewhat forgotten marketing technique, but it can still be highly effective. While some people may believe that cold calling has become obsolete, it is not necessarily a outdated or ineffective method. In fact, cold calls can be a powerful way to reach interested buyers and can be more effective than contacting them via email. Phone calls require an immediate response, unlike emails which can be easily ignored or forgotten. Therefore, placing calls to previous clients can be a more successful method of communication.

It is important to remember that previous clients can be valuable customers, and you do not want to risk losing their interest. When contacting them, be mindful of the time you choose to make the call. Avoid calling after office hours, as this may irritate them and lead to a loss of their business. Plan your call in advance and choose a time that is convenient for them to ensure a positive outcome.

In addition to being a useful way to reconnect with previous customers, cold calls can also be a good way to identify potential business partners. By making these calls, you may be able to find individuals or companies interested in working with your black-owned business. It is worth taking the time to go through your old contacts and see what opportunities may be waiting for you.

PRINT PUBLICATIONS

Print publications, such as magazines, journals, and newspapers, can still be a valuable marketing tool for some black-owned businesses. If you are able to secure prominent placements in relevant publications, you may be able to attract a large number of potential customers for your product.

It is undeniable that print publications can help increase your brand visibility and showcase your expertise. Therefore, it is important to seek out as many opportunities for print publications as you can, but be selective about which ones you pursue. Look for opportunities that are relevant to your brand and will be beneficial to your business. Be mindful of your budget and avoid wasting resources on unnecessary publications. By being selective and strategic in your use of print publications, you can effectively increase your brand awareness and visibility.

It is important to try to target only interested readers through print publications. While it may not be possible to reach only this audience with complete accuracy, this approach can still yield good results.

TRADE SHOWS/ASSOCIATIONS

Trade shows are a great way to connect with people in similar industries and fields. These events are often attended by industry leaders and potential buyers who may be ready to place orders. Participating in trade shows involves more than just setting up a booth and giving out promotional items – it can also provide an opportunity to secure bulk orders and grow your business on a larger scale.

Trade shows are widely considered to be the most effective offline marketing method. This is because they combine several other marketing techniques, such as networking, print publications, and speaking engagements, into one powerful approach. At trade shows, you have the opportunity to communicate with people in person and share printed materials with them, which can help them learn more about your product and become interested in it. Overall, trade shows offer a comprehensive marketing strategy that can be highly effective in promoting your black-owned business.

PRINT ADVERTISING

Print advertising is similar to print publications, except that it involves promoting your product directly rather than printing articles or other materials. This can include placing advertisements in newspapers or magazines, or using billboards to display your message to a large audience. While print advertising may not be as popular or require as much investment as other methods, it can still be effective and may be more targeted than television advertising. However, it can be difficult to track the impact of print advertising on interest in your product.

TRACK YOUR RESULTS
It's important to track the effectiveness of your offline marketing efforts and make adjustments as needed. Use tools like customer surveys and sales data to measure the success of your campaigns and inform your future marketing decisions.

USES OF OFFLINE MARKETING

Offline marketing techniques, such as billboards, flyers, and printed materials, can be effective in reaching individuals who are not as active on the internet and prefer to be contacted through non-digital means. These methods, while not necessarily outdated, are still widely utilized by black business owners and representatives to reach their target audience.

One major advantage of offline marketing is the opportunity for black-owned businesses to reach potential customers at the right place and time. For example, if you are on your way to the grocery store and see a billboard advertising a particular brand of meat or bread, you may be more likely to purchase that product when you reach the store. This demonstrates how offline marketing methods, such as billboards, can effectively influence consumer behavior and drive sales for a company.

It is not necessary to choose between online and offline marketing, as both can be effectively utilized simultaneously. Neither can completely replace the other, as both offer unique benefits and opportunities for black-owned businesses to reach their target audience.

IN SHORT

Offline marketing can be a valuable tool for black-owned businesses looking to reach and engage with customers in the real world. By considering their target audience and goals, businesses can develop effective offline marketing strategies that include tactics such as events, promotions, and advertising in traditional media channels.

In addition, businesses can leverage the power of word-of-mouth marketing by providing excellent customer service and encouraging satisfied customers to recommend the business to their friends and family. By combining offline marketing with a strong online presence, black-owned businesses can create a well-rounded marketing strategy that helps them reach and engage with customers in both the physical and digital worlds.

OFFLINE MARKETING IS ABOUT USING TRADITIONAL MARKETING TACTICS TO REACH AND ENGAGE WITH YOUR AUDIENCE IN THE PHYSICAL WORLD AND CAN BE A POWERFUL TOOL FOR BUILDING BRAND AWARENESS AND DRIVING SALES.

CHAPTER 15

CUSTOMER RELATIONS MANAGERS (CRM)

Now that we have discussed various strategies for generating leads through digital marketing, let's discuss how to effectively manage, track, and retain them. A Customer Relationship Manager (CRM) can be a valuable tool for maximizing the benefits of today's technology and gaining a competitive advantage. As your black-owned business grows and the volume of leads increases, a CRM can help streamline and organize the process of managing and retaining clients.

Some well-known CRM options include Salesforce, Hubspot, Insightly, and Agile. There are many other options available in this competitive market.

SO WHAT IS A CRM?

A CRM is a cloud-based software platform that stores data from customer interactions. It allows for various methods of data input and integrates with various communication channels, such as email, phone calls, contact forms, and third-party inquiries. It also allows teams to set specific goals, such as sales targets, sign-ups, phone calls, or point-of-sale data, and track them in real-time on the cloud. CRMs are useful for setting and achieving tangible goals as a team.

HOW TO USE A CRM

Most CRMs are easy to use and navigate, but some advanced features, such as automations and integrations, may require training or assistance from an experienced web programmer. In my experience, it is helpful to explore as many functions as possible while getting accustomed to a new software. This allows you to gain familiarity with the interface and become more efficient while using it.

By using customized fields, CRM users can track customer information and log key details upon initial interaction. This creates a file on the customer that allows you to track and analyze their journey as a customer. By inputting as much information as desired into the contact categories, you can create a comprehensive profile of each customer's experience with your black-owned business.

It is important to properly record all interactions with customers in the CRM in order to effectively utilize the tool. Failing to do so can result in lost opportunities and valuable information not being recorded. This can hinder the ability to follow up on or reference past interactions with customers, which can be detrimental to the business. Properly updating customer files ensures that key data is not overlooked or forgotten.

One of the benefits of a CRM is the ability to classify and segment customers in any way desired. For example, you can create a rewards program for your most loyal clients by setting rules on the CRM to identify them. You can also categorize customers based on the products, services, or subscriptions they receive. As a growing black-owned business, this can be particularly useful because it allows any team member to follow up with clients, rather than relying on a dedicated individual.

CHOOSE THE RIGHT CRM SOFTWARE
It's important to choose the one that best meets the needs of your business. Consider factors such as the size of your business, the type of customer data you need to track, and your budget when selecting a CRM software.

FIND A CRM TAILORED TOWARDS YOUR INDUSTRY

If you are in a specialized industry such as medical, real estate, financial, or manufacturing, you may want to consider using a CRM tailored to your specific needs. If you choose to use a major platform, make sure to research whether it supports the data collection that you require. Some CRMs, for example, have the ability to integrate with a hospital's healthcare system or an automated manufacturing production report. Keep in mind that not all CRM companies offer the same integrations, and some advanced features may come at a higher cost. It is important to choose the right CRM for your business needs.

BEST PRACTICES

It is important to keep a record of as many customer interactions as possible in order to get a sense of how engaged your clients are as a group. By analyzing CRM data, you can identify trends such as slow business periods, underperforming agents, and popular products or services. This information can be valuable in improving and growing your business.

CRM data can provide valuable insights to black business owners and managers. It allows you to gather actionable data and make adjustments to improve business performance.

Using a CRM, you can create sales leaderboards, assess leads based on scores or deal amounts, or compare performances over a specific time period. Many CRMs also allow you to generate reports with this data, which can be downloaded or printed for presentation purposes.

SALES

CRM systems are increasingly being adopted by sales teams as their primary tool for selling. When a lead or prospect is received, sales professionals can use the CRM to input all relevant information, set appointments, create follow-up alerts, and track progress and deal amounts. This helps to streamline the sales process and ensure that all relevant information is easily accessible.

CRMs are particularly useful for businesses that receive a high volume of phone calls or leads. When a client expresses a specific need, they can be referred to a specialist who will have access to a wealth of customer information already stored in the CRM. This helps to ensure that the client receives personalized and informed service.

Using a CRM allows you to monitor activity and document negotiations with clients. You can create custom stages in the CRM to reflect your company's sales process, such as negotiations, audits, or application in process. This helps to track the progress of each sale and ensures that important information is recorded and easily accessible.

> **T-IP**
> **USE DATA TO INFORM YOUR MARKETING EFFORTS**
> Your CRM software can provide valuable insights into your customers, including their preferences, needs, and behaviors. Use this data to inform your marketing efforts and create targeted campaigns that are more likely to resonate with your target audience.

EMAILS

If your sales team relies on sending emails to prospects and clients, integrating your email with a CRM can be helpful. In the past, you could only log that you sent an email and possibly include a summary of its contents. Today, it is easy to integrate most email platforms, such as Outlook, Gmail, or G-Suite, with a CRM. If you are using a customized mail server, you may need assistance from your IT team to integrate the accounts.

Integrating your email with a CRM allows you to create a more comprehensive timeline of client communications. You will also be able to track emails and receive alerts when a message is read and how many times it has been opened. This can be valuable in understanding how your emails are being received and engaging with clients.

CRMs have provided sales teams with a range of powerful tools that were previously unavailable.

AS A SALES FUNNEL

A CRM system can be customized to fit your specific needs. It can be integrated into your current sales process, or it can serve as the main method of managing and tracking sales.

Many CRM systems allow you to automatically import data from forms on your website or other sources. This feature is commonly available in most major CRM solutions. To fully integrate it into your workflow, you may need the assistance of a web developer. Some CRM systems also include the ability to create lead capture forms within the system itself. These forms can be embedded into your website or given their own dedicated URL for collecting leads.

LANDING PAGES

Many CRM platforms, such as Agile and HubSpot, offer the ability to design web pages within the platform itself. This feature is becoming increasingly prevalent among popular CRM solutions. With this feature, you can create customized landing pages that include lead capture forms linked directly to your contact database.

Although some options may only provide a few templates, they generally allow you to customize the elements and add your own personal touch through the use of text, photos, and videos.

If you are considering using this method, it is advisable to conduct an A/B test alongside your other lead generation forms. This will allow you to determine which form is more effective and appealing to your target market.

MOBILE APPS

Many CRM platforms now offer mobile apps, allowing professionals to manage their client affairs and pending cases outside of the office. This may be a convenient feature for some, but it may also be overwhelming depending on your level of commitment. These apps typically offer a high degree of control over which alerts you receive.

With customizable settings, you can choose to receive push notifications for various events such as new leads, emails, urgent matters, tasks, or appointments. You can enable or disable these notifications as desired. This feature can be especially useful for salespeople, who can be immediately notified when a new lead is received.

In the crowded field of CRM systems, the quality of their phone apps can vary. For instance, HubSpot's app includes a scanner that allows you to create a contact by scanning a business card with your phone's camera. Most of these apps also allow you to send and receive messages and emails. A common feature among these apps is the ability to update customer data and statuses in the database.

AS PART OF EMAIL MARKETING CAMPAIGNS

CRM systems are closely related to email marketing, which was discussed in the previous chapters. This is because a CRM platform can be an extremely valuable tool for building and organizing a strong email list. The thorough notes taken by your staff will be instrumental in the success of your email list.

As a black business owner who is fully committed to using a customer relationship management (CRM) system, you can expect to see an increase in the number of customers in your database. You can easily export all of your contacts and import them into your email marketing platforms, such as Constant Contact or MailChimp. Some CRM providers even offer built-in email clients or allow you to design and send newsletters using their platform. With these options, you can create and send newsletters to a large recipient list with ease.

HOW TO DECIDE ON A CRM

The appropriate CRM for your black-owned business will depend on the specific needs of your industry and which CRM options available offer the most suitable solution.

It is a good idea to take advantage of free trial periods offered by various CRM providers to test out their software and determine which one is the best fit for your business. From my own experience, each CRM system has its own strengths and weaknesses, so it is important to thoroughly evaluate the options before making a decision.

It is important to note that CRM systems may not be necessary or beneficial for all businesses, especially smaller ones that have not yet reached a certain level of growth. If you are unsure if a CRM would be useful for your black-owned business, it can be helpful to try out a free trial offered by many CRM providers. By testing out the basic features of the platform, you can quickly determine whether it will help you save time and/or money. However, it is worth noting that CRM systems are typically more beneficial for larger black-owned businesses that have reached a certain level of growth.

CUSTOMER RELATIONSHIP MANAGEMENT (CRM) IS ABOUT BUILDING AND MAINTAINING STRONG, LONG-TERM RELATIONSHIPS WITH YOUR CUSTOMERS BY UNDERSTANDING THEIR NEEDS AND DELIVERING PERSONALIZED AND VALUABLE EXPERIENCES.

CHAPTER 16
CREATING A DIGITAL MARKETING PLAN

Digital marketing planning involves creating a marketing plan within the context of the online business world. This type of planning involves adapting traditional marketing strategies and techniques to the digital media environment, and incorporating new digital marketing communication methods such as listening to customer feedback. This chapter explains how to develop a comprehensive and integrated digital marketing plan.

BENEFITS OF PLANNING

Having a plan in place is crucial because it allows you to avoid constantly putting out fires, frantically seeking financial resources, and making rushed decisions that may result in higher costs. A well-thought-out plan gives you control, reduces stress, provides direction, and promotes a sense of organization and effective management that allows your team to work together seamlessly.

> **T-IP**
> **DEFINE YOUR BUSINESS GOALS**
> Before you start creating your digital marketing plan, it's important to have a clear understanding of what you hope to achieve with your marketing efforts. Consider your business goals and how digital marketing can help you reach them.

MANY TYPES OF PLANS

There are various types of plans that organizations can use to guide their operations. Business plans outline the overall corporate strategy and include information about diversification and acquisition efforts, systems, and funding. Marketing plans are designed to support the business's overall objectives, while digital marketing plans integrate online and offline marketing efforts. Additionally, there are smaller, more specific campaign plans, such as an integrated social media campaign.

Digital marketing strategies are most successful when they are integrated with traditional offline marketing channels, such as print ads, public relations, telemarketing, direct mail, and face-to-face selling. These online and offline channels should work together to support the entire customer journey, from pre-sale to post-sale, and to foster ongoing relationships with customers.

HOW DIFFERENT PLANS FIT TOGETHER

The digital marketing plan focuses on acquiring and retaining customers using digital means, but it must align with the broader marketing plan's objectives and align with the overall business plan, which may include plans for growth such as acquiring other businesses, introducing new products, or discontinuing existing products.

In a traditional business, a corporate or business plan includes the systems, procedures, resources, and structure of the company, while a marketing plan focuses on the customer experience, including online and offline interactions, sales, distribution, communication, delivery of products or services, and ongoing improvement of the products, services, and overall customer experience.

A digital marketing plan can identify and analyze opportunities for business growth by targeting new audiences, expanding into new geographic markets, or introducing new products and services. Companies that have successfully used digital marketing to increase sales have often done so by creating a cost-effective online presence and investing in digital media to take advantage of new opportunities.

LONG-TERM PLANS VS SHORT-TERM PLANS

Many black-owned businesses have both short-term and long-term plans or roadmaps that outline the goals, timeframes, and resources required. These plans can be divided into four categories: 90-day plans, short-term (one-year) plans, medium-term (two- to three-year) plans, and longer-term (three- to five-year) plans.

Long-term digital marketing plans should focus on three main areas: first, identifying significant changes and trends in the external environment and changes to the competitive landscape; second, developing and communicating value propositions to customers in order to achieve commercial goals from digital channels; and third, defining the changes to resources, processes, and structures needed to support digital marketing, including the skills and expertise of people, technology infrastructure, and database architecture.

In large organizations, the third aspect is often outlined in a separate digital transformation plan or roadmap, which focuses on facilitating the change management required to shift from traditional marketing operations to a new process with digital at the center. Digital transformation plans are a series of business improvements that involve people, processes, and tools used for integrated digital marketing, with the aim of maximizing the potential contribution of digital technology, media, and new business models to business growth.

Technology projects that involve integrating data-driven customer relationship management (CRM) systems and delivering customized communications can take several years to plan, select, and implement, and therefore should be included in long-term roadmaps. Decisions related to databases, CRM, digital business architecture, and business processes are also long-term considerations when making plans.

The short-term operational digital marketing plan deals with the mix of communication techniques, such as search marketing and online advertising, used to attract new customers, as well as the tools used to engage and retain customers online, such as incentive programs and customer contact strategies delivered through opt-in email marketing that is integrated with traditional direct media like phone and direct mail. Now, let's examine the digital marketing planning process.

DIGITAL MARKETING PLANNING

A Situation Analysis is a way of understanding the current state of a business or organization. It involves answering questions such as "Where are we now?" and "What is the growth forecast?" For black-owned businesses, it is important to consider how many customers are buying or being influenced online. A full customer analysis helps to answer questions about the characteristics of your customers, such as "Who are they?" and "Why do they make purchases?" It is also important to consider what your competitors are doing and the impact of new intermediaries in the market. In addition, it is useful to examine what has been successful both online and offline, as well as any changes occurring in the online world. This information can be useful in making informed decisions about the future of the business. It is recommended to devote at least half of your plan to this section.

Objectives refer to the goals or desired outcomes that we hope to achieve. When considering going online, it is important to consider the benefits and purpose of the effort, as well as how it aligns with the 5Ss (Sell, Serve, Speak, Save, and Sizzle). Additionally, it is useful to consider key performance indicators (KPI) such as return on investment (ROI), market share, sales, inquiries, and visitors. Effective objectives should be specific and measurable, with clear timeframes for completion.

Strategy refers to the plan or approach for achieving the objectives. It is a crucial element of the overall plan as it provides direction for the tactics that will be employed. The strategy should outline how sales will be delivered, how the business will respond to trends, what positioning will be adopted, which customer segments will be targeted, and what communication and media strategies will be used to support customer acquisition, conversion, and retention. It should also consider the contact strategy for customer retention and increasing customer spending.

Tactics refer to the specific actions or steps that will be taken to execute the strategy. The marketing mix, communications mix, and channel mix are tactical tools that can be used to implement the strategy. Tactics may include specific activities such as the execution of Pay Per Click ads or a series of opt-in emails. It is also important to consider how various tools, databases, and customer relationship management systems will be integrated in the implementation of the tactics. Essentially, tactics explain how the strategy will be put into practice.

Action is the detailed working out of tactics. his may involve creating and optimizing a website, developing a Pay-Per-Click campaign, or creating an opt-in email campaign. However, executing these tactics can be a challenge for many black-owned businesses. Internal marketing, including motivation, communication, and training, is necessary to ensure that tasks are completed effectively. This is often an area that is overlooked, as managers may not allocate sufficient time and resources to ensuring that their staff understands and is motivated to complete their tasks with care and enthusiasm.

The Control Aspect of a plan involves identifying the metrics that need to be monitored, determining the frequency of monitoring, and defining what actions should be taken in response to any deviations from expected values. This typically involves using analytics systems to track key online metrics such as visitor traffic, duration of visits, enquiries, subscriptions, sales, conversion rates, churn rates, and loyalty levels. It is important to establish a system for regularly reporting on and evaluating these control criteria, including tasks such as usability testing and external trend analysis, in order to ensure that the plan is on track and any necessary adjustments can be made in a timely manner.

It is important to regularly review and revise your digital marketing plan in order to ensure that it is effective and up-to-date. If you notice that something is not working as intended, it is important to identify the problem and make necessary changes. It is also recommended to review your overall plan at least once every quarter and present any updates to senior management every six months. It is important to be proactive and continually strive to improve your digital marketing efforts.

It is important to allocate resources to your plan in order to ensure its success. Make sure to budget for the three key resources, often referred to as the "3Ms." Without these resources, your plan is likely to fail.

These are:

- **Men** (and women) – human resources
- **Money** – budgets
- **Minutes** – timescales and time horizons for production, delivery, service, etc.

THE KEY COMPONENTS OF STRATEGY

There are nine elements to consider when developing your digital marketing plan. You don't have to include all of them in your strategy, but you should at least think about each one. You can rearrange these elements to fit your plan.

Let's go through each of the nine components to help you create a clear and concise digital marketing strategy:

- **Target Markets** (essential)
- **Objectives** (it's helpful to summarize what objectives the strategy should deliver)
- **Positioning** (essential)
- **Processes** (strategy can involve new processes like Marketing Automation or developing a Beta testing culture). Some of these will overlap with integration.
- **Partnership** (strategic alliances and marketing marriages can make marketing easy)
- **Sequence** (or stages, e.g. develop credibility before raising visibility)
- **Integration** (of data – this may overlap with 'Processes' – major opportunity here)
- **Tactical tools** (or channels: list the priority tools PPC, SEO, email or PR and content)
- **Engagement** (what level of the Ladder of Engagement is required?)

Let's take a look at each of these briefly.

Target Markets

It is important to clearly define your target market. There are various tools and factors that can help black-owned businesses identify their ideal audience. Investing time and effort in carefully analyzing and identifying your target market is a valuable use of resources.

Objectives

It is essential to ensure that your strategy aligns with your overall goals and objectives, including your mission and vision. It is also important to track key performance indicators such as sales, market share, and return on investment. Without reference to your objectives, your strategy may not be effective in achieving them. Some black-owned businesses prefer to explicitly mention their main objectives when presenting their strategies. Deciding which is a priority, whether it be acquiring new customers or retaining existing ones, is a strategic decision.

Positioning

Positioning is a crucial aspect of your strategy and should not be changed frequently. It refers to how you want to be perceived by your target customers. It is the foundation for your brand proposition (the benefits for the customer) and customer experience. Defining your brand, online value proposition, and customer experience are all part of your strategy. These elements also influence your marketing mix, which includes tactical decisions such as exclusive online products, different pricing, online promotions, prioritized channels, and online distribution partners.

Process

Introducing new approaches, processes, systems, or ways of thinking can be strategic, such as implementing marketing automation, using analytics to inform decisions, fostering a culture of continuous improvement, or integrating multiple channels for customer service. Examples could include introducing a new customer service process that combines telephone, Twitter, and Facebook, or insisting on the use of analytics to measure and understand all future decisions.

Partnerships

Partnerships can be a strategic element of your marketing plan. This can include forming new partnerships, strengthening existing ones, or reducing the number of partnerships you have. Consider whether there are potential partners whose customers would be interested in your black-owned business products or services. Choosing the right partner can give you access to a larger target market and strengthen your brand. However, partnerships must benefit both parties and should have clear goals, roles, and responsibilities.

Sequence Or Stages

It is important to establish credibility before increasing visibility. For example, many TV ad campaigns drive traffic to websites that are not functional. There may also be other steps involved in building a successful campaign, such as increasing awareness and brand preference before seeking sales. Other stages of a campaign could include acquiring endorsements, establishing relationships and advocates, and then rolling out the campaign.

Integration

Integrating customer data from various sources, both online and offline, is a strategic decision. This can include data such as click behavior, registration information, social media data, customer relationship management data, purchase behavior, and post-purchase contact data. Combining this data with external data from third-party databases can also be valuable. It is important to have a process in place for integrating social data with your CRM or contact database, and for integrating customer profiling into both outbound and inbound campaigns.

Tactical Tools

Your marketing strategy should identify the major tactics or channels that you will use. Your brand, customer experience goals, target audience, and overall strategy will determine which tactics to use in your campaigns. For example, you may decide to launch a major pay-per-click ad campaign, cultivate an affiliate marketing program, or create social media campaigns based on high-quality marketing content. Content marketing, which involves providing free content, has largely replaced traditional sales promotion techniques. Depending on how it supports your brand and desired customer experience, content marketing may be a significant strategic component.

Engagement

There are various levels of engagement that you can aim for with your visitors and customers, ranging from encouraging them to leave ratings and reviews to collaborating with them on ideas and products. This is known as the Ladder of Engagement, with low-level engagement at the bottom and collaborative co-creation at the top. However, it is also important to recognize that not everyone wants to engage all the time; sometimes, visitors simply want to complete a task, find information, or make a purchase and leave your site. Therefore, it is crucial to have properly tested, quick, and easy-to-use websites and apps.

A digital marketing strategy helps to determine the target markets and positioning, which in turn influence the choice of tactics, such as a company website, opt-in email, e-sponsorship, social media, and content marketing. It can also guide the sequence of stages, such as the evolution of a website from a brochureware site to a fully integrated e-business system. Regardless of how a customer comes into contact with the company, they should be treated as an individual with unique preferences. This affects customer retention, which is itself a strategic decision. Improving customer retention levels may require a comprehensive, integrated database and contact strategy. The strategy can also determine the use of social media.

Actions

The Action section outlines the tasks that need to be completed based on the strategies and tactics outlined in the plan. How can you ensure that your team executes the plan with professionalism and enthusiasm?

If you do not have an Action section in your plan, you may end up with a website that does not function properly, apps with negative reviews, and offers that are poorly targeted and irritate customers. This can harm your brand, cause you to lose sales, and undermine your credibility. As a result, you could be spending money on marketing efforts that actually damage your brand.

USE A MIX OF MARKETING CHANNELS
Digital marketing includes a variety of channels, including social media, email marketing, search engine optimization, and paid advertising. Consider using a mix of channels to reach your target audience in different ways.

HOW DO YOU ENSURE EXCELLENT EXECUTION

To ensure that staff are able to effectively carry out a social media, social CRM, or marketing automation integrated campaign, it is important to have processes in place to guide them and prevent common mistakes. This may include training programs and checklists, and should be included in the budget and planning for the campaign.

The success of a plan often relies on its execution, and it is important to have a process in place to manage this. For instance, if a social media presence is meant to be "always on," it is important to consider staffing and scheduling in order to maintain this. Options for managing this could include scheduling auto-releases through tools like WordPress and HootSuite, using AI bots to respond to messages, or hiring real people with pre-written responses to interact with social media users outside of regular business hours. It is important to carefully consider the best approach for setting up these processes and actions to ensure a smooth and effective execution of the plan.

Tactics are comprised of a series of actions that must be carefully managed in order to be successful. It is important to create a detailed project plan for each tactic, including specific tasks that are assigned to specific people and deadlines. Although it may not be necessary to create a mini-project plan for every tactic in a digital marketing plan, it is important to have a clear understanding of how each tactic will be executed. The plan should outline the steps that will be taken to ensure that the tactics are carried out effectively.

To ensure that tactics are executed effectively, it is necessary to create detailed action plans that outline the specific steps that need to be taken. Tactics are based on the overall strategy, and the success of the strategy depends on the ability to translate it into specific, well-executed tactics. Good implementation requires careful planning and efficient use of resources, including project management schedules, meeting deadlines, and communication through meetings, memos, phone calls, and other channels. It also requires a focus on details and internal marketing, as well as constant monitoring and follow-up to ensure that everything is running smoothly.

INTERNAL MARKETING

To achieve excellence in execution, it is important to ensure that staff are motivated and aware of the purpose and goals of the new digital strategy and tactics. They should also be familiar with any new systems and tools, such as e-CRM, social media, split testing, Google Analytics, and marketing automation, and have the necessary training to use them effectively. Internal marketing, which includes motivating, communicating, and training staff and external partners, is crucial in this process. It is important to assess whether staff are knowledgeable, capable, passionate, and motivated to succeed in their roles and contribute to the overall success of the campaign.

RISK MANAGEMENT & CONTINGENCY PLANNING

Effective implementation also involves anticipating and preparing for potential problems, such as cyber libel, viruses, mail bombs, hackers, hijackers, and cybersquatting. Contingency planning is necessary to address these issues and ensure that the campaign can continue smoothly in the face of unexpected challenges. This may involve making changes to the plan or the tactics being used if something is not working or generating the desired results. It is important to have a plan in place for addressing server downtime or other technical issues that may arise.

Risk management involves:

- Brainstorming a list of all the significant things that could go wrong (server crashes to being blacklisted by Google)
- Assessing their impact and likelihood
- Creating contingency plans for the highest impact and most probable risks
- Continuous review, revising and refining during campaign execution
- Post-implementation reviews to learn from the successes and failures for the next project.

DIGITAL MARKETING PLAN SUMMARY

Effective execution is crucial for the success of your plan, and can be achieved through careful attention to detail, well-defined processes and procedures, and the use of checklists. Proper internal communication, training, and motivation of staff is also important for successful execution. Strong project management skills are necessary during the implementation phase to ensure smooth progress. By including control mechanisms in your digital marketing plan, you can take control of your own success.

Digital marketing can be uncertain without control mechanisms in place. It's like trying to throw darts in the dark, not knowing if you're hitting the target or just shooting blindly. To truly understand your customers and make informed decisions, it's important to have control over various aspects of your marketing strategy, such as identifying your target audience, understanding their preferences, measuring the success of your campaigns, and analyzing the cost and return on investment of your digital marketing tools. By the end of this section, you'll learn how to gain control over your marketing efforts and track your competitors.

CREATING A DIGITAL MARKETING PLAN INVOLVES DEFINING YOUR GOALS, IDENTIFYING YOUR TARGET AUDIENCE, AND MAPPING OUT A STRATEGY TO REACH AND ENGAGE WITH THEM EFFECTIVELY.

CHAPTER 17
TRACKING YOUR DIGITAL MARKETING PLAN

Measuring and analyzing your digital marketing results is an important step in the marketing process for black-owned businesses. It helps you understand the effectiveness of your campaigns and make informed decisions about your marketing strategy.

There are several key metrics that you can track to measure and analyze your digital marketing results:

Traffic

This measures the number of visitors to your website or app. You can use tools like Google Analytics to track your traffic and understand where it's coming from (e.g. search engines, social media, referral sites).

Conversion Rate

This measures the percentage of visitors who complete a desired action on your website or app (e.g. making a purchase, filling out a form). A high conversion rate indicates that your marketing efforts are effective at attracting and converting visitors.

Cost Per Acquisition (CPA)

This measures the cost of acquiring a new customer through your marketing efforts. It's calculated by dividing the total cost of your marketing campaign by the number of new customers acquired.

Return On Investment (ROI)

This measures the profitability of your marketing efforts. It's calculated by dividing the revenue generated from your marketing campaign by the cost of the campaign.

TRAFFIC

Tracking key metrics allows you to gauge the effectiveness of your digital marketing campaigns and make informed decisions about how to optimize your strategy. Let's delve into more detail about each metric.

Traffic refers to the number of visitors to a website or app. It's a key metric for measuring the reach and popularity of a digital marketing campaign.

There are several ways to track traffic, including:

Web Analytics Tools:

Tools like Google Analytics allow you to track the number of visitors to your website, as well as where they're coming from (e.g. search engines, social media, referral sites). You can also see how long visitors spend on your site, which pages they visit, and what actions they take (e.g. making a purchase, filling out a form).

Server Logs

Some hosting providers offer access to server logs, which provide detailed information about the traffic to your website. This includes the IP address of each visitor, the pages they visit, and the time they spend on the site.

Social Media Analytics

If you're using social media to promote your website or app, you can use the analytics tools provided by each platform (e.g. Facebook Insights, Twitter Analytics) to track the number of visits to your site from social media.

 USE WEB ANALYTICS TOOLS
Web analytics tools, such as Google Analytics, allow you to track the performance of your website and marketing efforts. These tools can provide valuable insights into your website traffic, customer behavior, and conversion rates.

CONVERSION RATE

The conversion rate is the percentage of visitors to a website or app who complete a desired action. It's a key metric for measuring the effectiveness of a digital marketing campaign. For example, if 100 people visit a website and 10 of them make a purchase, the conversion rate would be 10%.

There are several ways to improve the conversion rate of a website or app:

Optimize The User Experience

A smooth and intuitive user experience can increase the likelihood of visitors completing a desired action. This includes making it easy to navigate the site, displaying clear calls to action, and reducing loading times.

Test Different Designs

A/B testing allows you to compare different versions of a website or app and see which one has a higher conversion rate. This can help you identify design elements that are most effective at converting visitors.

Target The Right Audience

By targeting the right audience with your marketing efforts, you'll be more likely to attract visitors who are interested in what you have to offer and are therefore more likely to convert.

Offer Incentives

Offering incentives (e.g. discounts, free shipping) can encourage visitors to complete a desired action.

COST PER ACQUISITION (CPA)

Cost per acquisition (CPA) is a metric that measures the cost of acquiring a new customer through marketing efforts. It's calculated by dividing the total cost of a marketing campaign by the number of new customers acquired. For example, if a marketing campaign costs $1,000 and results in 100 new customers, the CPA would be $10.

CPA is an important metric because it helps you understand the efficiency of your marketing efforts. A low CPA indicates that you're able to acquire new customers at a low cost, while a high CPA may indicate that you need to optimize your marketing strategy to reduce costs.

There are several ways to reduce the CPA of a marketing campaign:

Target The Right Audience

By targeting the right audience with your marketing efforts, you'll be more likely to attract customers who are interested in what you have to offer and are therefore more likely to make a purchase.

Optimize Your Marketing Channels

Different marketing channels (e.g. search advertising, social media, email marketing) can have different CPAs. By identifying the channels that are most cost-effective, you can allocate more budget to those channels and reduce the overall CPA of your campaign.

Test Different Marketing Tactics

A/B testing allows you to compare the performance of different marketing tactics and identify the ones that are most effective at driving conversions at a low cost.

RETURN ON INVESTMENT (ROI)

Return on investment (ROI) is a financial metric that measures the profitability of an investment. It's calculated by dividing the revenue generated by an investment by the cost of the investment. For example, if an investment costs $100 and generates $200 in revenue, the ROI would be 100%.

ROI is an important metric for digital marketing campaigns because it helps you understand the profitability of your marketing efforts. A high ROI indicates that your marketing campaigns are generating a good return on investment, while a low ROI may indicate that you need to optimize your marketing strategy to improve profitability.

There are several ways to improve the ROI of a digital marketing campaign:

Optimize The Conversion Rate

By improving the conversion rate of your website or app, you can increase the revenue generated by your marketing efforts.

Reduce The Cost Of Acquisition

By reducing the cost per acquisition (CPA) of your marketing campaigns, you can increase the profitability of your marketing efforts.

Target The Right Audience

By targeting the right audience with your marketing efforts, you'll be more likely to attract customers who are interested in what you have to offer and are therefore more likely to make a purchase.

Test Different Marketing Tactics

A/B testing allows you to compare the performance of different marketing tactics and identify the ones that are most effective at driving conversions and generating revenue.

Now that we've covered the importance of tracking key metrics to measure and analyze your digital marketing results and how it can benefit your company, let's delve into how to make use of data using Google Analytics (which is free). With Google Analytics, you can create clear and useful reports that you can learn from and share with your team or clients. These reports can help you make informed decisions about your marketing strategy.

UTILIZING THE 5 GOOGLE ANALYTICS REPORT SUITES

Google Analytics is a widely used website statistics service that helps you make informed marketing and business decisions by tracking traffic to your site. It can track visitors from search engines, social media, and direct visits, and offers both a free basic service and a premium version. To learn more about Google Analytics or how to install it on your site, visit the Google Analytics Help Center.

Google Analytics offers five report suites that allow you to analyze your data in more detail. These reports can be accessed from the left side of the website.

Real Time Suite

The Real-Time report provides instant data on what is happening on your site, such as the number of visitors, which pages they are on, and their geographical location.

Audience Suite

This report provides insight into the characteristics of the people visiting your site, including their demographics, interests, behaviors, and the devices and browsers they use to access your site.

Acquisition Suite

Use this report allows you to understand how users arrived at your site, such as through a referral from another website or by searching for a specific keyword.

Behavior Suite

The Behavior Reports provide information on what users do once they arrive on your site, such as which pages they visit, how long they stay on those pages, and how many people leave those pages.

Conversions Suite

The Conversion Reports help you determine whether users are achieving your desired goals, such as making a purchase or subscribing to a newsletter, by tracking their actions on your site.

Each of the report suites in Google Analytics offers multiple reports that can provide increasing levels of detail. For example, the Mobile Devices report in the Audience Report suite allows you to view how visitor behavior differs on desktop, mobile, and tablet devices, and you can also drill down to view behavior by service provider and operating system. By clicking on one of the operating systems, you can even view behavior by specific versions of the operating system. This level of granularity allows you to understand visitor behavior in great detail and make informed decisions about your marketing strategy.

ANALYZING THE SOURCES OF YOUR TRAFFIC

There are many different ways that people can find and access your website, such as through ads, search queries, and bookmarking.

According to Google Analytics, the following are common sources of traffic:

Email

Visits to your website from individuals who have clicked on the links in your email promotions and newsletters.

Organic Search

Visits to your website from people who have entered specific search terms or phrases into search engines like Google or Bing.

Direct

Direct traffic refers to visits to your site that come from users typing in the exact domain of your site (e.g. GoBlackOwn.com) into their browser or accessing it through a bookmark they have saved. When someone navigates directly to your site in this way, it is counted as direct traffic.

Paid search

Paid search traffic refers to visits to your site that come from search engine ads that you have paid for, such as pay-per-click ads. This is traffic that you have purchased in order to drive more visitors to your site.

Referral

Visitors from sites that link to your website, such as blogs and forums.

Social

Visits from social channels, such as Twitter or Facebook.

The Acquisition Overview report in the Acquisition Suite of Google Analytics is a valuable resource for understanding the performance and health of a website. It is the first report you should check when evaluating your site. This report provides important insights into your website's traffic and can help you identify areas for improvement.

IDENTIFYING THE SOURCE OF SITE VISITORS

Tools like Google Analytics can track the source of your site's visitors using default settings, but these may not provide detailed or meaningful data. To gather more specific and useful information, you can add UTM parameters to the links you share online. UTM stands for Urchin Tracking Module, and it is a tracking code that can be added to a URL. By adding UTM tags to your links, you can track where your visitors are coming from and get a better understanding of their origins. UTM parameters allow you to gain a more granular understanding of your website's traffic, enabling you to make informed decisions about your marketing and advertising efforts.

UTM parameters can be used to track specific actions or events that occur on your website, such as the number of leads generated through a particular link. To do this, you can add UTM tags to the end of a hyperlink and track the link using Google Analytics. For example, if you want to see how many leads are generated through a link shared with your Facebook followers, you can add a UTM tag to the link and track the results in Google Analytics. This allows you to understand where your visitors are coming from and what they do once they arrive on your site.

To track the source of traffic to your landing pages from your blog or social media channels, you can use UTM parameters in your hyperlinks. These parameters are a type of tracking code that you can add to the links you share. When someone clicks on the link, the UTM parameters will allow you to see where the visit came from. Each UTM consists of several different parameters.

Here are the UTM parameters that matter most:

- Campaign source (utm_source)
- Campaign medium (utm_medium)
- Campaign content (utm_content)
- Campaign name (utm_campaign)

We explain each of these parameters in the sections that follow.

Campaign Source (utm_source)

Typically, the source of a UTM indicates the origin of your visitors. It specifies the location where the referring link was shared, such as

- An email promotion
- A social network
- A referring website

Common sources include:

- Facebook
- Email newsletter
- Twitter
- Google
- YouTube

By tracking the source of your UTMs, you can see which email, search engine, or Facebook ad (or other source) a user was referred from. Understanding the sources of your traffic can provide valuable insights into what your users are responding to and engaging with.

Campaign Medium (utm_medium)

The medium parameter in a UTM identifies the platform or method through which the link was accessed, such as email. This parameter helps you understand how visitors arrived at your site.

Some of the most common mediums include:

- Email
- Pay per click (PPC)
- Banner-ads
- Direct (which tells you users directly typed in your site address)

Campaign Content (utm_content)

The campaign content parameter in a UTM specifies the specific ad, banner, or email that was used to share the link. This information can be useful for A/B testing or targeted advertising, and can help you determine which marketing materials are most effective at promoting offers or distributing content.

It is important to be as detailed as possible when naming the campaign content parameter in a UTM, so that you can easily identify which email or ad the UTM refers to.

Campaign Name (utm_campaign)

The campaign name parameter in a UTM is used to identify a specific product or promotional campaign, such as a spring sale or other promotion. Its primary purpose is to highlight promotional offers or content distribution strategies, allowing you to easily compare their performance over time and across platforms.

To make it easier to analyze the overall performance of a campaign, it is important to use consistent UTMs across all sources and platforms for any given promotion.

Creating UTM Parameters For Your URLs

Google provides a free tool called the Google Analytics URL Builder that makes it easy to create UTM links. To use this tool, simply visit the page, follow the prompts, and input your information. The tool will automatically generate a hyperlink with UTM parameters that you can track with Google Analytics. If you don't already have a Google Analytics account set up, you can find instructions on how to use the different UTM parameters in the Google Analytics Help Center.

It may take some time to get used to creating hyperlinks with proper attribution, but the data they provide is valuable. To ensure consistency, you can create a document that tracks all the hyperlinks you use, which will make it easier to refer back to when analyzing data later.

Keep in mind that UTM parameters are case sensitive, so if you use different capitalization for your utm_campaign tags on different links, they will appear as separate campaigns in Google Analytics. For example, using 'abc' for some links and 'ABC' for others will be treated as two separate campaigns.

CREATING GOALS TO SEE WHO'S TAKING ACTION

With the UTM tag in place, you can track specific actions taken by groups of people on your website using goals in Google Analytics. These goals provide not only a count of the times an action was taken, but also insights into which groups of people took that action. While Google Analytics does not allow you to track personal identifiable information, such as names or emails, it does allow you to track details such as the device being used, the location of the user, and the other pages visited on your site. Using UTM parameters, you can see what individual users and groups of users do when they visit your site.

To track the effectiveness of an opt-in form on your website, you can use Google Analytics to monitor the number of visitors who reach the confirmation page after filling out the form. This can help you understand how many leads are being generated through the opt-in process. To set this up, you can configure Google Analytics to track visits to the confirmation page following a visit to the opt-in page.

To set up a form fill in Google Analytics, follow these steps:

1. **Click the Admin section of Google Analytics.**
    The Admin menu appears.
2. **Click Goals under All Website Data.**
    The Goals dialog box appears.
3. **Click the + New Goal button to create a new goal.**
    The Goal Setup page appears.

4. **Scroll down and select the Sign Up Goal type; then click the Continue button.**

    The Goal Description page appears. Google offers a variety of goal templates that should fit your specific needs (although you can create custom ones as well). Because you want to track opt-ins, Sign Up should be perfect in this case.

5. **Name your goal and then, under the Type field, select Destination and press the Continue button.**

    The final setup page, called the Goal Details page, appears.

6. **Set up the specifics for your goal.**

    For Destination field, change your rule to Begins With and add your Thank You page's URL string — that's where people who opt-in end up. Using Begins With helps to ensure that all opt-ins are properly credited. The other way to ensure that you're tracking actual opt-ins and not just accidental Thank You page visitors is to create a funnel. This involves adding the URL string of the opt-in page as well. To set up a funnel, you turn the Funnel option to ON and add a step with the page field, including the URL that precedes your destination page. Set this step to Required and you've added this rule! When you're done, verify your goal to make sure that you set it up correctly.

7. **Click Save.**

    You've built your first goal in Google Analytics!

For your URL strings, always use the text after your domain name, not the entire URL — Google already knows the root domain.

To review the collected data for a goal that you have set up in Google Analytics, you can go to the Conversions section of the Reporting menu and choose the Goals tab. This will display the Goal Overview report, which provides an overview of the performance of all the goals you have set up. You can also select a specific goal from the drop-down menu at the top of the page to view the performance of a particular goal. The report will show you the total number of goal completions and the conversion rate for that goal. You can use this information to understand how your customers are interacting with your website and which channels, such as Facebook, email, and your blog, are driving the most traffic.

By properly setting up campaign tracking in Google Analytics and applying proper attribution tagging, you can gain valuable insights into the effectiveness of your marketing efforts. This will provide a solid foundation for tracking the success of your campaigns and help you identify what is and isn't working. It is important for businesses to regularly assess and analyze their campaigns in order to make informed decisions about how to grow and improve. With the right tools and approach, you can use Google Analytics to gain a deeper understanding of your customers and optimize your marketing strategies for greater success.

SEGMENTING YOUR AUDIENCE WITH GOOGLE ANALYTICS

Now that you have a basic understanding of how to track success and identify the channels that are driving it using UTM parameters and goals in Google Analytics, you may be wondering how to use this information to improve your marketing efforts. One way to do this is to segment your audience based on the data you have collected.

Some possible segments you could create might include:

- Channel
- Traffic source
- Completed actions
- Conversions

In Google Analytics, a segment is a group of website visitors who share certain characteristics or behaviors. By creating segments within your audience, you can:

- Determine which group of people are most likely to be interested in a particular offer or message, so that you can target this group more effectively with your marketing efforts.
- Create customized marketing messages that are tailored to specific groups of people in order to improve the effectiveness of your ads and follow-up campaigns.

Segmenting your audience can be a powerful tool for maximizing the impact of your marketing efforts and understanding what is and isn't working. By creating segments and analyzing the data within them, you can gain a deeper understanding of your customers and make more informed decisions about how to allocate your resources. In the next section, we will discuss how to create useful segments and how to analyze the data within them to gain a better understanding of the people who are taking the desired actions on your website.

> **TIP**
>
> **USE CUSTOMER FEEDBACK**
> Customer feedback, such as reviews and surveys, can provide valuable insights into the effectiveness of your marketing efforts. Consider using tools like Google Reviews and SurveyMonkey to gather customer feedback and identify areas for improvement.

Creating Audience Segments

Segmenting your audience can be a valuable strategy for identifying and targeting the most valuable and highest-converting groups of people. By creating segments and analyzing the data within them, you can learn more about what motivates these individuals and tailor your marketing efforts to better meet their needs. In the next section, we will discuss how to create segments and what data you should be looking at to better understand your audience.

Creating segments in Google Analytics is a quick and easy process that allows you to focus on specific subsets of your audience, rather than all website visitors. By defining rules to include or exclude certain individuals, you can narrow down your analysis to specific groups, such as those who have opted in for a gated offer. Once you have created a segment, you can then analyze the behavior of this subset of visitors or learn more about who is in the subset, providing valuable insights that can inform your marketing efforts.

Follow these steps to create your own segments:

1. **In Google Analytics, navigate to the Reporting section.**
   The report suites appear.
2. **Select the Audience suite and click the Overview tab within the Audience suite.**
   The Audience Overview report appears.
3. **Click the + Add Segment field along the top of the page.**
   The Segment menu appears.
4. **Click the New Segment button to create a new segment.**
   The Segment menu opens, allowing you to set conditions for your segments to meet and exclusions you want your segment to ignore. For instance, you might set a condition for age or operating system.
5. **Set conditions for your segment by selecting any of the following check boxes or filling in the field within in the following categories:**
   - **Demographics:** Segment your users by demographic information, such as age, gender, location, and other details. These are check boxes and form fields, depending on the option within the Demographics category.

- **Technology:** Segment your users' sessions by their web and mobile technologies, such as browser, device category, and screen resolution. These are check boxes and form fields, depending on the option within the Technology category.
- **Behavior:** Segment your users by how often they visit (called a session) and conduct transactions, such as sessions, session duration, and days since last session. These are form fields.
- **Date of first session:** Segment your users (create cohorts) by when they first visited your site. This is a form field.
- **Traffic sources:** Segment your users by how they found you, such as the keyword they used, the ad campaign, and the medium used. These are form fields.
- **Conditions:** Segment your users, their sessions, or both according to single or multisession conditions, such as time, goal conversions, and custom variables. This is a form field.
- **Sequences:** Segment your users, their sessions, or both according to sequential conditions, such as the steps they took to reach your site. This is a form field.

6. **After setting your conditions for your segment, name your segment by filling out the empty name field.**
7. **Click the Save button to successfully complete this segment.**

Your new segment loads, and you can return to this segment at a later date when conducting future data research and analysis.

Once you have created a new segment in Google Analytics, the data for that segment will be displayed, allowing you to analyze and assess the performance of that group. The data displayed may include the number of users in the segment, as well as other statistics such as conversion rate and average session duration. You can use this information to understand the characteristics and behavior of the people in the segment, and to make informed decisions about your marketing efforts.

As a general rule, it is best to aim for a minimum of 3,000 people in each of your audience segments in Google Analytics. This will ensure that you have a large enough sample size to have confidence in your groupings and make reliable decisions. While you can experiment with smaller segments, the larger the segment size, the more trustworthy the data will be, allowing you to make informed business decisions.

In Google Analytics, you can create segments in any of the following suites: Audience, Acquisition, Behavior, or Conversion. Simply choose the suite that best meets your needs and select the Overview option within that suite. The process for creating a segment is the same regardless of the suite you choose, although the data that is measured will vary depending on the suite you select. You can use segments to gain a deeper understanding of your audience and make more informed decisions about your marketing efforts by analyzing data from any of these suites.

HORNING IN ON YOUR AUDIENCE

Once you have segmented your audience in Google Analytics, you can further analyze the data within those segments to gain a deeper understanding of your customers. By running reports and analyzing the data, you can learn more about who is and isn't taking desired actions, such as opting in, and use this information to optimize your marketing efforts. Reports can help you better understand your audience and identify opportunities to drive down ad costs or develop more effective strategies for monetizing leads. By gaining a deeper understanding of your audience, you can make more informed decisions about your marketing efforts and improve the return on your investment.

You should look for two main types of data:

- Demographic
- Psychographic

Demographic data refers to information about the characteristics and traits of people, such as their age, gender, location, and device type. This data can be useful in helping you understand who you are targeting with your marketing campaigns and how to tailor your messaging and targeting to better reach and engage your audience. Demographic information can help you get a better sense of who your audience is and what they are like, allowing you to more effectively design your marketing efforts.

Psychographic data refers to information about the interests, hobbies, and preferences of people, and it can provide insight into their personality and behavior. In contrast to demographic data, which describes what people are like, psychographic data focuses on what people like and helps to paint a more complete picture of their interests and motivations. This data can be particularly useful in shaping your marketing messaging and targeting to better connect with your audience. By understanding what people are interested in and what they like, you can create more relevant and engaging marketing campaigns that are more likely to resonate with your audience.

In the next sections, we will show you how to create reports that focus on demographic data and psychographic data in Google Analytics. By building these reports, you will be able to easily analyze these types of data for any audience segments you have created. This will allow you to get a better understanding of your audience and make more informed decisions about your marketing efforts.

ANALYZING DEMOGRAPHIC DATA IN DETAIL

Demographic data is often straightforward and easy to analyze, but it can provide valuable insights into your audience. In Google Analytics, you can view a demographics report on the Audience tab, which focuses on sessions (visits) as the key metric. However, to get a more detailed understanding of your users, you will need to create a custom report. This will allow you to delve deeper into the demographic data and gain a better understanding of your audience.

To make a custom report for demographics, follow these steps:

1. **Go to the Customization section in Google Analytics and select the + New Custom Report button.**
   The Create Custom Report page opens. Create as many separate reports as you want to examine for demographics. At our company, we make four reports when drilling down into demographics: one each for age, gender, location, and device type.
2. **In the Report Content section of the Create Custom Report page, create Report Tabs.**
   Name the tab based on the demographic you are drilling down on. For example, if you are measuring age, name the Age. If you plan to measure multiple demographics in this report, as we suggest in Step 1, you can create a new Report Tab by clicking the + Add Report Tab button under the Report Content section. Name each tab for the demographic you are measuring.
3. **On the same page, set the Metric Groups dimension to Users by clicking the + Add Metric button and then selecting Users from the drop-down menu for every Report Tab you create.**
   The word Users will now be displayed in the Metric Groups dimension. Users is the constant among all your tabs.
4. **On the same page, in the Dimension Drilldowns dimension, set the demographic for each Report Tab you create by clicking the + Add Dimension button.**

For Age, the Dimension Drilldown is Age; for Gender, it's Gender, and for Device, it's the Device Category. Your respective demographic now appears in the Dimension Drilldown dimension. Location is the only oddball; for the other demographics, you keep Type (located above the Metric Groups dimension) at the preselected Explorer Tab. For location, however, you set your Type to the Map Overlay tab, which will display the location data on a geographical map, and it replaces the need for a Dimension Drilldown.

5. **Click the Save button when you're done.**

    The report you created loads, and you now have a ready-made demographics report to use repeatedly.

This demographics report will provide you with important information to consider when analyzing the success of your campaign. The following sections will guide you on what to focus on in the report in order to gain valuable insights.

Age

One aspect to consider when evaluating the success of your campaign is the age of the individuals who are responding. Take a look at the age range of those who are opting in. Does this align with the customer profile you defined? If not, it may be necessary to revise the ad copy for your campaign to better target that age group. This will allow you to create a more tailored campaign, potentially resulting in higher opt-in rates and a reduction in cost per click. Keep an eye out for any unexpected patterns in the age range of those who are responding to your campaign.

Gender

If the gender of the users who opted in to your campaign is heavily skewed towards a particular gender, it may be beneficial to create a version of the campaign that specifically targets that gender. This could potentially increase clicks and ad relevance, while also reducing the cost-per-click (CPC).

Location

Using location data can be helpful for expanding into new regions or scaling in other areas. For example, if you see from a location report that your campaign is performing well in a particular city, state, or country that you hadn't previously targeted, you may want to allocate more of your ad budget to this location. This can allow you to take advantage of regional interests.

Device

The Device report allows you to see which device people used to opt into your campaign, such as a mobile phone, tablet, or desktop. This information can help you design your campaign effectively. For example, if you see that your gated offer is popular with mobile users, it may be important to design your conversion funnel with mobile users in mind in order to turn gated offer downloaders into buyers.

Drilling Into Psychographics

Using the information from the previous sections, you can optimize your campaign targeting based on factual data about your audience. However, in order to determine the most effective messaging and follow-up strategy, it can be helpful to consider psychographic data. Psychographic data pertains to an individual's personality, values, attitudes, interests, and lifestyles.

To gather more information about your audience, you can create a custom report that includes data on Affinity Categories and In-Market Segments. Affinity Categories provide insight into users' likes and interests, while In-Market Segments reveal what products or services this audience is interested in purchasing or has recently purchased.

This process follows many of the same steps as when you created your custom demographic report:

1. **Go to Customization in Google Analytics and select + New Custom Report.**
   The Create Custom Report page opens.
2. **In the Report Content section of the Create Custom Report page, create Report Tabs: one for Affinity Categories and another for In-Market Segments.**
   You add a tab by clicking the + Add Report Tab button under the Report Content section. Name one tab for your In-Market Segments and one for your Affinity Categories.
3. **On the same page, set the Metric Groups dimension to Users by clicking the + Add Metric button and then selecting Users from the drop-down menu for every Report Tab you create.**
   The word Users will now be displayed in the Metric Groups dimension. Users is the constant among all your tabs.
4. **On the same page, in the Dimension Drilldowns dimension, set the demographic for each Report Tab you create by clicking the +Add Dimension button.**

The Dimension Drilldowns that you select are Affinity Category and In-Market Segment, respectively.
5. **Click the Save button when you're done.**

After creating a report, you can now access it at any time to analyze the interests of the users who have opted into your campaign.

AFFINITY CATEGORY REPORT

The Affinity Category report provides information on what your users are interested in, which can help you create more targeted campaigns. When reviewing this data, it is best to set the data view type to Comparison. This view allows you to see interests more clearly, with the most popular listed at the top and the least popular listed at the bottom. This can be more helpful than just looking at raw numbers.

Using Affinity reports can help you refine your marketing message and make your ad copy more targeted as you optimize your campaign.

IN-MARKET REPORT

In-Market Segments provide information on what products or services your audience is interested in purchasing or has recently purchased. This can be valuable for targeting your market based on specific products and services. As with the Affinity report, it is best to set the data view type to Comparison when reviewing this data, as it allows you to see interests more clearly than raw numbers do.

You can use In-Market reports to gather information about your users' income range by looking at the type of products and services they are interested in purchasing. For example, if you see that they are interested in luxury goods, it may indicate that they have a higher income. This can help you get a sense of your target market's income range.

By using this strategy, you can gain another perspective on your users' income and the types of products they may be interested in. For instance, if you find that only a small percentage of your audience for this campaign falls within any of the In-Market Segments related to wealth, you can conclude that the people opting into your campaign are not likely to have a high income. As a result, following up with a campaign for a high-priced item may not be as effective as a campaign with more modest, discounted offers.

PUTTING IT ALL TOGETHER

Using the data from your custom reports, you can create a detailed profile of the audience that is opting into your campaign. This includes both demographic and psychographic data. This information allows you to make informed decisions about optimizing and scaling your campaign, rather than relying on guesses. By using data-driven strategies, you can potentially increase opt-ins, improve ad relevancy, and reduce the cost-per-click (CPC). This demonstrates the value of using data to guide business decisions.

Here is an example of what your customer profile might look like after combining all the data points that you have gathered about your audience:

- **Gender:** Male
- **Age:** Late 20s, early 30s
- **Preferred Device:** Smartphone
- **Estimated Average Income:** Under $100k Annually
- **Role at Work:** Supervisor
- **Likes and Interests:** Movies, Business News, Hip-Hop Music, Education, Career Consulting, Dating Services
- **Dislikes:** Sports, Horror Films, Board Games, Videogames, Automobile Accessories

With this detailed profile of your ideal candidate, you can create a more targeted campaign or expand it to other traffic platforms. You can use this information to approach your campaign from a new angle and speak more directly to your target audience. With this level of detail about your target audience, your paid traffic team can be more effective in their efforts.

 MONITOR YOUR BRAND MENTIONS
It's important to track how your brand is being mentioned online. Consider using tools like Google Alerts or Brand24 to track mentions of your brand and identify opportunities for engagement.

The data strategies discussed in this chapter can be applied not only to people who opt in, but also to purchasers or membership site users, depending on the type of targeting you use. These strategies can be used on any platform that generates a sufficient amount of traffic.

TRACKING THE SUCCESS OF YOUR DIGITAL MARKETING PLAN INVOLVES REGULARLY MEASURING AND ANALYZING KEY PERFORMANCE INDICATORS TO UNDERSTAND WHAT'S WORKING AND WHAT'S NOT.

CHAPTER 18
CONCLUSION & CONSULTING

The process of creating this book has been similar to my career in that it has involved a wide range of tested experiences, just as a journey would. For black business owners, from small startups to established entrepreneurs, my advice is to embrace the journey of building and growing your business. Don't waste time looking for a quick fix or magic solution for success in digital marketing. It's a process that requires effort and creativity, and there is no one-size-fits-all approach. Treat it as an art form and enjoy the ride.

Achieving success in your black-owned business requires dedication and perseverance. If you want to accelerate your progress, you may consider investing money in your digital marketing efforts. One way to do this is by seeking the guidance of an expert or partnering with a reputable digital marketing agency. When selecting a team to work with, it's important to do your research and choose wisely based on their experience, reputation, and track record. By putting great minds together, you can work towards a common goal effectively.

One of the benefits of digital marketing is that it allows you to connect and collaborate with people from all around the world. As a black-owned business owner, you have the power to make a big impact through the use of these tactics. By implementing a diverse range of strategies, you can expect to see significant returns in terms of revenue for your business in the future.

REVIEWING WHAT WE'VE LEARNED

To summarize what we have learned in this book, let's revisit how all of the information fits together:

DIGITAL MARKETING

Digital marketing refers to the use of online platforms and channels to promote and sell products or services. It includes a wide range of tactics and strategies, such as search engine optimization (SEO), social media marketing, email marketing, and content marketing, that can help businesses reach and engage with their target audience.

For black-owned businesses, digital marketing can be a particularly effective way to reach and connect with potential customers. It allows businesses to target specific audiences and track the success of their marketing efforts in real-time, which can help them make more informed decisions about their marketing strategy.

There are several key tactics that black-owned businesses can use as part of their digital marketing efforts.

These include:

1. **SEO:** By optimizing their websites and content for relevant keywords and phrases, businesses can improve their rankings on search engines like Google and make it easier for potential customers to find them.
2. **Social media marketing:** By creating and maintaining a presence on social media platforms like Facebook, Instagram, and Twitter, businesses can reach and engage with their target audience and build brand awareness.
3. **Email marketing:** By collecting email addresses and sending targeted emails to their subscribers, businesses can keep their customers informed about new products and promotions, and encourage them to make purchases.

4. **Content marketing:** By creating and sharing valuable, informative, and entertaining content, businesses can attract and retain a clearly defined audience and build trust and credibility with their customers.

CREATING A CUSTOMER PROFILE

Creating a customer profile, also known as a buyer persona, is an important step for any business, including black-owned businesses. A customer profile is a fictional representation of your ideal customer, based on market research and real data about your existing customers. It helps you understand your target audience and tailor your marketing and sales efforts to better meet their needs and preferences.

To create a customer profile for your black-owned business, you should start by gathering as much information as possible about your existing customers. This may include demographic information, such as age, gender, and location, as well as information about their interests, needs, and purchasing habits. You can also conduct market research to gather additional insights into your target audience.

Once you have a good understanding of your existing customers, you can use this information to create a customer profile that represents your ideal customer. This profile should include details such as the customer's age, gender, location, occupation, and income level, as well as their interests, values, and goals. You should also include information about their pain points and challenges, as well as how your business can help address these issues.

Once you have created a customer profile, you can use it to guide your marketing and sales efforts. For example, you can use it to develop targeted messaging and marketing campaigns that speak directly to the needs and interests of your target audience. You can also use it to create more effective sales materials, such as pitch decks and product demos, that are tailored to the specific needs and preferences of your ideal customer.

Overall, creating a customer profile is an important step for any business, including black-owned businesses, as it helps you understand your target audience and create more effective marketing and sales efforts. By taking the time to research and understand your ideal customer, you can better meet their needs and build stronger, more profitable relationships with them.

BUILDING AN ONLINE PRESENCE

Having an online presence is essential for businesses of all sizes and industries, and this is especially true for Black-owned businesses. An online presence allows Black-owned businesses to reach a wider audience, showcase their products and services, and establish their brand identity.

Here are some steps to consider when building an online presence for a Black-owned business:

1. **Create a website:** A website is the cornerstone of any online presence. It allows customers to learn about your business, view your products and services, and contact you. There are many website builders available that make it easy to create a professional-looking website, even if you don't have any coding experience.
2. **Use social media:** Social media platforms like Facebook, Instagram, and Twitter are great tools for promoting your business and connecting with customers. Create accounts on the platforms that are most relevant to your business and start posting updates, pictures, and other content that showcases your products and services.
3. **Use email marketing:** Email marketing allows you to send targeted messages to your customers and potential customers. Use email marketing to keep your customers informed about new products, sales, and other special offers.
4. **Optimize your website for search engines:** To attract more visitors to your website, it's important to optimize your website for search engines like Google. This involves using relevant keywords in your website's content and meta tags, as well as building high-quality backlinks from other websites.
5. **Use online advertising:** Online advertising allows you to reach a specific audience by placing ads on websites, social media platforms, and other online channels. There are many different types of online advertising, including pay-per-click ads, display ads, and social media ads.
6. **Engage with your customers:** Building an online presence is not just about promoting your business – it's also about engaging with your customers. Respond to customer inquiries and complaints in a timely manner, and use social media to connect with your customers and build a community around your business.

SEO & SERP

SEO, or search engine optimization, is the process of improving the ranking of a website on search engines like Google. It involves optimizing various elements of a website, such as its content, technical infrastructure, and user experience, to make it more appealing to search engines and users.

SERP, or search engine results page, is the page that a search engine returns with the results of a query. It typically consists of a list of web pages, along with other types of content such as images and videos, that are relevant to the search query.

For black-owned businesses, SEO and SERP can be particularly important as they may not have the same level of visibility as larger, more established businesses. By optimizing their websites and improving their rankings on search engines, black-owned businesses can increase their chances of being found by potential customers and grow their online presence.

There are a number of strategies that black-owned businesses can use to improve their SEO and SERP.

Some of these strategies include:

1. **Keyword research:** Identifying the keywords and phrases that potential customers are using to search for businesses like yours can help you optimize your website's content and make it more visible to search engines.
2. **On-page optimization:** This involves optimizing various elements of your website, such as the title tags, headings, and meta descriptions, to make it more attractive to search engines and users.
3. **Technical SEO:** This involves optimizing the technical infrastructure of your website, such as its loading speed and mobile-friendliness, to make it more appealing to search engines.
4. **Off-page optimization:** This involves building links from other websites to your own, as well as using social media and other online platforms to promote your business and drive traffic to your website.

PR MARKETING

Public relations (PR) marketing is a strategic communication process that helps businesses, organizations, and individuals build and maintain a positive reputation with their target audience. For black-owned businesses, PR marketing can be a powerful tool for building brand awareness, establishing credibility, and attracting new customers.

Here are some key points to consider when developing a PR marketing strategy for a black-owned business:

1. **Identify your target audience:** The first step in any PR marketing campaign is to identify the specific group of people you want to reach. This could include potential customers, industry influencers, the media, or other key stakeholders.
2. **Develop a clear and consistent message:** To effectively communicate with your target audience, it's important to develop a clear and consistent message that conveys the unique value and benefits of your business. This message should be reflected in all of your PR materials, including press releases, social media posts, and any other communication channels you use.
3. **Build relationships with the media:** Establishing relationships with journalists, editors, and other media professionals can be a valuable way to get your message out to a wider audience. This can be achieved through press releases, media kits, and other PR materials that highlight the unique aspects of your business and its offerings.
4. **Utilize social media:** Social media platforms can be a powerful tool for promoting your business and engaging with your target audience. Use platforms like Instagram, Twitter, and Facebook to share updates about your business, highlight positive reviews and testimonials, and engage with your followers.
5. **Leverage partnerships and sponsorships:** Partnering with other businesses or organizations can help to amplify your message and reach a larger audience. Consider sponsorships or partnerships that align with your business goals and values, and be sure to showcase these relationships in your PR materials.
6. **Monitor and measure your PR efforts:** To understand the effectiveness of your PR marketing efforts, it's important to track and measure key metrics such as website traffic, social media engagement, and media coverage. This will help you to determine what is and isn't working, and make any necessary adjustments to your strategy.

ONLINE REPUTATION MANAGEMENT

Online reputation management is the process of monitoring and improving the online presence of a business or individual. This can be particularly important for black-owned businesses, as online reviews, social media posts, and other online content can significantly impact the perceived credibility and reputation of the business.

Here are some key considerations for online reputation management for black-owned businesses:

1. **Monitor your online presence:** It's important to regularly monitor your online presence to stay aware of what is being said about your business. This can be done through a variety of tools, such as Google Alerts, which notify you of any new content that includes your business name or specific keywords.
2. **Respond to customer feedback:** If you receive negative feedback or reviews online, it's important to respond in a timely and professional manner. This shows customers that you care about their experiences and are willing to address any issues that may arise.
3. **Manage negative content:** If you come across negative content about your business, it's important to address it promptly. This could involve responding to the individual or reviewing the content to see if there are any actionable steps you can take to resolve the issue.
4. **Encourage positive reviews:** Encouraging customers to leave positive reviews can help to offset any negative content that may exist online. Consider offering incentives for customers who leave positive reviews, or make it easy for them to do so by providing links to review sites on your website or social media accounts.
5. **Use social media to your advantage:** Social media platforms can be a valuable tool for managing your online reputation. Use platforms like Twitter and Facebook to engage with customers and address any concerns they may have in real-time.
6. **Seek professional help if necessary:** If you're struggling to manage your online reputation on your own, it may be worth seeking out the help of a professional reputation management firm. These companies specialize in helping businesses and individuals improve their online presence and can provide valuable guidance and support.

Overall, effective online reputation management is crucial for black-owned businesses looking to build and maintain a positive reputation online. By monitoring and managing your online presence, responding to customer feedback, and encouraging positive reviews, you can help to ensure that your business is perceived in the best light possible.

PAID ADVERTISING

Paid advertising refers to the use of paid media channels to promote a product, service, or brand. This can be a powerful marketing tool for black-owned businesses looking to reach a specific target audience and drive sales.

Here are some key considerations for paid advertising for black-owned businesses:

1. **Identify your target audience:** The first step in any paid advertising campaign is to identify the specific group of people you want to reach. This could include potential customers, industry influencers, or other key stakeholders.
2. **Determine your budget:** It's important to determine how much you're willing to spend on your paid advertising campaign before you get started. This will help you to make informed decisions about which channels to use and how to allocate your budget.
3. **Choose the right channels:** There are many different channels available for paid advertising, including social media platforms, search engines, and traditional media outlets. It's important to choose the channels that will most effectively reach your target audience and align with your business goals.
4. **Develop compelling ad copy:** The text and visuals used in your ads should be engaging and compelling, and should clearly communicate the value and benefits of your business.
5. **Use analytics to track your results:** It's important to track and measure the success of your paid advertising efforts to understand what is and isn't working. Use tools like Google Analytics to track key metrics such as website traffic, conversion rates, and cost-per-click.
6. **Test and optimize:** Don't be afraid to test different ad copy, visuals, and targeting to see what works best for your business. Use the data you collect to optimize your campaigns and improve their effectiveness over time.

SOCIAL MEDIA MARKETING

Social media marketing is the process of using social media platforms to promote a product, service, or brand. This can be a powerful marketing tool for black-owned businesses looking to reach a wide audience and build brand awareness.

Here are some key considerations for social media marketing for black-owned businesses:

1. **Choose the right platforms:** There are many different social media platforms available, each with its own unique features and audience. It's important to choose the platforms that will most effectively reach your target audience and align with your business goals.
2. **Develop a content strategy:** To effectively use social media for marketing, it's important to have a clear content strategy in place. This should include a mix of content types, such as informative posts, promotional offers, and engaging visuals.
3. **Engage with your audience:** Social media is a two-way communication channel, so it's important to engage with your followers and respond to their comments and questions in a timely and professional manner.
4. **Use hashtags and tagging:** Hashtags and tagging can help to increase the reach of your content and make it more discoverable to a wider audience. Research relevant hashtags and consider tagging other businesses or individuals in your posts to help increase visibility.
5. **Use paid advertising:** While organic reach on social media can be limited, paid advertising can help to increase the visibility of your content and reach a wider audience. Consider using paid advertising on platforms like Facebook, Instagram, and Twitter to amplify your message.
6. **Track and measure your results:** To understand the effectiveness of your social media marketing efforts, it's important to track and measure key metrics such as website traffic, social media engagement, and conversions. This will help you to determine what is and isn't working and make any necessary adjustments to your strategy.

VIDEO MARKETING

Video marketing can be an effective way for black-owned businesses to reach and engage with their target audience.

Here are some key points to consider when developing a video marketing strategy for a black-owned business:

1. **Identify your target audience:** The first step in any marketing campaign is to identify your target audience. This will help you tailor your messaging and content to appeal to the right people.
2. **Determine your goals:** Before you start creating videos, it's important to have a clear understanding of what you hope to achieve with your video marketing efforts. Do you want to increase brand awareness, drive sales, or generate leads? Having specific goals will help you measure the success of your campaigns and make adjustments as needed.
3. **Choose the right platforms:** There are many different platforms you can use to share your videos, including social media platforms like YouTube, Facebook, and Instagram, as well as video hosting platforms like Vimeo and Wistia. Consider where your target audience is most likely to be found and choose the platforms that will reach them most effectively.
4. **Create engaging and informative content:** The key to successful video marketing is creating content that resonates with your audience. This might include informational videos that teach viewers about your products or services, or more personal, behind-the-scenes videos that give them a glimpse into your company culture and values.
5. **Use video in email marketing:** In addition to sharing your videos on social media and other platforms, you can also use video in your email marketing campaigns. This can help you grab your audience's attention and increase the chances that they will engage with your content.
6. **Analyze and optimize your efforts:** As with any marketing campaign, it's important to track the success of your video marketing efforts and make adjustments as needed. Use tools like Google Analytics and social media analytics to track the performance of your videos and see what's working and what's not. This will help you optimize your strategy and get the most out of your video marketing efforts.

CUSTOMER RELATIONS MANAGERS (CRM)

A customer relationship manager (CRM) is a professional responsible for managing the interactions and relationships between a business and its customers. This can be particularly important for black-owned businesses, as building strong relationships with customers can be key to attracting new business and maintaining loyalty.

Here are some key considerations for CRM for black-owned businesses:

1. **Understand customer needs:** To effectively manage customer relationships, it's important to have a deep understanding of your customers' needs and preferences. This can be achieved through customer surveys, focus groups, and other research methods.
2. **Use customer data effectively:** A CRM system can be a valuable tool for collecting and analyzing customer data, such as purchase history, demographics, and preferences. This data can help you to understand your customers better and tailor your marketing and customer service efforts accordingly.
3. **Foster customer loyalty:** Building customer loyalty is key to the success of any business. Consider offering incentives for repeat business, such as loyalty programs or special promotions, and make an effort to provide excellent customer service at every touchpoint.
4. **Respond to customer feedback:** It's important to actively listen to customer feedback and use it to make improvements to your products, services, and overall customer experience. Consider implementing a system for collecting and responding to customer feedback, such as online reviews or a customer feedback form.
5. **Use customer data to personalize marketing efforts:** Personalized marketing efforts can be more effective at converting leads into customers. Use customer data to tailor your marketing efforts to the specific needs and preferences of your audience.
6. **Monitor and measure customer satisfaction:** To understand the effectiveness of your CRM efforts, it's important to track and measure key metrics such as customer satisfaction and loyalty. This will help you to determine what is and isn't working and make any necessary adjustments to your strategy.

EMAIL MARKETING

Email marketing is a form of digital marketing that involves sending promotional messages or advertisements to a large group of people via email. It can be a powerful tool for black-owned businesses, as it allows them to reach a large audience in a cost-effective and measurable way.

There are several key steps to effective email marketing for black-owned businesses:

1. **Build an email list:** The first step in any email marketing campaign is to build a list of email addresses to send your messages to. There are several ways to do this, including offering a sign-up form on your

website, collecting emails at events or through social media, or purchasing a list from a reputable vendor.
2. **Create a compelling subject line:** The subject line of your email is the first thing that recipients will see, so it's important to make it as compelling as possible. Keep it short, informative, and relevant to the content of your email.
3. **Personalize your emails:** Personalization is key to effective email marketing. Include the recipient's name in the subject line or body of the email, and segment your list so that you can send more targeted messages to specific groups.
4. **Use a clear and visually appealing layout:** Your email should be easy to read and visually appealing. Use clear headings, bullet points, and images to break up the text and make it more appealing to readers.
5. **Include a call to action:** Your email should always include a call to action, whether it's asking readers to visit your website, make a purchase, or sign up for a newsletter. Make it easy for them to take the desired action by including links or buttons.
6. **Test and track your emails:** It's important to test and track your emails to see how they are performing. Use tools like A/B testing to see which subject lines or layouts perform best, and track your open and click-through rates to see how your emails are resonating with your audience.

MOBILE MARKETING

Mobile marketing is a form of digital marketing that utilizes mobile devices and platforms to reach and engage with customers. It can be an effective way for black-owned businesses to reach their target audience and build brand awareness.

Here are some key strategies for implementing a successful mobile marketing campaign for a black-owned business:

1. **Create a mobile-friendly website:** With more and more people accessing the internet from their smartphones, it's important to ensure that your website is optimized for mobile. This includes having a responsive design that adjusts to different screen sizes and devices, as well as fast loading times.
2. **Use QR Codes:** QR codes (short for Quick Response codes) are a type of barcode that can be scanned by a smartphone or other device to access information or perform an action. QR codes can be

incorporated on business cards, promotional materials, product packaging, in-store signage, in email, and SMS marketing campaigns.
3. **Use SMS marketing:** SMS marketing involves sending promotional messages to customers via text message. This can be a great way to reach a large audience quickly and efficiently. Make sure to get permission from customers before sending them any promotional messages, and provide an opt-out option.
4. **Utilize social media:** Social media platforms like Facebook, Instagram, and Twitter can be powerful tools for reaching and engaging with customers. Make sure to create profiles on these platforms and regularly post updates, promotions, and content that will appeal to your target audience.
5. **Leverage email marketing:** Email marketing involves sending newsletters, promotional emails, and other types of marketing messages to a list of subscribers. This can be a great way to keep in touch with customers and promote your products or services.
6. **Use mobile advertising:** Mobile advertising involves placing ads on mobile websites or apps. This can be an effective way to reach a specific target audience and drive traffic to your website or social media profiles.
7. **Implement mobile apps:** Developing a mobile app for your business can be a great way to engage with customers and provide value. For example, you could create a loyalty program or offer exclusive discounts to app users.

MERCH (MERCHANDISE) MARKETING

Merchandise marketing can be a powerful tool for black-owned businesses to promote their brand, engage with customers, and generate revenue.

Here are some key considerations for black-owned businesses looking to incorporate merchandise marketing into their strategy:

1. **Identify your target audience:** The first step in developing a successful merchandise marketing strategy is to understand who your target audience is. Consider factors such as age, gender, location, interests, and values when determining who you want to reach with your merchandise.
2. **Choose the right merchandise:** The type of merchandise you offer will depend on your target audience and the overall image you want to project for your brand. Popular options for black-owned

businesses include t-shirts, hats, mugs, and stickers, but you can also consider more unique items such as tote bags, scarves, or keychains.

3. **Develop a consistent brand identity:** Your merchandise should reflect your brand's values and aesthetic. Choose colors, fonts, and graphics that align with your brand's image and make sure to use them consistently across all of your merchandise.
4. **Utilize social media:** Social media platforms such as Instagram and Facebook can be great tools for promoting your merchandise and engaging with your audience. Consider creating a dedicated hashtag for your merchandise and encouraging customers to share photos of themselves wearing or using your products.
5. **Partner with influencers:** Influencer marketing can be an effective way to reach a larger audience and drive sales of your merchandise. Look for influencers who align with your brand's values and who have a following that includes your target audience.
6. **Offer discounts and promotions:** Offering discounts and promotions can be a great way to drive sales of your merchandise. Consider offering special discounts to first-time buyers or to customers who purchase a certain amount of merchandise.
7. **Consider using print-on-demand services:** Print-on-demand services allow you to offer a wide range of merchandise without having to invest in large quantities of inventory. This can be a great option for black-owned businesses looking to test the waters with merchandise marketing.

OFFLINE MARKETING

Offline marketing refers to promotional tactics that do not involve the use of the internet.

Here are some key considerations for black-owned businesses looking to incorporate offline marketing into their strategy:

1. **Identify your target audience:** As with any marketing strategy, it is important to understand who your target audience is and where they can be found. Consider factors such as age, gender, location, interests, and values when determining your target audience and the best ways to reach them.
2. **Develop a consistent brand identity:** Your offline marketing materials should reflect your brand's values and aesthetic. Choose colors, fonts, and graphics that align with your brand's image and

make sure to use them consistently across all of your marketing materials.
3. **Utilize print materials:** Print materials such as business cards, flyers, and brochures can be effective for promoting your business and reaching potential customers. Consider distributing these materials at events, through direct mail, or by leaving them in high-traffic areas.
4. **Attend local events and trade shows:** Participating in local events and trade shows can be a great way to promote your business and connect with potential customers. Consider exhibiting your products or services, giving presentations, or hosting demonstrations to showcase your offerings.
5. **Partner with other businesses:** Collaborating with other businesses, particularly those that serve a similar target audience, can be a great way to reach new customers. Consider offering joint promotions, hosting events together, or cross-promoting each other's products or services.
6. **Utilize word-of-mouth marketing:** Word-of-mouth marketing can be a powerful tool for black-owned businesses. Encourage satisfied customers to share their experiences with others, and consider offering incentives for referrals.
7. **Use traditional advertising:** Traditional advertising methods such as print, radio, and television can be effective for reaching a large audience. Consider the type of audience you want to reach and the best channels for reaching them.

CREATING A DIGITAL MARKETING PLAN

Creating a digital marketing plan is essential for black-owned businesses looking to reach and engage with their target audience online.

Here are some key considerations for developing a successful digital marketing plan:

1. **Identify your target audience:** As with any marketing strategy, it is important to understand who your target audience is and where they can be found online. Consider factors such as age, gender, location, interests, and values when determining your target audience and the best ways to reach them.
2. **Develop a consistent brand identity:** Your digital marketing efforts should reflect your brand's values and aesthetic. Choose colors, fonts, and graphics that align with your brand's image and make sure to use them consistently across all of your digital marketing channels.

3. **Define your goals:** What do you hope to achieve with your digital marketing efforts? Some common goals include increasing brand awareness, driving traffic to your website, generating leads, or increasing sales. Clearly defining your goals will help you measure the success of your marketing efforts and make any necessary adjustments.
4. **Choose the right channels:** There are many different channels available for digital marketing, including social media, email marketing, search engine optimization (SEO), and pay-per-click (PPC) advertising. Consider which channels are most likely to reach your target audience and align with your goals.
5. **Create a content marketing plan:** Content marketing involves creating and sharing valuable, relevant, and consistent content with the goal of attracting and retaining a clearly defined audience. Consider what types of content will be most effective for your target audience and how you will distribute it.
6. **Utilize data and analytics:** Collecting and analyzing data from your digital marketing efforts can help you understand what is working and what is not. Tools such as Google Analytics can help you track website traffic, conversions, and other important metrics.
7. **Monitor and adjust your plan:** Digital marketing is an ongoing process, and it is important to regularly monitor and adjust your plan as needed. Keep an eye on your data and analytics to understand what is working and what is not, and be open to trying new tactics as needed.

TRACKING YOUR DIGITAL MARKETING PLAN

Tracking a digital marketing plan for a black-owned business involves monitoring and measuring the effectiveness of marketing efforts in order to make informed decisions about how to allocate resources and optimize future campaigns.

There are several key steps involved in tracking a digital marketing plan:

1. **Set clear goals and objectives:** Before you start tracking your marketing efforts, it's important to have clear goals and objectives in place. This could include things like increasing website traffic, generating leads, or improving brand awareness.
2. **Identify key performance indicators (KPIs):** Once you have your goals and objectives in place, you need to identify the specific metrics that will help you measure your progress. These are your KPIs.

Common KPIs for digital marketing include website traffic, social media followers, email subscribers, and conversion rates.
3. **Implement tracking tools:** There are a wide variety of tools available for tracking the effectiveness of your digital marketing efforts. These include Google Analytics, which allows you to track website traffic and conversions, and social media analytics tools, which allow you to track engagement and reach on platforms like Facebook, Instagram, and Twitter.
4. **Regularly review and analyze data:** It's important to regularly review and analyze the data you are collecting in order to identify trends and patterns. This will allow you to see what is and isn't working, and make adjustments to your marketing plan as needed.
5. **Use data to optimize campaigns:** Once you have a good understanding of what is and isn't working, you can use the data you have collected to optimize your marketing campaigns. This could involve testing different strategies or targeting specific audiences in order to improve the effectiveness of your marketing efforts.

FINAL RECOMMENDATION

My final recommendation is to use a combination of the strategies we have discussed. Some may be more effective for your specific industry, but all of them can contribute to your financial success when used correctly. Utilizing multiple approaches together can be especially beneficial.

If you are interested in digital marketing but not in the business world, it is important to set clear, measurable goals. For black business owners, it is also important to have specific goals and identify your key performance indicators. Then, you can test different strategies to see which ones work best for your black-owned business, whether you are selling products or services. By using the tracking methods mentioned in this book, you can easily monitor your progress and key metrics.

If you have studied our various digital marketing techniques and strategies and have successfully implemented them, you may be experiencing an increase in sales, growth in your business, and an ability to attract new customers through effective digital marketing efforts.

Alternatively, you may recognize the value of using these methods but lack the time or motivation to consistently apply them. In this case, it may be helpful to seek the assistance of a consultant.

To put it simply, if running your black-owned business that requires all of your attention and leaves no time for marketing, it may be advisable to hire a digital marketing agency. Many black-owned businesses require a lot of time and effort for things like creativity, research, and development, and may not have the resources to also focus on marketing activities. If this is the case for your business, a consultant can be a useful resource.

DO YOU NEED A CONSULTANT

There are a few ways to determine whether hiring a digital marketing agency is right for your black-owned business, depending on where you are in your business's life cycle. If you are in the early stages, you may need guidance on how to grow your business and invest in marketing in a way that doesn't inhibit growth. A consultant can provide this kind of advice and coaching.

For established businesses, it may be helpful to bring in an outside consultant to assess the internal operations of the company. In these cases, it is often the head of the marketing department or the entire team that seeks out a consultant for guidance. It can be challenging to determine appropriate goals and performance indicators when different people are focusing on their own metrics, so it is important to identify the key decision maker to determine the direction to take.

HOW DOES CONSULTING WORK

Obtaining professional business consultation can benefit businesses of any size by providing an outside perspective on their internal operations. This can be helpful for evaluating marketing campaigns and identifying areas for improvement. As a general rule, it is advisable to allocate about 10% of gross revenues to marketing efforts. However, determining how to allocate the remainder of this budget can be challenging, as there is no one-size-fits-all solution. Consulting with a professional and asking relevant questions can help you make informed decisions about your marketing strategy.

It may be necessary to carefully consider different strategies for merchandising and advertising budgets. From my experience in providing digital marketing advice to various black-owned business owners, I have observed that many have set up their digital advertising in a manner that is financially draining. If this is the case, hiring a digital marketing agency may be a suitable solution.

Black business owners may sometimes feel that their marketing efforts are ineffective. Often, a little bit of guidance or a few changes can make a significant difference. When we get involved, we often recommend diversifying the marketing portfolio by implementing the strategies discussed in previous chapters. This can help to introduce new sources of feedback and identify areas where marketing efforts and budgets should be focused.

TO BRING IT HOME

In closing, digital marketing is an essential tool for black-owned businesses to reach new customers, promote their products and services, and build their brand. By implementing a variety of strategies and tactics, such as search engine optimization, social media marketing, email marketing, and pay-per-click advertising, businesses can effectively market themselves online and achieve their marketing goals.

However, it is important for black-owned businesses to also consider the unique challenges and opportunities they may face in the digital marketing landscape. This includes overcoming potential biases and discrimination, as well as leveraging the power of supportive communities and networks.

Overcome Biases & Discrimination

Unfortunately, black-owned businesses may face biases and discrimination in the digital marketing space, whether it be from algorithms or individuals. It is important for you to be aware of these potential challenges and take steps to overcome them. This can include diversifying the types of platforms and channels used for marketing, as well as monitoring and addressing any negative feedback or reviews.

Leverage Supportive Communities & Networks

Black-owned businesses can also find support and resources through various online communities and networks. This can include joining industry groups or forums, connecting with other black business owners, and participating in events and conferences focused on diversity and inclusion in the digital marketing world.

Stay Up-To-Date On Trends & Best Practices

Digital marketing is constantly evolving, so it is important for black-owned businesses to stay up-to-date on the latest trends and best practices. This can include following industry blogs and social media accounts, attending webinars and conferences, and continuing to educate oneself on new technologies and strategies.

Test & Refine Strategies

As with any marketing efforts, it is important for black-owned businesses to continuously test and refine your digital marketing strategies. This can include experimenting with different tactics and platforms, analyzing data and metrics, and making adjustments based on what is and isn't working. By regularly reviewing and adjusting your strategies, you can optimize your efforts and achieve the best results possible.

WE ARE GRATEFUL

Thank you for reading our book on the digital marketing revolution for black-owned businesses! We hope that you have found the information and strategies shared within to be valuable and helpful in growing your business online.

As a black-owned business, it is important to have a strong online presence in today's digital age in order to reach new customers and build your brand. By implementing the strategies and tactics outlined in our book, we hope that you have gained the knowledge and confidence to effectively market your business online and achieve your marketing goals.

We appreciate your support and are grateful that you have chosen to invest in your business by reading our book. We hope that you will continue to refer back to it as a valuable resource as you navigate the ever-evolving world of digital marketing.

Thank you again for your support and we wish you the best of luck in your business endeavors.

FOLLOW US
ON SOCIAL MEDIA

Follow The Company **Follow The Movement**
@GoBlackOwn   @GoBlackly

On All Social Media Platforms

RESO- URCES

Go Black Own has compiled a list of widely available and easily accessible resources to help black-owned businesses grow and succeed. Our company is dedicated to providing the support black-owned businesses need to thrive.

A digital marketing checklist can be a valuable tool for black-owned businesses to ensure you are taking all necessary steps to effectively market yourself online. This checklist include tasks such as setting up a professional email address, creating a responsive website, utilizing social media platforms, and implementing search engine optimization (SEO) strategies. It also include tasks related to email marketing, mobile marketing, and paid advertising. By following our comprehensive digital marketing checklist, black-owned businesses can effectively reach and engage with your target audience and drive growth and success.

Also choosing the right tools is crucial for successful digital marketing for black-owned businesses and in the online resource section, we will guide you through the types of tools needed for running digital marketing campaigns and which tools are best for each job.

Hashtags can be a powerful way to increase the reach and visibility of a business's social media posts, and there are many hashtags specifically for black-owned businesses, such as #GoBlackly, #BlackOwnedBusiness, #SupportBlackBusiness. We have included these hashtags in our resources to help increase visibility for black-owned businesses.

Black news outlets and directories of black-owned businesses can be valuable sources of information and support for black business owners. These resources can help you connect with other entrepreneurs, share experiences and ideas, and seek advice and support. There are also many organizations and networks specifically for black business owners, such as the National Black Business Association and the Black Business Network. These organizations can provide resources, training, and networking opportunities to help your black-owned businesses succeed. We have included a list of black-owned news outlets, directories, and organizations in this resource section.

In addition to these resources, there are also grants and financial assistance programs available to support black-owned businesses. Some banks and financial institutions also have programs and services specifically designed to support black business owners. We have included a list of black-owned banks and grants for black-owned businesses in this resource section.

Last but not least, if you are feeling overwhelmed by the information provided or have questions about digital marketing, our free interactive webinar on how black-owned businesses can grow using digital marketing may be able to help. This webinar is a convenient and cost-effective way for black-owned business owners to learn about and stay up-to-date on the latest digital marketing trends and techniques. Participating in this webinar can provide valuable insights and knowledge that can help your business grow and succeed in the digital world.

By leveraging these resources, black-owned businesses can gain access to the support and tools they need to grow and succeed.

The resources mentioned in this section are also available here at:

GoBlackly.com/resources

DIGITAL MARKETING CHECKLIST

- What are the goals of the digital marketing campaign?
- Who is the target audience?
- What channels will be used for the campaign (e.g. social media, email, website, paid advertising)?
- How will the success of the campaign be measured?
- Have clear calls to action been defined for the audience?
- Has a budget been established for the campaign?
- Has keyword research been conducted to inform the marketing efforts?
- Have targeted and relevant landing pages been created for the campaigns?
- Has the website been optimized for search engines (SEO)?
- Have marketing automation or analytics tools been set up to help track and analyze the results?

CREATE A CUSTOMER PROFILE CHECKLIST

- Who is the target customer for your business?
- What are the demographics of the target customer (e.g. age, gender, location)?
- What is the target customer's income level?
- What are the interests and hobbies of the target customer?
- What are the pain points or challenges faced by the target customer?
- What are the goals and aspirations of the target customer?
- How does the target customer prefer to receive communication (e.g. email, phone, social media)?
- What is the target customer's preferred purchasing process (e.g. online, in-store, phone)?
- What motivates the target customer to make a purchase?
- What are the values and beliefs of the target customer?

BUILDING AN ONLINE PRESENCE CHECKLIST

- Do you have a website?
- Is your website mobile-friendly?
- Does your website have clear and concise content?
- Is your website visually appealing?
- Is your website easy to navigate?
- Do you have a strong social media presence?

- Which social media platforms are you active on?
- Are you active on review sites like Yelp or Google Reviews?
- Do you have a Google My Business listing?
- Do you have a professional email address?

SEO & SERP CHECKLIST

- Have you identified relevant keywords for your website and content?
- Have you included those keywords in the title tags, meta descriptions, and headings on your website?
- Have you optimized your website's loading speed?
- Have you made sure your website is mobile-friendly?
- Have you set up Google Search Console and Bing Webmaster Tools?
- Have you claimed and verified your business on Google My Business?
- Have you set up and regularly updated your business's profile on relevant directories and review sites?
- Have you obtained high-quality backlinks from reputable websites?
- Have you used alt tags to describe images on your website?
- Have you created a sitemap and submitted it to search engines?

PR MARKETING CHECKLIST

- What is the goal of your PR campaign?
- Who is your target audience?
- What is the key message you want to communicate?
- Have you identified relevant media outlets and journalists to target?
- Have you created a press release or other promotional materials?
- Have you considered any potential legal issues or compliance requirements?
- Have you established a budget for your PR campaign?
- Have you set up media monitoring tools to track coverage of your campaign?
- Have you prepared talking points and materials for interviews or press events?
- Have you followed up with media outlets to ensure they received your materials and to answer any questions they may have?

ONLINE REPUTATION MANAGEMENT CHECKLIST

- Have you set up Google Alerts to monitor mentions of your business online?

- Have you claimed and optimized our business's profiles on review sites like Yelp and Google Reviews?
- Have you responded to customer reviews, both positive and negative, in a timely and professional manner?
- Have you addressed any negative reviews or complaints by trying to resolve the issue and prevent similar issues in the future?
- Have you promoted positive customer reviews and testimonials on your website and social media channels?
- Have you established guidelines for employees on how to handle negative reviews or complaints online?
- Have you considered using online reputation management tools to monitor and manage our online reputation?
- Have you evaluated the SEO impact of your online reputation, and taken steps to improve your rankings if necessary?
- Have you considered the potential impact of negative news or press on your online reputation, and prepared a plan to address it if necessary?
- Have you regularly monitored and updated your online reputation to ensure it accurately reflects your business and brand?

PAID ADVERTISING CHECKLIST

- What is the goal of your paid advertising campaign?
- Who is your target audience?
- Which platforms will you use for your campaign (e.g. Google Ads, Facebook Ads, Instagram Ads)?
- Have you defined clear calls to action for your audience?
- Have you established a budget for your campaign?
- Have you conducted keyword research to inform your ad targeting?
- Have you created targeted and relevant landing pages for your ads?
- Have you set up conversion tracking to measure the success of your campaign?
- Have you A/B tested different ad copy and creative to find what works best?
- Have you regularly monitored and analyzed the performance of your ads, and made adjustments as needed?

SOCIAL MEDIA MARKETING CHECKLIST

- What are the goals of your social media marketing campaign?
- Who is your target audience?

- What platforms will you use for your campaign?
- How often will you post?
- What types of content will you share?
- How will you measure the success of your campaign?
- Have you defined clear calls to action for your audience?
- Have you established a budget for your campaign?
- Have you considered any potential legal issues or compliance requirements?
- Have you set up social media management tools to help schedule and analyze your content?

VIDEO MARKETING CHECKLIST

- What is the goal of your video marketing campaign?
- Who is your target audience?
- What platforms will you use to share your videos (e.g. YouTube, Facebook, Instagram)?
- Have you identified the key message you want to communicate through your videos?
- Have you created a script or outline for your video?
- Have you considered the visual elements of your video (e.g. lighting, composition, branding)?
- Have you recorded and edited the video using professional equipment and software?
- Have you optimized the video for search engines by including relevant keywords and a descriptive title and description?
- Have you set up tracking and analytics to measure the success of your video campaign?
- Have you promoted your video through other marketing channels, such as social media and email marketing?

EMAIL MARKETING CHECKLIST

- What is the goal of your email marketing campaign?
- Who is your target audience?
- Have you segmented your email list to ensure you are sending relevant messages to the right people?
- Have you created a clear and compelling subject line for your emails?
- Have you designed your emails to be visually appealing and mobile-friendly?
- Have you included a clear call to action in your emails?

- Have you proofread and tested your emails for spelling and grammar errors?
- Have you set up tracking and analytics to measure the success of your email campaign?
- Have you established a schedule for sending emails (e.g. weekly, monthly)?
- Have you obtained permission to send emails to your list (e.g. through opt-in forms)?

MOBILE MARKETING CHECKLIST

- What is the goal of your mobile marketing campaign?
- Who is your target audience?
- Have you optimized your website and marketing materials for mobile devices?
- Have you considered using mobile-specific advertising platforms (e.g. Google AdWords mobile, Facebook mobile ads)?
- Have you created mobile-friendly email marketing campaigns?
- Have you considered using SMS or MMS marketing to reach your audience?
- Have you created mobile apps or used mobile app advertising to reach your audience?
- Have you set up tracking and analytics to measure the success of your mobile marketing campaign?
- Have you considered the potential privacy and security issues with mobile marketing?
- Have you adapted your mobile marketing strategy to account for the unique features and capabilities of different mobile devices?

MERCHANDISE "MERCH" MARKETING CHECKLIST

- What is the goal of your merch marketing campaign?
- Who is your target audience?
- Have you identified the types of merch that will appeal to your target audience?
- Have you considered the price points and profit margins for your merch?
- Have you created eye-catching and cohesive branding for your merch?
- Have you identified the channels through which you will sell your merch (e.g. online store, physical retail locations, events)?

- Have you set up a system for fulfilling orders and handling returns or exchanges?
- Have you set up tracking and analytics to measure the success of your merch marketing campaign?
- Have you considered the potential legal and compliance issues with selling merch (e.g. trademark and copyright considerations)?
- Have you promoted your merch through other marketing channels, such as social media and email marketing?

OFFLINE MARKETING CHECKLIST

- What is the goal of your offline marketing campaign?
- Who is your target audience?
- Have you identified the most effective channels for reaching your target audience (e.g. print ads, radio commercials, events)?
- Have you created marketing materials that are visually appealing and effectively communicate your message (e.g. flyers, brochures, business cards)?
- Have you considered the logistics of executing your offline marketing campaign (e.g. budget, timeline, staffing)?
- Have you set up tracking and analytics to measure the success of your offline marketing campaign?
- Have you considered any potential legal or compliance issues with your offline marketing efforts?
- Have you incorporated offline marketing into your overall marketing strategy and integrated it with your online marketing efforts?
- Have you sought out partnerships or sponsorships that can support and enhance your offline marketing efforts?
- Have you regularly evaluated and adjusted your offline marketing strategy based on data and feedback?

CUSTOMER RELATIONS MANAGERS (CRM) CHECKLIST

- Have you chosen a CRM system that meets the needs of your business and your customer base?
- Have you migrated all relevant customer data into the CRM system?
- Have you trained your team on how to use the CRM system effectively?
- Have you set up processes for regularly updating and maintaining customer data in the CRM system?

- Have you set up automation and integration with other marketing and sales tools (e.g. email marketing, lead management)?
- Have you established a system for tracking and managing customer inquiries and complaints through the CRM system?
- Have you set up reporting and analytics to track the performance of our customer relationship management efforts?
- Have you considered data privacy and security when using the CRM system?
- Have you established a system for periodically reviewing and optimizing your use of the CRM system?
- Have you considered how the CRM system can be used to improve customer retention and loyalty?

CREATING A DIGITAL MARKETING PLAN CHECKLIST

- What are the goals of your digital marketing plan?
- Who is your target audience?
- What channels will we use to reach your audience (e.g. website, social media, email, paid advertising)?
- Have you defined clear calls to action for your audience?
- Have you established a budget for your digital marketing efforts?
- Have you conducted market research to inform your strategy?
- Have you identified and targeted relevant keywords for search engine optimization (SEO)?
- Have you created targeted and relevant landing pages for your campaigns?
- Have you set up tracking and analytics to measure the success of your digital marketing efforts?
- Have you integrated your digital marketing plan with our overall marketing and business strategy?

TRACKING YOUR DIGITAL MARKETING PLAN CHECKLIST

- Have you set up tracking and analytics for all relevant channels (e.g. website traffic, social media engagement, email open and click-through rates)?
- Have you defined key performance indicators (KPIs) to measure the success of your digital marketing plan?
- Have you set up regular reporting to monitor the performance of your digital marketing efforts?

- Have you identified any areas of our digital marketing plan that are underperforming, and taken steps to improve them?
- Have you considered how to use data and insights from your tracking and analytics to inform future digital marketing strategies?
- Have you integrated your tracking and analytics with your overall business and marketing metrics to gain a complete picture of your performance?
- Have you considered the potential limitations and biases of your tracking and analytics tools, and taken steps to mitigate them?
- Have you regularly reviewed and optimized your tracking and analytics setup to ensure it is meeting the needs of your business?
- Have you considered the privacy and security implications of your tracking and analytics efforts?
- Have you established a system for sharing tracking and analytics data with relevant stakeholders within your organization?

ONLINE RESOURCES

The success of black-owned businesses' digital marketing efforts often depends on choosing the right tools for the job at the right time. With so many software and applications available online, it can be challenging to select the most effective ones.

At Go Black Own, we test and use a variety of tools to grow our businesses and in this section, we will guide you through tools you need to run your digital marketing campaigns and specifically, which tools are best suited for each job.

DOMAIN REGISTRATION

Domain registration is the process of purchasing and reserving a unique web address, or domain name, for a website. For black-owned businesses, registering a domain name is an important step in building an online presence and establishing a professional image.

There are many companies that offer domain registration services, and it is typically a relatively straightforward process. To register a domain name, a business owner will need to choose a domain name that is available and meets the requirements of the domain registrar. The business owner will then need to pay a fee to register the domain name for a certain period of time, typically one to three years.

Once the domain name is registered, the business owner can use it to create a website, set up email addresses, and establish an online presence. Having a unique domain name can help black-owned businesses stand out online and make it easier for customers to find and connect with them.

We recommend the following domain registrar.

Go Black Own Domain Registrar

GoBlackly.com/domain-registration

WEBSITE SECURITY

An SSL (Secure Sockets Layer) certificate is a type of digital certificate that is used to establish a secure connection between a website and a user's web browser. For black-owned businesses, an SSL certificate is an important tool for protecting sensitive information, such as credit card numbers, personal data, and login credentials, and for establishing trust with customers.

SSL certificates work by encrypting the data that is transmitted between a website and a user's web browser, making it difficult for anyone to intercept or access this information. When a website has an SSL certificate, it is typically indicated by a padlock icon in the web browser and the "https" prefix in the website's URL.

To get an SSL certificate, a business owner will need to purchase one from a trusted certificate authority (CA) and install it on their website's server. Many hosting providers offer SSL certificates as an add-on service, and some even offer them for free.

Having an SSL certificate is important for black-owned businesses that handle sensitive information online, as it helps to protect their customers' data and build trust with their audience. It is also increasingly important for search engine optimization (SEO), as Google and other search engines tend to rank websites with SSL certificates higher in search results.

We recommend the following SSL certificate provider.

Go Black Own SSL Certificate

GoBlackly.com/ssl

PROFESSIONAL EMAIL

A professional email address is an email address that is used for business communication and is typically in the format of "name@businessname.com." For black-owned businesses, a professional email address can help establish a professional image and make it easier for customers and clients to contact the business.

To set up a professional email address, a business owner will need to register a domain name and sign up for an email hosting service. There are many companies that offer email hosting services, and they typically provide tools and resources for setting up and managing professional email accounts.

Once the business owner has set up a professional email address, they can use it to communicate with customers, clients, and partners, and to send and receive important business emails. Having a professional email address can help black-owned businesses establish credibility and professionalism, and can make it easier for customers to find and connect with them.

We recommend the following professional email provider.

Go Black Own Professional Email

GoBlackly.com/professional-email

BUILDING A WEBSITE

Gone are the days when building a website required custom coding from scratch. Today, even those with little to no technical expertise can create and publish text, images, video, and audio to the web using a content management system (CMS). A CMS is a software application used to manage the digital content and design of a website. For black-owned businesses, choosing the right CMS is an important decision that can have a significant impact on the success of their online presence.

Following are some CRMs that we recommend:

Go Black Own Website Builder

Go Black Own's website builder is a user-friendly online tool that allows users to create responsive websites without needing any technical expertise. With the website builder, black-owned businesses can easily create an online store, accept orders, and build a seamless shopping experience for customers, complete with features like Apple Pay and Google Pay.

GoBlackly.com/website-builder

WordPress.org

This free, open source platform began as a blogging platform and has evolved into a full-blown CMS. It is extremely modular and search-engine friendly, and it allows for multiple users with various levels of permissions. The difference between WordPress.com and WordPress.org is that WordPress.org is a self-hosted platform, whereas WordPress.com is hosted on WordPress' servers. As a business owner, you want to use the self-hosted WordPress.org CMS so that you have complete ownership of your website. If you're looking for a low budget, flexible CMS, WordPress.org is a great choice.

Wordpress.org

Shopify

Whether you're selling physical products completely online or you're a brick-and-mortar retailer looking to sell your wares online, Shopify is worth your consideration. Shopify handles the design and layout of your store, but it also manages payments, shipping, inventory, and more.

Shopify.com

HOSTING A WEBSITE

Website hosting is a service that allows businesses to store and publish their website online, making it accessible to users around the world. For black-owned businesses, website hosting is an important component of building and maintaining an online presence.

There are many companies that offer website hosting services, and they vary in terms of features, pricing, and support. Some common types of website hosting include shared hosting, VPS (Virtual Private Server) hosting, and dedicated hosting.

To use website hosting, a business owner will typically need to purchase a hosting plan from a hosting provider and set up their website on the provider's servers. The hosting provider will then manage the technical aspects of hosting the website, such as ensuring that it is available and accessible to users.

Website hosting is important for black-owned businesses because it enables them to publish and maintain their website online, and to reach and engage with customers around the world. It is also important for website performance, as a reliable and fast hosting provider can help ensure that a website loads quickly and performs well.

We recommend the following website hosts.

Go Black Own Hosting

If you choose to use WordPress as your CMS, Go Black Own Hosting is a great choice as your web host. This company is known for exceptional uptime, lightning-fast page load speeds, and unprecedented security.

GoBlackly.com/hosting

EMAIL MARKETING SOFTWARE

Email marketing software is a tool that allows businesses to create and send email campaigns to their customers and prospects. For black-owned businesses, email marketing software can be an effective way to reach and engage with their audience, promote products or services, and grow their business.

Email marketing software typically provides features such as email templates, list management, segmentation, and tracking and reporting tools. It can be used to create newsletters, promotional emails, transactional emails, and other types of email campaigns.

Here are some email service providers that we recommend.

Go Black Own's Email Marketing

Go Black Own's email marketing service has a sterling reputation for deliverability, and the software integrates seamlessly with other popular tools like WordPress. If your budget is tight, Go Black Own's email marketing service is an outstanding choice.

GoBlackly.com/email-marketing

Maropost

Maropost provides enterprise-level email marketing software with the capability to handle complex email automation campaigns and advanced email segmentation.

Maropost.com

Klaviyo

Klaviyo offers solid email marketing software for businesses that sell physical products. The software integrates with your shopping cart, payment platform, customer relationship management (CRM), and more.

Klaviyo.com

CUSTOMER RELATIONSHIP MANAGEMENT (CRM) SOFTWARE

Customer relationship management (CRM) software is a tool that helps businesses manage and analyze customer interactions and data throughout the customer lifecycle. For black-owned businesses, CRM software can be an effective way to manage customer relationships, improve customer service, and drive sales and growth.

CRM software typically provides features such as contact management, sales tracking, marketing automation, and customer service tools. It can be used to store and organize customer information, track customer interactions and interactions, and analyze customer data to identify trends and patterns.

Here are some CRM Software providers that we recommend.

Keap

With this CRM, you have the capability to manage products, record customers' and prospects' data, process payments, send emails, and more all from one system.

Keap.com

Salesforce

Salesforce is a cloud-based CRM that offers solutions for every business, from small to enterprise level. Salesforce is known for its robust integration with thousands of applications, from QuickBooks to Evernote.

Salesforce.com

ADDING A PAYMENT SOLUTION

An online payment solution is a tool that allows businesses to accept payments from customers online, typically through a website or mobile app. For black-owned businesses, an online payment solution can be an effective way to process transactions, expand their customer base, and grow their business.

There are many online payment solutions available, and they vary in terms of features, pricing, and compatibility with different types of businesses and payment methods. Some popular online payment solutions include PayPal, Stripe, and Square.

To use an online payment solution, a business owner will typically need to sign up for an account and choose a plan that meets their needs. They can then integrate the payment solution into their website or mobile app, and start accepting payments from customers. Online payment solutions can be a convenient and cost-effective way for black-owned businesses to process transactions and expand their customer base.

We encourage you to try the following payment processors.

Stripe

Offering dependable, easy-to-configure payment processing with a rich feature set, Stripe handles recurrent billing and integrates with applications such as WordPress, Shopify, and FreshBooks.

Stripe.com

Square

If you want customers to be able to swipe credit or debit cards in your store or on the go, consider Square. The Square app turns your smartphone or tablet into a credit card processing machine.

SquareUp.com

SOURCING & EDITING IMAGES

As the web becomes more visual, black-owned businesses are finding it increasingly important to create visually appealing images for use on social media platforms like Pinterest and Instagram, as well as text-based platforms like Twitter. Adobe Photoshop is considered the gold standard for image creation, but there are also many low-cost and user-friendly options available for producing high-quality images for marketing purposes. As a black-owned business owner, it is essential to have the skills and tools necessary to create visually appealing images that will help your business stand out and connect with your audience.

Following are image-editing tools that we recommend.

Canva

Canva is a cloud-based drag-and-drop design application that comes with millions of images, layouts, icons, shapes, and fonts to choose from.

Canva.com

SnagIt

Capture any type of image on your computer screen and use SnagIt's dynamic editor to crop, resize, add callouts and text, and much more.

Techsmith.com/screen-capture.html

Pixlr

This application enables you to open an image and make changes to it by rotating, cropping, or resizing it in the cloud-based editor. Add effects, overlays, stickers, and more with this free image editor.

Pixlr.com

MANAGING SOCIAL MEDIA

There are many social media management tools available that allow black-owned businesses to monitor and publish to the social web. These tools come in a range of prices, depending on the size of the organization and the features required. However, there are also many low-cost options available that can help black-owned businesses manage their social media presence without breaking the bank.

We recommend the following social media tools.

Hootsuite Pro

The best cloud-based, low-cost application for managing Twitter is Hootsuite. This tool also manages Facebook and LinkedIn, but you'll find it most useful for organizing your Twitter activity. You can use the free version, but Hootsuite Pro adds solid reporting and the capability to easily append UTM parameters to links.

Hootsuite.com

Buffer

Buffer helps you build an audience organically. They are a values-driven company that provides affordable, intuitive, marketing tools for ambitious people and teams.

Buffer.com

Mention

Find conversations about your brands, people, competitors, and more with this reasonably priced social-listening and reputation-management application.

Mention.com

MEASURING YOUR PERFORMANCE DATA & ANALYTICS

There are many vendors that claim to have the solution to all of a black-owned business's data and analytics problems, but luckily, many of the best tools are offered for free by Google. These tools are user-friendly and provide the functionality needed by most black-owned businesses. By utilizing these tools, businesses can easily track and analyze their data to inform their marketing and business decisions.

Try the following data analytics applications.

Google Analytics

Google Analytics tracks and reports website traffic. We've tried the more expensive analytics solutions, and we keep coming back to good old Google Analytics.

Google.com/analytics/

Google Data Studio

Use this application to create stunningly beautiful and informative, interactive reports and graphs that you can share with others. Pull data from sources like Google Analytics, Google AdWords, and Google Docs.

DataStudio.google.com

Google Tag Manager

Google Tag Manager is a powerful tool that allows users to update website tags and add scripts to their website, even if they don't have coding expertise. While there is a bit of a learning curve, once users get the hang of it, they may wonder how they ever managed without it. This tool can be particularly useful for black-owned businesses looking to optimize their website and track user behavior.

Google.com/analytics/tag-manager/

OPTIMIZING YOUR MARKETING

There are many powerful tools available that can help black-owned businesses generate more leads, sales, and engagement from their existing website traffic. Many of these tools are affordably priced and offer free trials, so black-owned businesses can test them out before making a commitment. These tools can be an effective way to maximize the impact of a business's online presence and drive growth.

The optimization applications that we recommend follow.

Visual Website Optimizer

For intuitive set up and configuration of split and multivariate website tests we recommend Visual Website Optimizer. Its point-and-click interface and support documentation make it easy to get started testing.

Vwo.com

TruConversion

TruConversion is a multipurpose optimization tool that offers heat maps, session recordings, user surveys, and more in a single tool.

TruConversion.com

MOBILE MARKETING

When choosing a mobile marketing company for your black-owned business, it's important to consider a few key factors. First, you'll want to look for a company that has experience developing mobile apps and websites specifically for small businesses or startups. This will ensure that they understand the unique needs and challenges of your business and can deliver a high-quality product.

Next, you should look for a company that offers a range of services, including mobile app development, digital business cards, QR code generation, mobile website development, and mobile advertising. This will give you the flexibility to choose the services that best meet your needs and budget.

NOTE: This is the company that developed the Go Black Own App.

We recommend the following black-owned mobile marketing company.

MobileFusionSoft.com, Inc

MobileFusionSoft.com, Inc is an expert in mobile marketing and provides a variety of services to assist black-owned businesses in reaching their target audience via mobile devices. These services include creating mobile ads, developing mobile websites and apps, offering digital business cards, implementing SMS text message marketing campaigns, and generating QR codes. These resources enable black-owned businesses to connect with their target audience where they spend most of their time, on mobile devices, resulting in increased sales and app downloads.

MobileFusionSoft.com

PRINT ON DEMAND COMPANIES FOR MERCH

Print on demand allows you to create and sell products without having to hold your own inventory. However, selecting the best paid or free print on demand company to work with can require extensive research, as each platform has its own unique set of products, shipping options, and features that should be considered. It is important to carefully evaluate these factors in order to bring your vision to life.

We recommend the follow print on demand companies.

Printful

Printful is one of the best print on demand companies, offering a wide range of products to customize and features to help you get started that range from product and t-shirt mockup generators to services like logo design.

Printful.com

SPOD

SPOD is one of the best print on demand businesses and is owned by Spreadshirt. It boasts one of the fastest fulfillment times in the industry, 95% of orders ship within 48 hours, which makes for a satisfying experience for the end customer.

Spod.com

HASH TAGS TO INCLUDE IN YOUR SOCIAL MEDIA POST

Here are a few different hashtags that can be used to promote and support black-owned businesses:

- #blackownedbusiness
- #blackbusiness
- #supportblackbusiness
- #buyblack
- #blackentrepreneur
- #blackbusinessowner
- #blackpride
- #blackgirlmagic
- #blackwomeninbusiness
- #blackmeninbusiness
- #blackcommunity
- #blackexcellence
- #goblackly
- #goblackown

These hashtags can be used on social media platforms like Twitter, Instagram, and Facebook to help promote and support black-owned businesses. By using these hashtags, businesses can connect with a wider audience and build a sense of community and support within the black business community. They can also be used by individuals looking to discover and support black-owned businesses in their area or online.

BLACK NEWS OUTLETS

There are many black-owned and operated news outlets that provide coverage of issues and events relevant to the black community.

Some examples include:

The Root

A daily news website that provides analysis and commentary on politics, race, and culture from a black perspective.

TheRoot.com

Blavity

A digital media company that produces news and lifestyle content for a black millennial audience.

Blavity.com

The Grio

A digital news and opinion website that provides coverage of issues affecting the black community, as well as news and analysis on politics, entertainment, and culture.

TheGrio.com

Black Press USA

A national news organization that serves the black community with news and information from a black perspective.

BlackPressUSA.com

The Final Call

A national news organization that provides coverage of issues affecting the black community, as well as news and analysis on politics, culture, and social justice.

New.FinalCall.com

The African American News & Information Consortium

A national news organization that provides coverage of issues affecting the black community, as well as news and analysis on politics, culture, and social justice.

Aaprc.org

The New Tri-State Defender

A weekly newspaper that provides coverage of issues affecting the black community in the Mid-South region of the United States.

Tri-StateDefender.com

The Amsterdam News

A weekly newspaper that provides coverage of issues affecting the black community in New York City.

AmsterdamNews.com

The Michigan Chronicle

A weekly newspaper that provides coverage of issues affecting the black community in Detroit and the surrounding area.

MichiganChronicle.com

The Dallas Examiner

A weekly newspaper that provides coverage of issues affecting the black community in Dallas and the surrounding area.

DallasExaminer.com

Black Enterprise

A magazine and website that provides resources and support for black-owned businesses.

BlackEnterprise.com

News One

A news website that provides coverage of issues and events relevant to the black community.

NewsOne.com

Black Business

A site features the latest success stories for and about African American entrepreneurs, executives, and CEOs.

BlackBusiness.com

Black America Web

A site features all things black America, breaking national news, entertainment news, celebrity news, Black-owned businesses, and Black history facts.

BlackAmericaWeb.com

Black News

A site features daily news for and about African American culture, businesses, entertainment and more.

BlackNews.com

Black Voice News

A newspaper that publishes in the spirit of the Black Press, the Black Voice News has given voice to the voiceless and shined a light on systemic inequities.

BlackVoiceNews.com

BLACK-OWNED BUSINESS DIRECTORIES

There are several directories and platforms that aim to support and promote black-owned businesses.

Some examples include:

Black Owned Business Directory

A directory of black-owned businesses in the United States, with listings organized by industry and location.

TheBlackOwnedBusiness.org

Buy Black Directory

A directory of black-owned businesses in the United States, with listings organized by industry and location.

BuyBlack.org

Black Business Green Book

A directory of black-owned businesses in the United States, with listings organized by industry and location.

BlackBusinessGreenBook.com

Black Business Network

A directory of black-owned businesses in the United States, with listings organized by industry and location.

BlackBusinessNetwork.online

Black Enterprise

A magazine and website that provides resources and support for black-owned businesses, including a directory of black-owned businesses.

BlackEnterprise.com

Black Owned Association

A platform that connects consumers with black-owned businesses, including a directory of businesses organized by industry and location.

BlackOwnedAssociation.com

Black Wall Street

A platform that connects consumers with black-owned businesses, including a directory of businesses organized by industry and location.

Obws.com

Black Woman Owned

A platform that connects consumers with black women owned businesses, including a directory of businesses organized by industry and location.

BlackWomanOwned.co

By Black

A platform that connects consumers with black-owned businesses, including a directory of businesses organized by industry and location.

ByBlack.us

Eat Okra

A platform that connects consumers with black food.

EatOkra.com

Go Black Own

A platform that connects consumers with black-owned businesses, including a directory of businesses organized by industry and location.

GoBlackOwn.com

I Am Black Business

A platform that connects consumers with black-owned businesses, including a directory of businesses organized by industry and location.

IamBlackBusiness.com

Support Black Owned

A platform that connects consumers with black-owned businesses, including a directory of businesses organized by industry and location.

SupportBlackOwned.com

The National Black Chamber of Commerce

A national organization that supports and promotes black-owned businesses, including through a directory of member businesses.

Nationalbcc.org

The National Minority Supplier Development Council

A national organization that supports and promotes minority-owned businesses, including through a directory of member businesses.

Nmsdc.org

The National Association of Black Owned Broadcasters

A national organization that supports and promotes black-owned radio and television stations, including through a directory of member stations.

Nabob.org

The National Black MBA Association

A national organization that supports and promotes black business professionals, including through a directory of member businesses.

Nbmbaa.org

The National Black Nurses Association

A national organization that supports and promotes black nurses and nursing students, including through a directory of member businesses.

Nbna.org

The Nile List

A platform that connects consumers with black-owned businesses, including a directory of businesses organized by industry and location.

TheNileList.com

We Buy Black

A platform that connects consumers with black-owned businesses, including a directory of businesses organized by industry and location.

WeBuyBlack.com/blog/

BLACK BUSINESS ORGANIZATIONS

There are several organizations that support and promote black-owned businesses.

Some examples include:

National Black Chamber of Commerce

A national organization that supports and promotes black-owned businesses through advocacy, research, and networking opportunities.

Nationalbcc.org

National Minority Supplier Development Council

A national organization that supports and promotes minority-owned businesses through procurement and business development opportunities.

Nmsdc.org

Black Business Association

A California-based organization that supports and promotes black-owned businesses through networking, education, and advocacy.

Bbala.org

National Association of Black Owned Broadcasters

A national organization that supports and promotes black-owned radio and television stations through advocacy and networking opportunities.

Nabob.org

National Black MBA Association

A national organization that supports and promotes black business professionals through education, networking, and career development opportunities.

Nbmbaa.org

National Black Nurses Association

A national organization that supports and promotes black nurses and nursing students through education, networking, and leadership development opportunities.

Nbna.org

National Association of Colored Women's Clubs

A national organization that supports and promotes black women entrepreneurs through education, networking, and advocacy.

Nacwc.com

National Black Child Development Institute

A national organization that supports and promotes black child care professionals through education, networking, and advocacy.

Nbcdi.org

National Black Dental Association

A national organization that supports and promotes black dental professionals through education, networking, and advocacy.

Ndaonline.org

National Association of Black Accountants

A national organization that supports and promotes black accounting professionals through education, networking, and career development opportunities.

Nabainc.org

National Association of Real Estate Brokers

A national organization that brings together the nation's minority professionals in the real estate industry to promote the meaningful exchange of ideas about their business and how best to serve their clientele.

Nareb.com

National Business League

A national organization that supports and promotes black business professional and trade associations.

NationalBusinessLeague.org

Black Girl Ventures

A national organization dedicated to creating access to capital for Black and Brown women entrepreneurs.

BlackGirlVentures.org

Black Founders

A national organization dedicated to diversity in tech.

BlackFounders.com

The Black Upstart

A national organization that teaches aspiring Black entrepreneurs how to start a successful and profitable business through an intense, culturally-relevant popup school.

TheBlackUpStart.com

GRANTS FOR BLACK-OWNED BUSINESSES

There are several organizations and initiatives that offer grants to support and promote black-owned businesses.

Some examples include:

The National Black Chamber of Commerce

The NBCC offers a variety of grants and funding opportunities for black-owned businesses through its Small Business Capital Access program.

Nationalbcc.org

The National Minority Supplier Development Council

The NMSDC offers a variety of grants and funding opportunities for minority-owned businesses through its Minority Business Enterprise program.

Nmsdc.org

The Black Business Association

The BBA offers a variety of grants and funding opportunities for black-owned businesses in California through its Financial Assistance and Access to Capital program.

Bbala.org

The National Association of Black Owned Broadcasters

The NABOB offers a variety of grants and funding opportunities for black-owned radio and television stations through its Broadcast Diversity Development program.

Nabob.org

The National Black MBA Association

The NBMBAA offers a variety of grants and funding opportunities for black business professionals through its Entrepreneurial and Business Development program.

Nbmbaa.org

The National Black Nurses Association

The NBNA offers a variety of grants and funding opportunities for black nurses and nursing students through its Health Disparities and Education grant program.

Nbna.org

The National Association of Colored Women's Clubs

The NACWC offers a variety of grants and funding opportunities for black women entrepreneurs through its Business and Economic Development program.

Nacwc.com

The National Black Child Development Institute

The NBCDI offers a variety of grants and funding opportunities for black child care professionals through its Early Childhood Education grant program.

Nbcdi.org

The National Black Dental Association

The NBDA offers a variety of grants and funding opportunities for black dental professionals through its Education and Research grant program.

Ndaonline.org

The National Association of Black Accountants

The NABA offers a variety of grants and funding opportunities for black accounting professionals through its Scholarships and Grants program.

Nabainc.org

We Back Black Businesses

A coalition to Back Black Businesses is a multi-year grantmaking and training initiative to help support Black-owned small businesses.

WeBackBlackBusinesses.com

It's worth noting that grant programs can have specific eligibility requirements, such as being a member of the organization or operating a business in a certain industry or location. It's important to carefully review the requirements and application process for any grant program you are considering applying for.

BANKS FOR BLACK-OWNED BUSINESSES

There are several black-owned banks in the United States that serve the financial needs of the black community.

Some examples include:

OneUnited Bank

OneUnited Bank is the largest black-owned bank in the United States, with branches in Boston, Los Angeles, and Miami.

OneUnited.com

Broadway Federal Bank

Broadway Federal Bank is a community development financial institution that serves the black community in Los Angeles.

CityFirstBank.com

City First Bank

City First Bank is a community development financial institution that serves the black community in the Washington, D.C. metropolitan area.

CityFirstBank.com

Capital City Bank Group

Capital City Bank Group is a financial services company that serves the black community in Tallahassee, Florida.

Ccbg.com

Liberty Bank and Trust

Liberty Bank and Trust is a community development financial institution that serves the black community in New Orleans.

LibertyBank.net

Carver Federal Savings Bank

Carver Federal Savings Bank is a community development financial institution that serves the black community in New York City.

CarverBank.com

Freedom First Credit Union

Freedom First Credit Union is a credit union that serves the black community in Roanoke, Virginia.

FreedomFirst.com

Industrial Bank

Industrial Bank is a community development financial institution that serves the black community in Washington, D.C.

Industrial-Bank.com

FREE: HOW TO GROW YOUR BLACK OWNED BUSINESS USING DIGITAL MARKETING WEBINAR

During this webinar, we will demonstrate how you can use various digital marketing techniques to boost your sales. These techniques include search engine optimization, social media marketing, email marketing, pay-per-click advertising, content marketing, video marketing, PR marketing, mobile marketing, and analytics and measurement, as outlined in this book. By applying these strategies, you can effectively reach your target audience and achieve your business goals with digital marketing for your black-owned business.

In addition to these topics, we will also cover specific challenges and opportunities faced by black-owned businesses in the digital space. This will include discussions on overcoming biases and stereotypes, building a strong online presence, and connecting with customers and clients in a virtual environment. By addressing these issues, your business can gain a deeper understanding of the unique challenges and opportunities faced by black-owned businesses in the digital marketing world, and develop strategies to overcome these challenges and succeed.

This workshop-style presentation will involve your active participation, so come prepared with your book and ready to develop a customized action plan for using digital marketing to expand your black-owned business.

WARNING: LIMITED SPACE AVAILABLE

This is always our most popular webinar of the year and space is limited. Make sure to register now to secure your spot on this live & interactive webinar.

To Register Go To:

GoBlackly.com/webinar

GLOSSARY

Ad impressions: Ad impressions refer to the number of times an ad is displayed to a user.

Ad recall: Ad recall refers to the ability of a user to remember an advertisement that they have seen.

Ad relevance: Ad relevance refers to how closely the content of an advertisement aligns with the interests of the viewer. A highly relevant ad is more likely to be effective in terms of engagement and conversions.

Ad targeting: Ad targeting refers to the process of selecting specific audience segments to show an advertisement to. This can be based on various factors such as demographics, interests, location, and more.

Affiliate marketing: A type of performance-based marketing in which a business rewards affiliates for each customer brought to the company by the affiliate's own marketing efforts.

Affinity categories: Affinity categories refer to groupings of users based on their interests and preferences.

Algorithm: A set of instructions used by a computer to perform a task, such as searching for information or sorting data.

Analytics: The process of collecting, measuring, and analyzing data to gain insights and inform business decisions.

Blog: A website or section of a website that contains regular updates, often in the form of written articles or posts.

Call-to-action (CTA): A call-to-action is a message or button that encourages the user to take a specific action, such as making a purchase or filling out a form.

Click-through rate (CTR): CTR refers to the percentage of users who click on an ad or link out of the total number of users who see it.

Content marketing: A strategic approach to creating and distributing valuable, relevant, and consistent content to attract and retain a clearly defined audience, with the goal of driving profitable customer action.

Cookie: A small piece of data stored on a user's computer by a website, used to track the user's actions and preferences.

Cost-per-click (CPC): CPC refers to the amount of money that an advertiser pays each time a user clicks on their ad.

Conversion rate: The conversion rate is the percentage of visitors to a website who complete a desired action, such as making a purchase or filling out a form.

Customer journey: The customer journey refers to the series of steps that a customer goes through from awareness to purchase.

Customer profile: A customer profile is a detailed profile of the ideal customer for a business or product. It includes information on demographics, interests, pain points, and other factors that are relevant to marketing and sales efforts.

Customer relationship management (CRM): CRM refers to the process of managing and organizing customer interactions and data throughout the customer lifecycle.

Demographics: Demographics refer to the characteristics of a population, such as age, gender, income, education level, and geographic location.

Digital marketing: Digital marketing refers to the use of electronic media to promote products or services. This can include tactics such as search engine optimization, social media advertising, email marketing, and more.

Display advertising: Display advertising refers to the use of banner ads, video ads, and other forms of visual advertisements to promote products or services.

Email marketing: Email marketing refers to the use of email to promote products or services, or to nurture leads and customers.

In-market segments: In-market segments refer to groupings of users based on their current or recent search and purchase behavior.

Landing page: A landing page is a webpage specifically designed to capture leads or drive conversions. It usually has a specific call-to-action (CTA) and is optimized for conversions.

Metrics: Metrics refer to measurements or data points that are used to evaluate the performance of a campaign or website.

Opt-in: An opt-in is when a user actively signs up to receive emails or other communications from a business.

Pay-per-click (PPC): PPC refers to a form of advertising in which the advertiser pays each time a user clicks on their ad.

Psychographics: Psychographics refer to the psychological and behavioral characteristics of a population, such as values, attitudes, interests, and lifestyles.

Remarketing: Remarketing refers to the practice of targeting ads to users who have previously visited a website

Retargeting: Retargeting is a form of remarketing that involves displaying ads to users who have previously visited a website but have not completed a desired action, such as making a purchase.

Search engine optimization (SEO): SEO refers to the practice of optimizing a website to improve its visibility and ranking in search engine results pages (SERPs).

Search engine marketing (SEM): SEM refers to the practice of using paid advertising to improve a website's visibility and ranking in search engine results pages (SERPs).

Social media advertising: Social media advertising refers to the use of social media platforms to promote products or services. This can include sponsored posts, ads, and other forms of promoted content.

Targeting: Targeting refers to the process of selecting specific audience segments to show an advertisement to. This can be based on various factors such as demographics, interests, location, and more.

Traffic: Traffic refers to the number of visitors to a website.

User experience (UX): UX refers to the overall experience of a user when interacting with a website or app. A good UX is characterized by ease of use, efficiency, and overall satisfaction.

Video advertising: Video advertising refers to the use of video content to promote products or services.

Web analytics: Web analytics refers to the measurement, collection, analysis, and reporting of data about website traffic and user behavior.

Website conversion rate: The website conversion rate refers to the percentage of visitors to a website who complete a desired action, such as making a purchase or filling out a form

Made in the USA
Middletown, DE
02 October 2023

39902565R00170